The Best of COUNTRY COOKING
2009

Editor in Chief: Catherine Cassidy
Vice President, Executive Editor/Books: Heidi Reuter Lloyd
Creative Director: Ardyth Cope
Food Director: Diane Werner RD
Senior Editor/Books: Mark Hagen
Editor: Krista Lanphier
Art Director: Gretchen Trautman
Content Production Supervisor: Julie Wagner
Design Layout Artists: Kathy Crawford, Catherine Fletcher
Proofreader: Linne Bruskewitz
Recipe Asset Systems: Coleen Martin, Sue A. Jurack
Premedia Supervisor: Scott Berger
Recipe Testing & Editing: Taste of Home Test Kitchen
Food Photography: Taste of Home Photo Studio
Editorial Assistant: Barb Czysz

Chief Marketing Officer: Lisa Karpinski
Vice President/Book Marketing: Dan Fink
Creative Director/Creative Marketing: Jim Palmen

THE READER'S DIGEST ASSOCIATION, INC.
President and Chief Executive Officer: Mary G. Berner
President, RDA Food & Entertaining: Suzanne M. Grimes
President, Consumer Marketing: Dawn Zier

Taste of Home Books
©2009 Reiman Media Group, Inc.
5400 S. 60th St., Greendale WI 53129
International Standard Book Number (10): 0-89821-721-0
International Standard Book Number (13): 978-0-89821-721-6
International Standard Serial Number: 1097-8321
All rights reserved. Printed in U.S.A.

Taste of Home is a registered trademark of The Reader's Digest Association, Inc.

For other Taste of Home books and products, visit **www.ShopTasteofHome.com**.

PICTURED ABOVE AND ON FRONT COVER: Cheddar 'n' Pea Tossed Salad
(p. 30), Banana Cheesecake (p. 130) and Chicken 'n' Corn Bread Bake (p. 48).
Photography by Jim Wieland. Food styled by Jennifer Janz. Set styled by Melissa Haberman.

Country Cooking Prepared With Extra-Loving Care

HOME ON THE RANGE takes on a special meaning with *The Best of Country Cooking 2009*. This book is full of down-home dishes that will fill your home with the enticing aromas everyone looks forward to most. These tried-and-true recipes, which come straight from the heart, are the year's best-of-the-best, and will surely delight you and your loved ones.

This 12th edition in our popular series has a total of 332 recipes that were created by readers of our rural- and nostalgia-based magazines. That includes hundreds of home-style dishes that have been featured in recent issues of *Country Woman, Country, Country EXTRA, Reminisce* and *Reminisce EXTRA*.

This beautiful cookbook is full of recipes that were created by hundreds of home cooks just like you. They crave the same wholesome, heartwarming food as you, and understand the challenges of feeding a family.

What's more, every recipe was tested by our home economists as well. So you can be doubly confident each and every dish is a "keeper" that doesn't require a tryout first.

This book begins with an appealing assortment of "Snacks & Beverages" that will whet your appetite. You'll find savory appetizers like Spinach-Stuffed Portobellos (p. 5), Chorizo Bean Dip (p. 13) and Pizza Roll-Ups (p. 15). You'll also be able to whet your whistle with drinks like Orange Lemonade (p. 8) and refreshing Pink Rhubarb Punch (p. 15).

You can't go wrong with items from the "Soups, Salads & Sandwiches" chapter when you need to set a meal on the table fast. We've even highlighted a few incredible burger recipes (p. 24) and hand selected warm and hearty chowders (p. 36) that are simply too good to pass up.

"Main Dishes" is packed with 59 supper ideas in all! If you're looking for a weeknight meal, try Meatballs Stroganoff (p. 45) or Oven-Fried Parmesan Chicken (p. 48). For weekend guests, consider Spiced Pork Loin with Plums (p. 58) or Steaks with Shallot Sauce (p. 62).

It's easy to balance mealtime with recipes from "Side Dishes & Condiments." In addition to a variety of potato sides, good-for-you veggies and savory rice favorites, you'll also want to try Mock Hollandaise (p. 79), Grilled Chiles Rellenos (p. 82) and a host of robust side dish casseroles. And because nothing goes better with dinner like oven-fresh loaves and biscuits, "Breads & Rolls" offers plenty of baked goods.

Speaking of baking, you'll want to check out the 23 recipes in "Cookies, Bars & Brownies." Whether looking for simple snacks, bake-sale items or additions to holiday cookie trays, this is one chapter you'll turn to time and again. Treats like Peanut Butter Brownie Bars (p. 105) and Apple Spice Drops (p. 107) are sure to become family favorites.

In addition, *The Best of Country Cooking 2009* features more than 49 impressive after-dinner delights. See "Dazzling Desserts" for incredible recipes, such as Cherry Walnut Cake (p. 114) and Pear Praline Pie (p. 120). Special sections feature cupcakes (p. 116) and craft-oriented cakes (p. 126) as well.

You'll also find the standbys you've come to expect from this handy collection:

Cooking for Two—Dishes and dinners that are sized right for a pair.

Meals in Minutes—Four suppers that require a minimum of prep work.

Our Most Memorable Meals—A total of 24 recipes divided into six unforgettable menus.

Look for the blue ribbon icon, right, as you browse *The Best of Country Cooking 2009*. It identifies prize-winning recipes that earned high honors in national cooking contests sponsored by one of our magazines.

You'll also see heart-smart recipes marked with the check at right. These dishes use less fat, salt or sugar and all of them include Diabetic Exchanges.

So what are you waiting for? Grab a fork, then come and get it! It won't be long before you and your family realize why these dishes are simply the best in the country.

CONTENTS

Snacks & Beverages...4

Soups, Salads & Sandwiches...18

Main Dishes...42

Side Dishes & Condiments...72

Breads & Rolls...84

Cookies, Bars & Brownies...98

Dazzling Desserts...110

Cooking for Two...136

Meals in Minutes...152

Our Most Memorable Meals...160

Index begins on page 172

Snacks & Beverages

SPINACH-STUFFED PORTOBELLOS
(Pictured at left)

Diane Lombardo, New Castle, Pennsylvania

The meaty texture of portobello mushrooms will make you think you're eating steak. With a cheesy spinach filling, this truly is a marvelous dish. Red pepper flakes add color and a kick.

      4 large portobello mushrooms
      2 tablespoons olive oil
      1 can (14-1/2 ounces) diced tomatoes, drained
      1 package (10 ounces) frozen chopped spinach, thawed and squeezed dry
      3 tablespoons chopped green onions
      2 tablespoons grated Romano cheese
  1/4 teaspoon crushed red pepper flakes
  1/8 teaspoon salt
  1/2 cup shredded part-skim mozzarella cheese

Remove and discard the stems and gills from mushrooms. In a large skillet, cook mushrooms in oil over medium heat for 10-15 minutes or just until tender, turning once.

In a small bowl, combine the tomatoes, spinach, onions, Romano cheese, pepper flakes and salt. Spoon into mushroom caps. Sprinkle with mozzarella cheese.

Place on a baking sheet lined with heavy-duty foil. Bake at 375° for 10-15 minutes or until heated through and the cheese is melted. **Yield:** 4 servings.

CRAN-RASPBERRY ICED TEA

The fruity flavor of this refreshing ruby-red beverage from our Test Kitchen has just the right touch of sweetness. It's sure to brighten up any summer get-together you might host.

 This recipe includes Nutrition Facts and Diabetic Exchanges.

      4 cups water
      1 cup frozen unsweetened raspberries
      4 teaspoons sugar
      8 individual raspberry-flavored tea bags

      4 cups reduced-calorie reduced-sugar cranberry-raspberry juice

In a large saucepan, bring the water, raspberries and sugar to a boil. Reduce heat; cover and simmer for 10 minutes. Remove from the heat; strain and discard raspberry seeds. Add tea bags. Let stand for 4 minutes. Discard tea bags. Stir in the cranberry-raspberry juice. Serve over ice. **Yield:** 8 servings.

Nutrition Facts: 1 cup equals 38 calories, 0.55 g fat (0 saturated fat), 0 cholesterol, 48 mg sodium, 8 g carbohydrate, 1 g fiber, 0.55 g protein. **Diabetic Exchange:** 1/2 fruit.

CREAMY RED PEPPER DIP

Linda Murray, Allenstown, New Hampshire

Roasted red peppers and cream cheese create the perfect combination in this zesty dip. Serve it in a sweet yellow pepper half for a pretty presentation.

      1 garlic clove, peeled
      1 package (8 ounces) cream cheese, cubed
  1/2 cup roasted sweet red peppers, drained
      2 green onions, cut into 2-inch pieces
      2 tablespoons lemon juice
  1/2 teaspoon ground cumin
      1 medium sweet yellow pepper, halved
Assorted fresh vegetables

In a food processor, cover and process garlic until minced. Add the cream cheese, red peppers, onions, lemon juice and cumin; cover and process until smooth. Spoon into pepper halves. Serve with vegetables. **Yield:** about 1-1/2 cups.

HOW TO ROAST PEPPERS

Arrange the whole peppers on a broiler pan coated with cooking spray. Broil on the rack closest to the heat, rotating occasionally until the skins are blackened, about 10 minutes. Immediately place the peppers in a bowl; cover with plastic wrap and let stand for 15-20 minutes. Remove charred skin, stems and seeds.

BACON WATER CHESTNUT WRAPS

(Pictured below)

Laura Mahaffey, Annapolis, Maryland

The holidays just wouldn't be the same without having these classic, savory wraps around the house. Through the years, our Christmas Eve guests have proved it is impossible to eat just one.

  1 pound sliced bacon
  2 cans (8 ounces *each*) whole water
     chestnuts, drained
1/2 cup packed brown sugar
1/2 cup mayonnaise
1/4 cup chili sauce

Cut bacon strips in half. In a large skillet, cook bacon over medium heat until almost crisp; drain. Wrap each bacon piece around a water chestnut and secure with a toothpick. Place in an ungreased 13-in. x 9-in. baking dish.

In a small bowl, combine the brown sugar, mayonnaise and chili sauce; pour over the water chestnuts. Bake, uncovered, at 350° for 30 minutes or until hot and bubbly. **Yield:** about 2-1/2 dozen.

CATFISH SPREAD

(Pictured above)

Edna Carter, West Point, Virginia

Whenever we have a fish fry, we begin the meal with this dip. My children and grandchildren love it, and it gets rave reviews at picnics and potlucks. I receive many requests for this recipe.

  1 pound catfish fillets
  2 teaspoons water
  2 packages (8 ounces *each*) cream cheese,
     softened
  2 packages (5.2 ounces *each*) garlic-herb
     cheese spread
  4 green onions, thinly sliced
1/2 cup minced fresh parsley
  1 tablespoon lemon juice
  2 teaspoons Worcestershire sauce
1/8 teaspoon garlic powder
1/8 teaspoon cayenne pepper
Dash paprika
  1 can (6 ounces) crabmeat, drained,
     flaked and cartilage removed
  1 can (6 ounces) small shrimp, rinsed
     and drained
Assorted fresh vegetables

Place catfish in a 2-qt. microwave-safe dish; drizzle with water. Cover and microwave on high for 4-6 minutes or until fish flakes easily with a fork. Drain and discard cooking liquid. Using a fork, flake fish into small pieces; set aside.

In a large bowl, beat cream cheese and cheese spread until smooth. Add the onions, parsley, lemon juice, Worcestershire sauce and seasonings and mix well. Stir in the crab, shrimp and catfish. Cover and refrigerate for at least 2 hours. Serve with vegetables. **Yield:** 5 cups.

Editor's Note: This recipe was tested in a 1,100-watt microwave.

⬥⬥⬥⬥⬥⬥⬥⬥⬥⬥⬥⬥⬥⬥⬥⬥

FLAVORED MOCHA DRINK MIX
(Pictured below)

Edna Hoffman, Hebron, Indiana

I rely on vanilla and almond extracts to get two great flavors from one hot beverage mix. It's easy to package these flavorful and fun mixes in pretty jars, decorative tins or seasonal mugs to make great-tasting presents and hostess gifts.

  1-1/2 cups powdered nondairy creamer
      1 cup sugar
    1/2 cup instant coffee granules
    1/2 cup baking cocoa
Dash salt
    1/4 teaspoon vanilla extract
    1/4 teaspoon almond extract
ADDITIONAL INGREDIENTS:
    3/4 cup boiling water
Whipped cream, optional

In a bowl, combine the first five ingredients. Divide mixture in half. Stir in vanilla to one portion and almond extract to the other. Store in airtight containers in a cool dry place for up to 1 year. **Yield:** 14-16 servings (7-8 servings vanilla mocha mix; 7-8 servings almond mocha mix), about 3 cups dry mix.

    To prepare beverage: Dissolve about 3 tablespoons mix in water; stir well. Top with whipped cream if desired. **Yield:** 1 serving.

⬥⬥⬥⬥⬥⬥⬥⬥⬥⬥⬥⬥⬥⬥⬥

CAPRESE TOMATO BITES
(Pictured above)

Crystal Williams, Brooklyn, New York

I love the classic combination of tomatoes, mozzarella and basil in these bite-size appetizers. The juicy explosion you get when you pop one into your mouth is the genuine taste of springtime.

    1 pint cherry tomatoes, halved
    3 tablespoons heavy whipping cream
  1/2 pound fresh mozzarella cheese, sliced
    6 fresh basil leaves
    1 garlic clove, minced
    1 tablespoon balsamic vinegar

Scoop out and discard pulp of cherry tomatoes. Invert tomatoes onto paper towels to drain.

    In a food processor, combine the cream, mozzarella cheese, basil and garlic; cover and process until blended. Cut a small hole in the corner of a pastry or heavy-duty resealable plastic bag. Fill with cheese mixture.

    Turn tomato halves over; drizzle with vinegar. Pipe cheese mixture into tomatoes. Refrigerate until serving. **Yield:** about 3-1/2 dozen.

FRESH MOZZARELLA

Compared to the firm texture of commercially produced mozzarella, fresh mozzarella is soft and moist. The flavor is mild and delicate. After buying fresh mozzarella, refrigerate it in the brine and eat within a few days.

■▬■▬■▬■▬■▬■

ORANGE LEMONADE
(Pictured above)

Wendy Masters, Grand Valley, Ontario

This juice is a favorite at our place. I'll often double the batch and send a jar next door to my mother-in-law! I make it more often in summer, but we enjoy it year-round. It's good for special occasions also.

 1-3/4 cups sugar
 2-1/2 cups water
 1-1/2 cups fresh lemon juice
   (about 8 lemons)
 1-1/2 cups fresh orange juice
   (about 5 oranges)
   2 tablespoons grated lemon peel
   2 tablespoons grated orange peel
Water

In a large saucepan, combine sugar and water. Cook over medium heat until sugar is dissolved, stirring occasionally. Cool.

Add juices and peel to cooled sugar syrup. Cover and let stand at room temperature for 1 hour. Strain the syrup; cover and refrigerate.

To serve, fill glasses or pitcher with equal amounts of fruit syrup and water. Add ice and serve. **Yield:** 12 servings.

■▬■▬■▬■▬■▬■

FRUIT 'N' NUT SPREAD

Donna Peduto, Brandon, Vermont

This is a delicious appetizer, but it's also nice for breakfast or brunch spread on bagels, muffins or English muffins. With cranberries and pecans, it's perfect for the holidays.

   1 package (8 ounces) cream cheese,
     softened
 1/4 cup orange juice
 1/2 cup dried cranberries
 1/2 cup chopped pecans
Assorted crackers *or* breads

In a small bowl, beat cream cheese and orange juice until smooth. Fold in cranberries and pecans. Cover and refrigerate for at least 30 minutes. Serve with crackers or breads. **Yield:** 1-1/2 cups.

PEPPER JACK CHEESE STICKS

(Pictured at right)

Darlene Brenden, Salem, Oregon

If you see a group of people huddled around an appetizer table, it's probably because they're feasting on these fun snacks. The cornflakes give them a crisp coating, and the soft creamy center has just enough kick to liven up any party.

> 1 pound pepper Jack cheese
> 3 cups all-purpose flour
> 3 eggs, lightly beaten
> 3 cups crushed cornflakes

Oil for deep-fat frying
Salsa and guacamole

Cut cheese into 2-3/4-in. x 1/2-in. sticks. Place the flour, eggs and cornflakes in three separate shallow bowls. Coat cheese sticks with flour; dip in egg, then roll in cornflakes until well coated. Let stand for 5 minutes.

In an electric skillet or deep-fat fryer, heat oil to 375°. Cook cheese sticks in batches for 30 seconds or until golden brown. Drain on paper towels. Let stand for 3-5 minutes. Serve with salsa and guacamole. **Yield:** 2-1/2 dozen.

TURKEY CHEESE BALL

(Pictured below)

While the real bird is roasting, you can present your guests with this tasty Thanksgiving turkey. Our flock of clever Test Kitchen cooks dreamed up the recipe for this festive cheese ball centerpiece.

> 2 packages (8 ounces *each*) reduced-fat cream cheese

> 6 ounces deli smoked turkey, finely chopped
> 1 cup (4 ounces) shredded cheddar cheese
> 1 tablespoon finely chopped onion
> 1 tablespoon Worcestershire sauce
> 1/2 teaspoon garlic powder

DECORATIONS:

> 3 packages (3 ounces *each*) cream cheese, softened
> 2 tablespoons milk

Brown, orange and yellow paste food coloring

> 6 large oval crackers
> 1 large sweet red pepper
> 1 small yellow summer squash
> 1 cup pecan halves

Assorted crackers

In a small bowl, beat the first six ingredients until combined. Shape into a ball; wrap in plastic wrap. Refrigerate for 1 hour or until firm.

In another small bowl, beat cream cheese and milk until smooth. Divide among four small bowls. With food coloring, tint one bowl brown, one dark orange and one light orange (using yellow and orange); leave one bowl plain.

Transfer each mixture to a heavy-duty resealable plastic bag; cut a small hole in a corner of each bag.

For turkey tail feathers, decorate the top halves of large oval crackers with tinted cream cheese.

Using the red pepper, form the turkey head and neck. For beak, cut a small triangle from summer squash; attach with cream cheese. Add eyes, using brown and plain cream cheese. Insert pecan halves and decorated crackers into cheese ball. Serve with assorted crackers. **Yield:** 1 cheese ball (3 cups).

Editor's Note: This recipe was tested with Townhouse Oval Bistro crackers.

SHRIMP 'N' MUSHROOM LETTUCE WRAPS
(Pictured below)

Mary Beth Vultee, Ocean Beach, North Carolina

Here's a simple recipe for lettuce wraps that's a nutritious option for a luncheon or dinner party. For fun, serve the filling on a platter with lettuce leaves on the side, and let your guests wrap their own.

    1 tablespoon water
    1 tablespoon lime juice
    1 tablespoon cider vinegar
    1 tablespoon reduced-sodium soy sauce
 1/4 cup reduced-fat creamy peanut butter
    1 tablespoon chopped jalapeno pepper
 3/4 teaspoon minced fresh gingerroot
    1 garlic clove, peeled
 3/4 teaspoon sesame oil
 3/4 teaspoon honey
FILLING:
    1 pound uncooked medium shrimp, peeled, deveined and coarsely chopped
 1/4 teaspoon salt
 1/4 teaspoon pepper
    2 teaspoons canola oil, *divided*
    1 package (6 ounces) portobello mushrooms, coarsely chopped
 1/2 cup chopped red onion

    1 cup canned bean sprouts, rinsed and drained
 1/4 cup minced fresh cilantro
    2 tablespoons minced fresh basil
    4 green onions, sliced
    2 tablespoons chopped salted peanuts
    8 Bibb *or* Boston lettuce leaves

For sauce, in a blender, combine the first 10 ingredients; cover and process until smooth. Set aside.

Sprinkle shrimp with salt and pepper. In a large nonstick skillet, saute the shrimp in 1 teaspoon canola oil for 4-6 minutes or until shrimp turn pink; remove and keep warm.

In the same skillet, saute mushrooms and red onion in remaining oil for 5-8 minutes or until tender. Return shrimp to the pan. Add the bean sprouts, cilantro and basil; cook and stir for 1 minute or until heated through.

Remove from the heat; stir in green onions and peanuts. Divide among lettuce leaves; drizzle each with 1 tablespoon sauce. Fold lettuce over filling. **Yield:** 4 servings.

Editor's Note: When cutting hot peppers, disposable gloves are recommended. Avoid touching your face.

OYSTERS ROCKEFELLER

Beth Walton, Eastham, Massachusetts

My husband and I are Cape Cod oyster farmers and like to use them liberally in our cooking. Our guests are always delighted when we serve this classic dish. It's deliciously simple!

    3 dozen fresh oysters in the shell, washed
    1 medium onion, finely chopped
 1/2 cup butter, cubed
    1 package (9 ounces) fresh spinach, torn
    1 cup grated Romano cheese
    1 tablespoon lemon juice
 1/8 teaspoon pepper
    2 pounds kosher salt

Shuck the oysters, reserving the bottom shell; set aside. In a large skillet, saute the onion in butter until tender. Add spinach; cook and stir until wilted. Remove from the heat; stir in the cheese, lemon juice and pepper.

Spread kosher salt into two ungreased 15-in. x 10-in. x 1-in. baking pans. Lightly press the oyster shells down into the salt. Place one oyster in each shell; top each with 2-1/2 teaspoons spinach mixture.

Bake, uncovered, at 450° for 6-8 minutes or until oysters are plump. Serve immediately. **Yield:** 3 dozen.

PARTY PITAS

(Pictured above)

Janette Root, Ellensburg, Washington

Whenever the ladies of our church host a bridal shower, these pita sandwiches always appear on the menu. Not only are they easy and delicious, they look nice on the table too.

    1 package (8 ounces) cream
       cheese, softened
  1/2 cup mayonnaise
  1/2 teaspoon dill weed
  1/4 teaspoon garlic salt
    8 miniature pita pockets
   16 fresh spinach leaves
  3/4 pound shaved fully cooked ham
  1/2 pound thinly sliced Monterey
       Jack cheese

In a small bowl, beat the cream cheese, mayonnaise, dill and garlic salt until blended.

Cut each pita in half horizontally; spread 1 tablespoon cream cheese mixture on each cut surface. On eight pita halves, layer the spinach, ham and cheese. Top with remaining pita halves. Cut each pita into four wedges; secure with toothpicks. **Yield:** 32 sandwich wedges.

APPETIZER COUNT

For an appetizer buffet that serves as the meal, offer five or six different appetizers and plan on eight to nine pieces per guest. If you'll also be serving a meal, two to three appetizers per person is sufficient.

BLUEBERRY ORANGE SMOOTHIES

(Pictured below)

Nella Parker, Hersey, Michigan

Start out your mornings with one of these refreshing smoothies using low-fat dairy products and blueberries. To complete the meal, serve these with whole grain muffins, bagels or toast. I also like to serve these smoothies at dinner.

✓ This recipe includes Nutrition Facts and Diabetic Exchanges.

    2 medium navel oranges
    1 cup fat-free plain yogurt
  1/4 cup fat-free milk
  2/3 cup fresh or frozen blueberries
    4 teaspoons sugar
    1 to 1-1/3 cups ice cubes

Peel and remove the white pith from oranges; separate into sections. Place in a blender; add the yogurt, milk, blueberries and sugar. Cover and process until smooth. Add ice; cover and process until smooth. Pour into chilled glasses; serve immediately. **Yield:** 4 servings.

Nutrition Facts: 1 cup equals 92 calories, trace fat (trace saturated fat), 2 mg cholesterol, 43 mg sodium, 21 g carbohydrate, 2 g fiber, 4 g protein. **Diabetic Exchange:** 1-1/2 fruit.

BEAN AND PINEAPPLE SALSA
(Pictured below)

Anne Bennett, Delmar, Maryland

The flavors of this tasty salsa complement each other very nicely. I like to serve it over either fish or chicken. It's a pleasant and colorful change.

 1/2 cup canned black beans, rinsed and drained
 1/4 cup unsweetened pineapple tidbits, drained
 1/4 cup chopped green pepper
 1/4 cup chopped sweet red pepper
  2 tablespoons finely chopped sweet onion
  2 tablespoons chopped green chilies
 1/2 to 1 teaspoon chopped seeded jalapeno pepper
  1 tablespoon rice vinegar
1-1/2 teaspoons minced fresh cilantro
 1/2 teaspoon ground coriander
 1/2 teaspoon ground cumin
Tortilla chips

In a small bowl, combine the first 11 ingredients. Refrigerate until serving. Serve with tortilla chips. **Yield:** 1-1/4 cups.

 Editor's Note: When cutting hot peppers, disposable gloves are recommended. Avoid touching your face.

CALLA LILY TEA SANDWICHES
(Pictured above)

Leann Williams, Beaverton, Oregon

Your tea tray will be blooming with these beautiful and novel lily-shaped sandwiches. The tasty chicken, mayonnaise and herb filling will delight guests at your next luncheon or shower.

  1 can (4-1/2 ounces) chunk white chicken, drained
  1 celery rib, finely chopped
 1/4 cup mayonnaise
  1 teaspoon grated onion
 1/4 teaspoon dried tarragon
 1/8 teaspoon pepper
 18 slices white bread, crusts removed
  2 tablespoons butter, softened
  1 tablespoon minced fresh parsley
 18 pieces (1 inch *each*) julienned carrot

In a small bowl, combine the first six ingredients; set aside. With a rolling pin, flatten each slice of bread to 1/8-in. thickness; cut into 2-1/2-in. squares. Spread with butter. Roll up into a funnel shape, overlapping the two adjacent sides; secure with a toothpick.

 Spoon about 1 teaspoon of the chicken filling into each sandwich. Cover with plastic wrap; refrigerate for 1 hour.

 Remove toothpicks. Sprinkle sandwiches with parsley. For the center spike, insert a carrot piece in the center of each lily. **Yield:** 1-1/2 dozen.

CHORIZO BEAN DIP
(Pictured above)

Elaine Sweet, Dallas, Texas

With its zesty Mexican flavors and tempting toppings, this dish is the first one to be empty on the appetizer table. I serve it with extra-thick tortilla chips for some serious scooping.

1 pound ground sirloin
1/3 pound uncooked chorizo *or* bulk spicy pork sausage
1 medium onion, chopped
1 envelope taco seasoning
2 cans (16 ounces *each*) refried black beans
1 cup (4 ounces) shredded Monterey Jack cheese
1 jar (11 ounces) salsa
2 cans (2-1/4 ounces *each*) sliced ripe olives, drained
2 cups guacamole
6 green onions, thinly sliced
1 cup (8 ounces) sour cream
1/2 cup minced fresh cilantro
3/4 cup jalapeno-stuffed olives, sliced
Tortilla chips

In a large skillet, cook the beef, chorizo, onion and taco seasoning over medium heat until meat is no longer pink; drain.

Spread beans into a greased 13-in. x 9-in. baking dish. Layer with the meat mixture, cheese, salsa and ripe olives. Cover and bake at 350° for 20-25 minutes or until heated through.

Spread guacamole over the top. Combine the green onions, sour cream and cilantro; spread over guacamole. Sprinkle with stuffed olives. Serve immediately with tortilla chips. Refrigerate leftovers. **Yield:** 48 servings.

Editor's Note: When cutting hot peppers, disposable gloves are recommended. Avoid touching your face.

COLD VEGETABLE PIZZA
(Pictured below)

Leslie Hampel, Palmer, Texas

This is one of my favorite vegetable recipes. Even youngsters love it. I've served it as an hors d'oeuvre at get-togethers and even as a light lunch.

>   2 tubes (8 ounces *each*) refrigerated crescent rolls
>   1 cup mayonnaise
>   1 package (8 ounces) cream cheese, softened
>   1 tablespoon dill weed
> 2-1/2 cups assorted chopped fresh vegetables (cucumber, radishes, broccoli, onion, green pepper, carrots, celery *and/or* mushrooms)
>   1/2 cup sliced ripe olives
>   3/4 cup shredded cheddar cheese
>   3/4 cup shredded part-skim mozzarella cheese

Unroll the crescent rolls and place in an ungreased 15-in. x 10-in. x 1-in. baking pan. Flatten dough to fit the pan, sealing seams and perforations. Bake at 375° for 10 minutes or until golden brown. Cool.

In a small bowl, beat the mayonnaise, cream cheese and dill until smooth; spread over crust. Top with the vegetables of your choice. Sprinkle with olives and cheeses; press lightly. Cover and chill for at least 1 hour. Cut into squares. **Yield:** 12-15 servings.

PICKLED MUSHROOMS
(Pictured above)

Sandra Johnson, Tioga, Pennsylvania

As an appetizer or salad, these tangy mushrooms are a welcome addition to any party buffet table or meal It doesn't take long for a whole bowlful to be devoured.

>   2/3 cup tarragon vinegar
>   1/2 cup canola oil
>   2 tablespoons water
>   1 tablespoon sugar
> 1-1/2 teaspoons salt
>   1 garlic clove, minced
> Dash hot pepper sauce
>   1 pound fresh mushrooms
>   1 medium onion, thinly sliced and separated into rings
> Finely diced sweet red pepper

In a large serving bowl, combine the first seven ingredients. Add mushrooms and onion; toss to coat. Cover and refrigerate 8 hours or overnight. Sprinkle with red pepper before serving. **Yield:** 4 cups.

CITRUS CIDER PUNCH

Carolyn Beck, St. Johns, Michigan

I share this refreshing punch recipe with people who visit our apple cider mill. It's perfect for autumn and holiday gatherings.

>   1 gallon apple cider, chilled
>   1 can (12 ounces) frozen lemonade concentrate, thawed
>   1 medium lemon, sliced
>   4 spiced apple rings

In a large punch bowl, combine the cider and lemonade. Garnish with lemon slices and apple rings. **Yield:** 25 servings (4-3/4 quarts).

PIZZA ROLL-UPS

(Pictured at right)

Donna Klettke, Wheatland, Missouri

Since receiving this recipe through 4-H, it's been a regular after-school snack. These bite-size pizza treats, made with refrigerated crescent rolls, are especially good served with spaghetti sauce for dipping.

- 1/2 **pound ground beef**
- 1 **can (8 ounces) tomato sauce**
- 1/2 **cup shredded part-skim mozzarella cheese**
- 1/2 **teaspoon dried oregano**
- 2 **tubes (8 ounces *each*) refrigerated crescent rolls**

In a skillet, cook beef over medium heat until no longer pink; drain. Remove from the heat. Add the tomato sauce, mozzarella cheese and oregano.

Separate crescent dough into eight rectangles, pinching the seams together. Place about 3 tablespoons of meat mixture along one long side of each rectangle. Roll up jelly-roll style, starting with a long side. Cut each roll into three pieces. Place seam side down 2 in. apart on greased baking sheets. Bake at 375° for 15 minutes or until golden brown. **Yield:** 2 dozen.

PINK RHUBARB PUNCH

(Pictured below)

Rebecca Mininger, Jeromesville, Ohio

To get your garden party started, toast the arrival of guests and springtime with this blush-colored rhubarb punch. The recipe has a crisp and refreshing taste everyone will love.

- 8 **cups chopped fresh *or* frozen rhubarb**
- 8 **cups water**
- 2-1/2 **cups sugar**
- 2 **tablespoons strawberry gelatin powder**
- 2 **cups boiling water**
- 2 **cups pineapple juice**
- 1/4 **cup lemon juice**
- 6 **cups ginger ale, chilled**

In a Dutch oven, bring rhubarb and water to a boil. Reduce heat; simmer, uncovered, for 10 minutes. Drain, reserving liquid (save rhubarb for another use).

In a large bowl, dissolve sugar and gelatin powder in boiling water. Stir in pineapple and lemon juices. Stir in rhubarb liquid; refrigerate until chilled.

Just before serving, pour into a punch bowl and stir in ginger ale. **Yield:** about 5 quarts.

ORANGE CREME SODAS

Lillian Weir, Dartmouth, Nova Scotia

This treat is a hit with kids and adults alike. Serve it on National Creamsicle Day—August 14—or whenever the temperature calls for frosty flavor.

- 8 **scoops vanilla ice cream, softened**
- 4 **cups orange soda, chilled**
- 1/4 **teaspoon orange extract**

Place two scoops ice cream in each of four chilled 16-oz. glasses. In a large pitcher, combine the soda and extract. Pour over the ice cream. **Yield:** 4 servings.

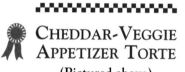

CHEDDAR-VEGGIE APPETIZER TORTE
(Pictured above)

Barbara Estabrook, Rhinelander, Wisconsin

A line forms quickly for this quiche-like torte at family gatherings. The wedges are easy to eat as finger food…plus, it's delicious hot or cold.

1-1/3 **cups finely crushed multigrain crackers**
  1/4 **cup butter, melted**
    2 **cups (8 ounces) shredded sharp cheddar cheese**
    1 **small zucchini, finely chopped**
    5 **small fresh mushrooms, sliced**
  1/3 **cup finely chopped red onion**
  1/4 **cup finely chopped sweet red pepper**
    1 **tablespoon olive oil**
    1 **carton (8 ounces) spreadable garlic and herb cream cheese**
    4 **eggs, lightly beaten**
    2 **tablespoons crumbled cooked bacon**
    2 **tablespoons grated Parmesan cheese**
    2 **fresh basil leaves, thinly sliced**

In a small bowl, combine the cracker crumbs and butter. Press onto the bottom of a greased 9-in. springform pan. Sprinkle with cheddar cheese. In a large skillet, saute the zucchini, mushrooms, onion and red pepper in olive oil until tender. Spoon over cheese.

In a large bowl, beat cream cheese until smooth. Add eggs; beat on low speed just until combined. Stir in bacon. Pour over vegetable mixture. Sprinkle with Parmesan cheese.

Place pan on a baking sheet. Bake at 375° for 30-35 minutes or until center is almost set. Cool on a wire rack for 10 minutes. Carefully run a knife around edge of pan to loosen; remove sides of pan. Garnish with basil. Serve warm or chilled. Refrigerate leftovers. **Yield:** 16 servings.

EASY SHREDDED CHEESE

When shredding a block of cheese, place the base of a box grater inside a rolled-down gallon-size plastic bag. Then pull out the grater, unroll the bag, seal it and refrigerate.

No-Bake Salted Pumpkin Seeds

Our Test Kitchen came up with this fast and easy pumpkin seed recipe! Crunchy, with just the right amount of salt, these are perfect for those busy sewing Halloween costumes or planning parties.

   1 cup fresh pumpkin seeds
   1/4 teaspoon salt

In a small bowl, toss the pumpkin seeds with salt. Spread half of the seeds in a single layer on a microwave-safe plate. Microwave, uncovered, on high for 1 minute; stir.

   Microwave 1-2 minutes longer or until seeds are crunchy and lightly browned, stirring after each minute. Repeat with remaining pumpkin seeds. Store in an airtight container. **Yield:** 1 cup.

   Editor's Note: This recipe was tested in a 1,100-watt microwave.

Pineapple Pecan Cheese Ball

(Pictured below)

June Stone, Brewton, Alabama

A blend of tastes—tangy cheese, tropical fruit and pecans—are featured in this cheese ball. This party starter keeps for days in the refrigerator.

   2 packages (8 ounces *each*) cream cheese, softened
   1 can (8 ounces) crushed pineapple, well drained
   1/2 cup chopped green pepper
   1/2 cup chopped green onions
   1 teaspoon lemon-pepper seasoning
   1 teaspoon seasoned salt

   2 cups chopped pecans, *divided*
   Assorted crackers

In a large bowl, beat the cream cheese until smooth. Stir in the pineapple, green pepper, onions, seasonings and 1/2 cup pecans. Place on a sheet of plastic wrap; shape into a ball. Refrigerate overnight.

   Just before serving, roll cheese ball in the remaining pecans. Serve with crackers. **Yield:** 3-1/3 cups.

Chili Chicken Strips

(Pictured above)

Instead of ordinary bread crumbs, our Test Kitchen used seasoned crushed corn chips to coat these slightly crunchy chicken fingers. If your family likes their food with extra zip, use the full 1-1/2 teaspoons of chili powder.

   3/4 cup crushed corn chips
   2 tablespoons dry bread crumbs
   1 tablespoon all-purpose flour
   1 to 1-1/2 teaspoons chili powder
   1/2 teaspoon seasoned salt
   1/2 teaspoon poultry seasoning
   1/4 teaspoon pepper
   1/4 teaspoon paprika
   1 egg
   1-1/2 pounds boneless skinless chicken breasts, cut into 1/2-inch strips
   4 tablespoons butter, *divided*

In a shallow bowl, combine the first eight ingredients. In another shallow bowl, beat egg. Dip chicken in egg, then roll in corn chip mixture.

   In a large skillet, cook half of the chicken in 2 tablespoons butter for 8-10 minutes or until the meat is no longer pink. Repeat with remaining chicken and butter. **Yield:** 6 servings.

EVERYTHING *you need for a hearty lunch or light dinner is right here, whether it's a warm bowl of soup, a satisfying sandwich or a savory salad!*

LOVELY LUNCH. Mediterranean Bulgur Salad and Roasted Red Pepper Soup (both on p. 19).

Soups, Salads & Sandwiches

ROASTED RED PEPPER SOUP

(Pictured at left)

If you like cream of tomato soup, try making it with purchased roasted red peppers like our experts in the Test Kitchen did. Using jarred roasted red peppers makes it extra easy and pureeing the soup in a blender gives it a nice smooth texture.

1 large sweet onion, chopped
2 garlic cloves, minced
2 teaspoons butter
2 jars (15-1/2 ounces *each*) roasted sweet red peppers, drained
2 cups vegetable broth
1/2 teaspoon dried basil
1/4 teaspoon salt
1 cup half-and-half cream

In a large saucepan, saute the onion and garlic in butter for 2-3 minutes or until tender. Add the red peppers, broth, basil and salt. Bring to a boil. Reduce heat; cover and simmer for 20 minutes. Cool slightly.

In a blender, cover and process soup in batches until smooth. Remove 1 cup to a small bowl; stir in cream. Return remaining puree to pan. Stir in the cream mixture; heat through (do not boil). **Yield:** 6 servings.

MEDITERRANEAN BULGUR SALAD

(Pictured at left)

Whether it's health or taste you're after, it doesn't get any better than this—bulgur, beans, tomatoes, pine nuts and olive oil team up in this vegetarian main dish salad that our Test Kitchen created.

3 cups vegetable broth
1-1/2 cups uncooked bulgur
6 tablespoons olive oil
2 tablespoons lemon juice
2 tablespoons minced fresh parsley
1/2 teaspoon salt
1/4 teaspoon pepper
1 can (15 ounces) garbanzo beans *or* chickpeas, rinsed and drained
2 cups halved cherry tomatoes

1 cup chopped cucumber
8 green onions, sliced
1 package (4 ounces) crumbled feta cheese
1/2 cup pine nuts, toasted

In a large saucepan, bring the broth and bulgur to a boil over high heat. Reduce heat; cover and simmer for 20 minutes or until tender and broth is almost absorbed. Remove from the heat; let stand at room temperature, uncovered, until broth is absorbed.

In a jar with a tight-fitting lid, combine the oil, lemon juice, parsley, salt and pepper; shake well.

In a large serving bowl, combine the bulgur, beans, tomatoes, cucumber and onions. Drizzle with dressing; toss to coat. Sprinkle with cheese and pine nuts. **Yield:** 9 servings.

ITALIAN BEEF SANDWICHES

Keith Sadler, Oran, Missouri

After a hectic day, our family loves coming home to the inviting smell of Italian beef wafting from our slow cooker. Use the broth from this recipe as an au jus sauce...perfect for dipping.

1 boneless beef sirloin tip roast (2 pounds), cut into 1/4-inch strips
2 jars (11-1/2 ounces *each*) sliced pepperoncinis, undrained
1 small onion, sliced and separated into rings
3 teaspoons dried oregano
1-1/2 teaspoons garlic salt
1 can (12 ounces) beer *or* nonalcoholic beer
Mayonnaise, optional
8 hoagie buns, split
8 slices provolone cheese

In a 5-qt. slow cooker, layer the beef strips, pepperoncinis and onion; sprinkle with the oregano and garlic salt. Pour beer over the top. Cover and cook on low for 6 hours or until the meat is tender.

Spread the mayonnaise on cut sides of rolls if desired. Place cheese on roll bottoms. With a slotted spoon, place meat mixture over cheese. **Yield:** 8 servings.

Toss greens with dressing; divide among seven serving plates. Top with chicken mixture, mango salsa and cheese. Serve immediately with tortilla chips. **Yield:** 7 servings.

Editor's Note: When cutting hot peppers, disposable gloves are recommended. Avoid touching your face.

■▪■▪■▪■▪■▪■▪■

SHREDDED VENISON SANDWICHES
(Pictured below)

Ruth Setterlund, Freyburg, Maine

My husband hunts for deer every November, so I'm always looking for new recipes that use venison. The whole family loves these slow cooker sandwiches, deliciously seasoned with soy sauce, brown sugar, ketchup and hot pepper sauce.

    1 boneless venison roast (4 pounds)
1-1/2 cups ketchup
    3 tablespoons brown sugar
    1 tablespoon ground mustard
    1 tablespoon lemon juice
    1 tablespoon soy sauce
    1 tablespoon Liquid Smoke, optional
    2 teaspoons celery salt
    2 teaspoons pepper
    2 teaspoons Worcestershire sauce
    1 teaspoon onion powder
    1 teaspoon garlic powder
  1/8 teaspoon ground nutmeg
    3 drops hot pepper sauce
   14 to 18 hamburger buns, split

Cut venison roast in half; place in a 5-qt. slow cooker. In a large bowl, combine the ketchup,

■▪■▪■▪■▪■▪■▪■

🏵 SPICY CHICKEN SALAD WITH MANGO SALSA
(Pictured above)

Jan Warren-Rucker, Clemmons, North Carolina

When I need a different weeknight meal, I pull out this salad recipe. To make it in record time, I use fully cooked chicken strips, jarred mango, bottled vinaigrette and packaged shredded cheese.

    2 cups chopped peeled mangoes
    1 medium red onion, chopped
  1/2 cup chopped sweet red pepper
  1/4 cup minced fresh cilantro
    1 jalapeno pepper, seeded and chopped
    2 tablespoons lime juice
    2 packages (9 ounces *each*) ready-to-use grilled chicken breast strips
    2 garlic cloves, minced
    2 teaspoons ground cumin
    1 teaspoon onion powder
    1 teaspoon chili powder
  1/4 teaspoon cayenne pepper
Dash salt
    2 tablespoons olive oil
    2 packages (8 ounces *each*) ready-to-serve European blend salad greens
  1/3 cup oil and vinegar salad dressing
    2 cups (8 ounces) shredded pepper Jack cheese
Tortilla chips

For salsa, in a large bowl, combine the first six ingredients; chill until serving. In a large skillet, saute the chicken, garlic, cumin, onion powder, chili powder, cayenne and salt in oil until chicken is heated through.

brown sugar, mustard, lemon juice, soy sauce, Liquid Smoke if desired and seasonings. Pour over venison. Cover and cook on high for 4-1/2 to 5 hours or until meat is tender.

Remove the roast; set aside to cool. Strain sauce and return to slow cooker. Shred meat, using two forks; stir into sauce and heat through. Using a slotted spoon, spoon meat mixture onto each bun. **Yield:** 14-18 servings.

FRESH MOZZARELLA TOMATO SALAD
(Pictured above)

Regina Wood, Mackenzie, British Columbia

It will only take you a few minutes to prepare this attractive salad and have it ready when a hungry bunch is coming in to eat. Basil is the finishing touch.

    3 medium tomatoes, sliced
    8 ounces fresh mozzarella cheese, thinly
      sliced
1/4 cup olive oil
    2 tablespoons minced fresh basil
1/4 teaspoon salt
1/4 teaspoon coarsely ground pepper

Alternate tomato and cheese slices on a platter. Drizzle with oil; sprinkle with the basil, salt and pepper. Serve immediately. **Yield:** 6 servings.

SLICING TOMATOES

The best way to cut through the skin of a tomato is with a serrated, not straight-edged, knife. Cut a tomato vertically, from stem end to blossom end, for slices that will be less juicy and hold their shape better.

SAUSAGE AND KALE SOUP
(Pictured below)

Dawn Rohn, Riverton, Wyoming

This is my family's absolute favorite soup, and I can have it on the table in 30 minutes. I usually double the recipe, as the flavors blend and make the soup even better the next day.

    3 medium Yukon Gold *or* red potatoes,
      chopped
    2 medium onions, chopped
    2 tablespoons olive oil
    1 pound fresh kale, trimmed and torn
    4 garlic cloves, minced
    1 carton (32 ounces) chicken broth
    1 pound smoked kielbasa *or* Polish
      sausage, cut into 1/4-inch slices
    1 can (15 ounces) garbanzo beans *or*
      chickpeas, rinsed and drained
    1 can (14-1/2 ounces) diced tomatoes,
      undrained
    2 bay leaves
1/4 teaspoon salt
1/4 teaspoon pepper

In a Dutch oven over medium-low heat, cook potatoes and onions in oil for 5 minutes, stirring occasionally. Add kale and garlic; cover and cook for 2-3 minutes or until kale is wilted.

Add the remaining ingredients. Bring to a boil. Reduce heat; cover and simmer for 9-12 minutes or until potatoes are tender. Discard bay leaves. **Yield:** 14 servings (3-1/2 quarts).

GREEN CHILI CHICKEN SANDWICHES
(Pictured below)

Paula Morigeau, Hot Springs, Montana

I enjoyed a sandwich similar to this in a restaurant and decided to try making it at home. The spicy chicken is a quick-and-easy alternative to hamburgers.

    4 boneless skinless chicken breast halves
      (4 ounces *each*)
  2/3 cup soy sauce
  1/4 cup cider vinegar
    2 tablespoon sugar
    2 teaspoons canola oil
    1 can (4 ounces) whole green chilies,
      drained and sliced lengthwise
    4 slices Pepper Jack cheese *or*
      Monterey Jack cheese
    4 kaiser *or* sandwich rolls, split

Flatten chicken to 1/4-in. thickness. Place in a large resealable plastic bag. In a bowl, combine the soy sauce, vinegar, sugar and oil. Set aside 1/4 cup for basting. Pour remaining marinade over chicken; seal bag and turn to coat. Refrigerate for 30 minutes.

Drain and discard marinade from chicken. Grill chicken, uncovered, over medium heat for 3 minutes. Turn and baste with reserved marinade; grill 3 minutes longer or until no longer pink. Top each with a green chili and cheese slice; cover and grill for 2 minutes longer or until cheese is melted. Serve on rolls. **Yield:** 4 servings.

RAINBOW PASTA SALAD
(Pictured above)

Benjamin and Sue Ellen Clark, Warsaw, New York

This colorful salad is hearty enough to be a light meal in itself. It's a great make-ahead dish, since the full flavors of the herbs and veggies need a little time to allow them to blend together.

    2 packages (12 ounces *each*)
      tricolor spiral pasta
    2 packages (16 ounces *each*) frozen
      California-blend vegetables, thawed
    2 pints grape tomatoes
    1 large zucchini, halved and thinly sliced
    1 large yellow summer squash, quartered
      and thinly sliced
    1 large red onion, finely chopped
    1 block (8 ounces) cheddar cheese, cubed
    1 block (8 ounces) Monterey Jack cheese,
      cubed
    2 packages (4 ounces *each*) crumbled
      tomato and basil feta cheese
    1 bottle (16 ounces) Italian salad dressing
    3 tablespoons minced fresh parsley
    1 tablespoon minced fresh basil
    1 teaspoon Italian seasoning
    1 teaspoon seasoned salt
  1/2 teaspoon pepper
    1 can (3.8 ounces) sliced ripe olives,
      drained
Grated Romano cheese, optional

Cook pasta according to package directions. Rinse with cold water; drain well. In two large bowls, combine the California vegetables, tomatoes, zucchini, yellow squash, onion, cheeses and pasta.

In a small bowl, combine the salad dressing, parsley, basil, Italian seasoning, seasoned salt and pepper. Pour over the pasta mixture; toss to coat. Stir in olives. Cover and refrigerate for 8 hours or overnight.

Toss before serving. Serve with Romano cheese if desired. **Yield:** 36 servings.

SWEET POTATO WALDORF SALAD
(Pictured below)

Lois Jeffery, Chesterland, Ohio

I came up with this recipe when I promised to bring a potato salad to a picnic but had no regular potatoes on hand. The sweet potatoes were there, so I revised my regular potato salad recipe and a new dish was born! Adding the apples was an extra touch, and everybody loved it. This version has been scaled down and is perfect for two.

    1 small sweet potato
    1 medium apple, cubed
    1/4 cup chopped celery
    2 tablespoons chopped walnuts
    2 tablespoons golden raisins
    2 tablespoons miniature marshmallows
    2 tablespoons mayonnaise
    2 tablespoons sour cream
    1/2 teaspoon lemon juice
Leaf lettuce, optional

Place the sweet potato in a small saucepan and cover with water. Bring to a boil. Reduce heat; cover and cook for 20 minutes or just until tender. Drain and cool completely.

Peel the potato and cut into cubes; place in a small bowl. Add the apple, celery, walnuts, raisins and marshmallows. In another bowl, combine the

mayonnaise, sour cream and lemon juice; pour over salad and toss gently. Cover and refrigerate for at least 1 hour.

Serve on lettuce-lined plates if desired. **Yield:** 2 servings.

HOMINY MEATBALL STEW
(Pictured above)

Diane Tennison, Lafayette, Louisiana

This stew is tasty served with crackers as well as corn bread, and it freezes well. For a less spicy version, substitute plain canned tomatoes for the Mexican blend.

    1 egg, lightly beaten
    1/2 cup cornmeal
    1/4 cup finely chopped onion
    1/2 teaspoon salt
    1/8 teaspoon pepper
    1 pound ground beef
    2 tablespoons canola oil
    2 cans (15-1/2 ounces *each*) hominy, rinsed and drained
    2 cans (14-1/2 ounces *each*) Mexican diced tomatoes, undrained
    2 cans (8 ounces *each*) tomato sauce
    2 cups water
    1 envelope taco seasoning

In a large bowl, combine the egg, cornmeal, onion, salt and pepper. Crumble beef over mixture and mix well. Shape into 3/4-in. balls. In a large skillet over medium heat, brown meatballs in oil in batches. Drain.

In a Dutch oven, combine the hominy, tomatoes, tomato sauce, water and taco seasoning. Cover and bring to a boil. Reduce heat; add meatballs. Cover and simmer for 30-40 minutes or until meat is no longer pink. **Yield:** 8 servings (2-1/2 quarts).

The Best Burgers in Town

THERE'S NOTHING quite like biting into a juicy burger to satisfy your hunger pains. Recipes for every taste and style of burger, from meatless to turkey, are right here.

***

BURGERS WITH GARDEN SAUCE

Debbie Buchholz, Amherst, New York

In western New York where I grew up, even the sunniest summer day can quickly turn ugly. So Mom came up with this recipe for burgers that are cooked indoors.

    1 large onion, diced
    2 medium carrots, diced
    1 medium green pepper, diced
    2 celery ribs, diced
    1 tablespoon minced fresh parsley
    1 tablespoon canola oil
    2 pints cherry tomatoes
1/2 cup ketchup
    2 tablespoons brown sugar
    2 tablespoons lemon juice
    2 tablespoons cider vinegar
    2 tablespoons prepared mustard
    1 tablespoon Worcestershire sauce
Salt and pepper to taste
BURGERS:
    4 slices bread
1/2 cup water
    2 eggs, lightly beaten
    1 medium onion, finely chopped
    2 teaspoons minced fresh parsley
    1 teaspoon salt
1/2 teaspoon pepper
    2 pounds ground beef
    8 sandwich rolls, split

In a Dutch oven, saute onion, carrots, green pepper, celery and parsley in oil until vegetables are tender. Add tomatoes, ketchup, sugar, lemon juice, vinegar, mustard, Worcestershire sauce, salt and pepper. Cover and simmer for 1-1/2 hours.

Meanwhile, soak bread in water; squeeze dry and crumble into a large bowl. Add the eggs, onion, parsley, salt and pepper. Crumble beef over mixture and mix well. Shape into eight patties.

Broil or pan-fry until a meat thermometer reads 160° and meat is no longer pink; drain. Add to sauce. Cover and simmer for 10 minutes or until heated through. Serve with rolls. **Yield:** 8 servings.

***

MUSHROOM BURGERS
(Pictured below)

Denise Hollebeke, Penhold, Alberta

Ready to turn over a new burger? I guarantee no one will miss the beef after they've tasted these vegetarian burgers. They're moist, tender and full of flavor.

    2 eggs, beaten
    2 cups finely chopped fresh mushrooms
1/2 cup dry bread crumbs
1/2 cup shredded cheddar cheese
1/2 cup finely chopped onion
1/4 cup all-purpose flour
1/2 teaspoon salt
1/4 teaspoon dried thyme
1/4 teaspoon pepper
    1 tablespoon vegetable oil
    4 whole wheat hamburger buns, split

In a large bowl, combine the first nine ingredients. Shape into four patties. In a large skillet, cook the patties in the oil over medium heat for 3 min-

utes on each side or until crisp and lightly browned. Serve on buns. **Yield:** 4 servings.

■■■■■■■■■■■■■■

RANCH TURKEY BURGERS

(Pictured above)

Sandy Umber, Springdale, Arkansas

A chopped jalapeno gives this interesting turkey burger a bit of a kick. Every bite is flavorful and cheesy. Top it off with ranch dressing sauce, and it's the best thing under a bun.

> 5 ounces sharp cheddar cheese, diced
> 1 small sweet onion, diced
> 4 teaspoons chili powder
> 1 jalapeno pepper, seeded, finely chopped
> 2 teaspoons ground cumin
> 2 garlic cloves, minced
> 3/4 teaspoon salt
> 1/4 teaspoon pepper
> 1-1/4 pounds ground turkey
> 3 tablespoons olive oil
> 1/4 cup sour cream
> 4-1/2 teaspoons prepared ranch salad dressing
> 4 hamburger buns, split

In a large bowl, combine the first eight ingredients. Crumble turkey over mixture and mix well. Shape into four patties; brush with oil.

Grill on a greased indoor grill for 2-3 minutes on each side or until a meat thermometer reads 165° and juices run clear. Meanwhile, combine sour cream and salad dressing. Serve burgers on buns with sauce. **Yield:** 4 servings.

Editor's Note: When cutting hot peppers, disposable gloves are recommended. Avoid touching your face.

■■■■■■■■■■■■■■

OPEN-FACED HAMBURGERS

(Pictured below)

Lois Sonderleiter, Port Ludlow, Washington

This kid-friendly recipe is one of my favorites. A Swedish friend passed it on to me when we worked together in Iowa.

> 1 cup (4 ounces) shredded cheddar cheese
> 1/4 cup chopped green pepper
> 1 tablespoon evaporated milk
> 1 tablespoon Dijon mustard
> 1 teaspoon salt
> 1 pound lean ground beef
> 3 hamburger buns, split
> 1 tablespoon butter, softened

In a large bowl, combine the cheese, green pepper, milk, mustard and salt. Crumble beef over mixture and mix well; shape into six patties.

Spread cut sides of buns with butter; top each with a patty. Bake on a baking sheet at 450° for 14-17 minutes or until a meat thermometer reads 160° and juices run clear. **Yield:** 6 servings.

LUNCHEON SALAD
(Pictured above)

Mrs. Leon Schleusener, Tomah, Wisconsin

Living In the heart of cranberry country, it is easy to stock up on cranberries, which are the key ingredients for this salad. If you can't find cranberry gelatin, raspberry or other red-colored flavors work, too.

- 2 cups orange juice, *divided*
- 1 cup water
- 2 packages (3 ounces *each*) cranberry gelatin
- 1 can (16 ounces) whole-berry cranberry sauce
- 1 can (15-1/4 ounces) sliced peaches, drained
- 3 cups cubed cooked chicken
- 2 celery ribs, chopped
- 1/2 cup mayonnaise
- 1 tablespoon cider vinegar
- 1/2 teaspoon salt
- 1/8 teaspoon pepper

Lettuce leaves
- 1/4 cup coarsely chopped pecans

In a small saucepan, bring 1 cup orange juice and water to a boil. Place gelatin in a large bowl; add juice mixture and stir until dissolved. Stir in the remaining orange juice. Chill until partially set, about 1-1/2 hours.

Stir in cranberry sauce. Pour into a 6-cup ring mold coated with cooking spray. Cover and refrigerate for 6 hours or overnight.

Set aside a few peach slices for garnish; cube the remaining peaches. In a large bowl, combine the cubed peaches, chicken, celery, mayonnaise, vinegar, salt and pepper. Cover and refrigerate for 1 hour or until chilled.

Invert gelatin mold onto a serving plate; line center of ring with lettuce leaves. Stir pecans into chicken salad; spoon into center of gelatin. Top with reserved peach slices. **Yield:** 10 servings.

ITALIAN STEW
(Pictured below)

Lorinda Pearson, Green Valley, Arizona

My niece shared this tasty dish with me, and whenever I have served it, I get requests for the recipe. The sausage, tortellini, tomatoes, zucchini and herbs make it different from typical stews that feature meat and potatoes. It's a robust one-dish meal that's simple to prepare.

- 1 pound bulk Italian sausage
- 1 small onion, chopped
- 1 garlic clove, minced
- 3 cups beef broth
- 1 can (14-1/2 ounces) stewed tomatoes, cut up
- 1 can (8 ounces) tomato sauce
- 1 medium carrot, thinly sliced
- 1 teaspoon dried basil
- 1 teaspoon dried oregano
- 1 package (9 ounces) refrigerated cheese tortellini
- 1 small zucchini, sliced
- 1/3 cup chopped green pepper
- 2 tablespoons minced fresh parsley

Grated Parmesan cheese

In a large saucepan or Dutch oven, cook sausage and onion over medium heat until meat is no longer pink; drain. Add garlic; cook and stir for 2 minutes. Stir in the broth, tomatoes, tomato sauce, carrot, basil and oregano. Bring to a boil. Reduce heat; simmer, uncovered, for 30 minutes.

Gently stir in the tortellini, zucchini, green pepper and parsley. Cover and simmer for 20-25 minutes or until tortellini is tender. Serve with Parmesan cheese. **Yield:** 6-8 servings (2 quarts).

GRILLED DELI SANDWICHES

(Pictured above)

Pat Stevens, Granbury, Texas

This outstanding sourdough sandwich is packed with a variety of deli meats, crispy bacon, two kinds of cheeses and sauteed vegetables. It's hearty enough to be a meal itself.

   1 medium onion, sliced
   1 cup sliced fresh mushrooms
   1 cup julienned green pepper
   1 cup julienned sweet red pepper
   2 tablespoons canola oil
  12 slices sourdough bread
 1/2 pound *each* thinly sliced deli ham,
     smoked turkey and pastrami
   6 bacon strips, cooked and crumbled
   6 slices process American cheese
   6 slices Swiss cheese

In a large skillet, saute the onion, mushrooms and peppers in oil until tender. Layer six bread slices with ham, turkey, pastrami, bacon, vegetables and cheeses; top with remaining bread. Wrap each sandwich in foil.

  Grill the sandwiches, covered, over medium heat for 4-5 minutes on each side or until heated through. **Yield:** 6 servings.

ZESTY GAZPACHO

Frances Dawson, Orlando, Florida

When I have a taste for something different, or something with a "zip," this soup always hits the spot.

   2 cans (28 ounces *each*) whole tomatoes
   1 medium cucumber, peeled, seeded and
     cut into chunks
   1 medium green pepper, cut into chunks
   1 small onion, cut into chunks
 1/3 cup red wine vinegar
   2 slices rye bread, cubed
   3 tablespoons olive oil
 1/2 teaspoon salt
 1/2 teaspoon garlic powder
 1/4 teaspoon pepper
 1/4 teaspoon hot pepper sauce

Drain the tomatoes, reserving juice. In a blender, cover and process the tomatoes, cucumber, green pepper and onion in batches until chopped. Transfer to a large bowl.

  Place the vinegar, bread cubes and reserved tomato juice in blender; cover and process until smooth. Pour over vegetable mixture. Stir in the oil, salt, garlic powder, pepper and pepper sauce. Cover and refrigerate for 1-2 hours before serving. **Yield:** 8 servings (2 quarts).

CURRIED TURKEY VEGETABLE SOUP
(Pictured below)

Virginia Anthony, Jacksonville, Florida

Chock-full of veggies, this aromatic soup has just the right hint of curry to give it a wonderful taste. It's a delicious way to use leftover turkey.

✓ This recipe includes Nutrition Facts and Diabetic Exchanges.

   2 medium onions, chopped
   2 tablespoons canola oil
   2 to 3 tablespoons all-purpose flour
   1 teaspoon curry powder
   3 cups reduced-sodium chicken broth
   1 cup diced red potatoes
   1 celery rib, sliced
 1/2 cup thinly sliced fresh carrot
   2 tablespoons minced fresh parsley
1-1/2 teaspoons minced fresh sage
   2 cups cubed cooked turkey breast
1-1/2 cups fat-free half-and-half
   1 package (9 ounces) fresh baby spinach, coarsely chopped
 1/4 teaspoon salt
 1/4 teaspoon pepper

In a Dutch oven, saute the onions in oil until tender. Stir in the flour and curry until blended. Gradually stir in broth. Add the potatoes, celery, carrot, parsley and sage. Bring to a boil. Reduce heat; cover and simmer for 10-12 minutes or until the vegetables are tender.

Stir in turkey, half-and-half, spinach, salt and pepper. Cook and stir until spinach is wilted and soup is heated. **Yield:** 6 servings (2 quarts).

Nutrition Facts: 1-1/3 cups equals 219 calories, 6 g fat (1 g saturated fat), 40 mg cholesterol, 534 mg sodium, 20 g carbohydrate, 3 g fiber, 20 g protein. **Diabetic Exchanges:** 2 very lean meat, 1 starch, 1 vegetable, 1 fat.

LEMON ARTICHOKE ROMAINE SALAD
(Pictured above)

Kathleen Law, Pullman, Washington

Fresh and vibrant, this signature side dish is my version of a crisp, lemony Caesar salad. It's unusual, healthy, great tasting and a "must" for warm-weather gatherings.

10 cups torn romaine
 4 plum tomatoes, sliced
 1 can (14 ounces) water-packed artichoke hearts, rinsed, drained and quartered
 1 can (2-1/4 ounces) sliced ripe olives, drained
 3 tablespoons water
 3 tablespoons lemon juice
 3 tablespoons olive oil
 2 garlic cloves, minced
 1 teaspoon salt
 1 teaspoon coarsely ground pepper
1/3 cup shredded Parmesan cheese

In a large salad bowl, combine the romaine, tomatoes, artichokes and olives. In a jar with a tight-fitting lid, combine the water, lemon juice, oil, garlic, salt and pepper; shake well. Pour over the salad and toss to coat. Sprinkle with cheese. **Yield:** 8 servings.

THREE-POTATO SALAD

Pamela Hershey, Parkesburg, Pennsylvania

This picnic-perfect potato salad is among the most popular in our deli. The addition of sweet potato and dill add great flavor.

 3 medium potatoes, peeled
 3 medium red potatoes, peeled
 1 large sweet potato, peeled and halved
 1 cup mayonnaise
 2 tablespoons sugar
 1 tablespoon white vinegar
 1 teaspoon salt
 3/4 teaspoon dill weed
 1/2 teaspoon pepper
 1 medium sweet onion, chopped

Place potatoes in a large saucepan and cover with water. Bring to a boil. Reduce heat; cover and cook for 30-40 minutes or until potatoes are just tender.

Meanwhile, in a small bowl, whisk the mayonnaise, sugar, vinegar, salt, dill and pepper. Drain the potatoes; cube and place in a large serving bowl. Cool slightly. Add onion and dressing; stir gently to coat. Cover and refrigerate for 2 hours or overnight. **Yield:** 12 servings.

CHICKEN SALAD POCKETS

Donna Poole, Marysville, Kansas

A nicely seasoned dressing gives plenty of herb flavor to these delicious sandwiches. The colorful filling is a great way to use up leftover chicken.

 2 cups cubed cooked chicken breast
 1 medium cucumber, seeded and chopped
 1 medium tomato, seeded and chopped
 3 green onions, thinly sliced
1/4 cup lemon juice
 3 tablespoons canola oil
 2 garlic cloves, minced
 1 teaspoon sugar
1/2 to 1 teaspoon dried basil
 2 cups shredded red leaf lettuce *or* romaine
 6 pita breads (6 inches), halved

In a large bowl, combine the chicken, cucumber, tomato and onions. In a small bowl, combine lemon juice, oil, garlic, sugar and basil. Pour over the chicken mixture and toss to coat. Cover and refrigerate for 2 hours.

Just before serving, add lettuce and toss to coat. Spoon about 1/2 cup into each pita half. **Yield:** 4 servings.

TOMATO SOUP WITH CHEESE TORTELLINI

(Pictured below)

Susan Peck, Republic, Missouri

Tortellini gives this unique tomato soup stick-to-your-ribs goodness. It's a staple on my table.

✓ This recipe includes Nutrition Facts and Diabetic Exchanges.

 1 large onion, chopped
 1 tablespoon butter
 2 pounds plum tomatoes, seeded and quartered
 3 cups reduced-sodium chicken broth *or* vegetable broth
 1 can (8 ounces) tomato sauce
 1 tablespoon minced fresh basil
1/4 teaspoon salt
Dash pepper
 1 cup dried cheese tortellini
1/3 cup shredded Parmesan cheese

In a large saucepan, saute onion in butter until tender. Add the tomatoes, broth, tomato sauce, basil, salt and pepper. Bring to a boil. Reduce heat; cover and simmer for 30 minutes. Cool slightly.

Cook the tortellini according to package directions; drain well and set aside. In a blender, cover and process the soup in batches until smooth. Return to the saucepan; add tortellini and heat through. Garnish with the Parmesan cheese. **Yield:** 8 servings (2 quarts).

Nutrition Facts: 1-1/3 cups equals 114 calories, 4 g fat (2 g saturated fat), 14 mg cholesterol, 609 mg sodium, 15 g carbohydrate, 2 g fiber, 6 g protein. **Diabetic Exchanges:** 2 vegetable, 1/2 starch, 1/2 fat.

CHEDDAR 'N' PEA TOSSED SALAD
(Pictured above)

Mandy Cmoc, Yorkton, Saskatchewan

My family says, "Yes!" when they see me preparing this easy no-cook side. We live on a farm...so in summer, our garden is a handy source for veggie salad ingredients.

    5 cups ready-to-serve salad greens
    1 medium cucumber, sliced
    1 medium tomato, chopped
    1 cup cubed cheddar cheese
    1/2 cup frozen peas, thawed
    2 tablespoons canola oil
    1 tablespoon white vinegar
    1/4 teaspoon sugar
    1/8 teaspoon onion powder
Dash salt and pepper

In a large bowl, combine the salad greens, cucumber, tomato, cheese and peas.

In a jar with a tight-fitting lid, combine the oil, vinegar, sugar, onion powder, salt and pepper; shake well. Drizzle over salad and toss gently. **Yield:** 8 servings.

FRESH & CRISP GREENS

To keep your salad greens extra crisp, after washing them, remove the water (a salad spinner works great) and transfer them to a serving bowl. Place a dampened paper towel over the top of the greens and refrigerate until serving.

HOT ITALIAN PATTIES
(Pictured below)

Brenda Jackson, Garden City, Kansas

I've been making these spicy and satisfying sandwiches for more than a dozen years. On occasion, I substitute country sausage for the Italian sausage, and they taste just as good. Served with a zesty sauce for dipping, they're my family's favorite.

    1 can (8 ounces) tomato sauce
    1/4 teaspoon dried basil
    1/4 teaspoon crushed red pepper flakes
    1/8 teaspoon garlic powder
    1 pound bulk Italian sausage
    1 medium onion, thinly sliced and
        separated into rings
    8 slices part-skim mozzarella cheese
    8 slices French bread (3/4 inch thick)
    1/4 to 1/2 cup butter, softened

In a saucepan, combine the tomato sauce, basil, red pepper flakes and garlic powder. Bring to a boil over medium heat. Reduce the heat; simmer for 15 minutes.

Meanwhile, shape sausage into four thin oval patties. In a skillet over medium heat, cook patties until no longer pink; remove and keep warm.

In the drippings, saute onion until tender. Place a slice of cheese on four slices of bread; layer each with a sausage patty, onion and remaining cheese. Top with remaining bread. Butter the outsides of sandwiches. On a griddle or in a large skillet, toast over medium heat until both sides are golden brown and cheese is melted. Serve with herbed tomato sauce for dipping. **Yield:** 4 servings.

LENTIL SOUP

(Pictured above)

Dorothy Webb, Estacada, Oregon

Legume lovers can easily fill up on this delectable and substantial soup without expanding their waistlines. Lentils lend taste and texture to the filling dish.

✓ This recipe includes Nutrition Facts and Diabetic Exchanges.

- 2 cups sliced fresh carrots
- 2 celery ribs, chopped
- 1 large onion, chopped
- 1 garlic clove, minced
- 2 tablespoons butter
- 7 cups reduced-sodium chicken broth *or* vegetable broth
- 1-1/2 cups dried lentils, rinsed
- 3 tablespoons medium pearl barley
- 1-1/2 cups chopped fresh tomatoes
- 2 tablespoons lemon juice
- 4-1/2 teaspoons molasses
- 1 tablespoon red wine vinegar
- 1/2 teaspoon pepper

Dash *each* dried thyme, basil and oregano

In a Dutch oven, saute the carrots, celery, onion and garlic in butter until crisp-tender. Add the broth, lentils and barley; bring to a boil. Reduce heat; cover and simmer for 25-30 minutes or until lentils and barley are almost tender.

Stir in remaining ingredients. Bring to a boil. Reduce heat; cover and simmer for 15 minutes or until the lentils and barley are tender. **Yield:** 8 servings (2 quarts).

Nutrition Facts: 1 cup equals 219 calories, 3 g fat (2 g saturated fat), 8 mg cholesterol, 601 mg sodium, 35 g carbohydrate, 14 g fiber, 14 g protein. **Diabetic Exchanges:** 2 starch, 1 lean meat, 1 vegetable, 1/2 fat.

NEXT-GENERATION GERMAN POTATO SALAD

(Pictured below)

Mary Shivers, Ada, Oklahoma

My quick-cooking German-style potato salad is a keeper for family reunions. Balsamic vinegar and bacon give it a different flavor twist.

- 4 pounds small red potatoes, quartered
- 10 bacon strips, chopped
- 1 large onion, chopped
- 3 tablespoons chopped celery
- 2 tablespoons chopped green pepper
- 1 tablespoon all-purpose flour
- 1 tablespoon sugar
- 1 teaspoon salt
- 1/2 teaspoon pepper
- 1 cup water
- 1/3 cup white balsamic vinegar

Place the potatoes in a Dutch oven and cover with water. Bring to a boil. Reduce heat; cover and simmer for 15-20 minutes or until tender.

Meanwhile, in a large skillet, cook bacon over medium heat until crisp. Using a slotted spoon, remove to paper towels. In the drippings, saute the onion, celery and green pepper until tender. Stir in the flour, sugar, salt and pepper until blended. Combine water and vinegar; stir into vegetable mixture. Bring to a boil; cook and stir for 2 minutes or until thickened.

Drain potatoes and place in a large serving bowl. Pour dressing over potatoes. Add bacon and toss to coat. Serve warm or at room temperature. Refrigerate leftovers. **Yield:** 14 servings.

BLT TORTILLAS
(Pictured below)

Darla Wester, Meriden, Iowa

I first sampled these tasty tortillas at a bridal lunch-eon years ago. Now I frequently make them for our weekly neighborhood dinners.

✓ This recipe includes Nutrition Facts and Diabetic Exchanges.

    1/2 cup mayonnaise
    1/2 cup sour cream
      2 tablespoons ranch salad dressing mix
    1/4 teaspoon crushed red pepper flakes
      8 flour tortillas (8 inches), room
         temperature
     16 bacon strips, cooked and drained
      2 to 3 cups shredded lettuce
      2 cups chopped tomato
Green and sweet red pepper strips, optional

In a large bowl, combine the mayonnaise, sour cream, salad dressing and red pepper flakes; spread on tortillas. Layer with the bacon, lettuce and tomato. Top with peppers if desired. Roll up the tortillas. **Yield:** 8 servings.

Nutrition Facts: 1 tortilla (prepared with fat-free mayonnaise and sour cream and three strips of green pepper) equals 232 calories, 9 g fat (0 saturated fat), 12 mg cholesterol, 511 mg sodium, 28 g carbohydrate, 0 fiber, 9 g protein.
Diabetic Exchanges: 1-1/2 starch, 1 vegetable, 1 fat, 1/2 meat.

CHIPOTLE BUTTERNUT SQUASH SOUP
(Pictured above)

Roxanne Chan, Albany, California

Using herbs and vegetables from the garden along with convenient pantry items makes this satisfying soup easy and fast to fix. Your family will devour it.

      2 cups diced peeled butternut squash
      1 small carrot, finely chopped
      1 green onion, sliced
      2 garlic cloves, minced
    1/2 teaspoon ground cumin
      1 tablespoon olive oil
      2 cups vegetable broth, *divided*
      1 can (14-1/2 ounces) diced tomatoes,
         undrained
      1 package (3 ounces) cream cheese,
         cubed
    1/4 cup minced fresh basil
      1 chipotle pepper in adobo sauce, chopped
      1 can (15 ounces) black beans, rinsed
         and drained
      1 can (11 ounces) Mexicorn, drained
      2 cups fresh baby spinach

In a large saucepan, saute the squash, carrot, onion, garlic and cumin in oil for 10 minutes. Add 1-1/2 cups broth; bring to a boil. Reduce heat. Cover and simmer for 10-12 minutes or until vegetables are tender; cool slightly.

Transfer the mixture to a blender; add the tomatoes, cream cheese, basil, chipotle pepper and remaining broth. Cover and process for 1-2 minutes or until smooth.

Return to the saucepan; stir in beans, corn and spinach. Cook and stir until spinach is wilted and soup is heated through. **Yield:** 5 servings.

Editor's Note: If garnish is desired, sprinkle butternut squash seeds with 1/8 teaspoon salt. Place on a baking sheet. Bake at 350° for 10-13 minutes or until golden brown.

GRANDMA'S POTATO SALAD

Karla Retzer, Grantsburg, Wisconsin

Our family get-togethers wouldn't be complete without this picnic-style potato salad. I get nothing but raves when I make it. Everyone agrees it's the best they've ever tasted.

- 10 pounds salad potatoes, cubed and cooked
- 12 hard-cooked eggs, chopped
- 4 celery ribs, chopped
- 5 radishes, sliced
- 1 medium onion, chopped
- 1/3 cup chopped green pepper
- Salt and pepper to taste
- 6 cups mayonnaise
- 1/4 cup packed brown sugar
- 1 tablespoon sugar
- 1-1/2 teaspoons vanilla extract
- 1/2 teaspoon prepared mustard
- 1/2 cup milk
- Leaf lettuce
- Paprika
- Minced fresh parsley

In a large bowl, combine the potatoes, eggs, celery, radishes, onion, green pepper, salt and pepper. In another large bowl, combine the mayonnaise, both sugars, vanilla and mustard. Stir in the milk. Pour over the potato mixture; gently toss to coat. Chill overnight.

Serve in a lettuce-lined bowl. Sprinkle with paprika and parsley. **Yield:** 6 quarts.

SPINACH SALAD WITH RED CURRANT DRESSING

Kaaren Yaku, Seattle, Washington

This pretty salad can be put together in less than 20 minutes. It adds lots of color to the table, and the sweet-tart dressing is a wonderful complement to the spinach and fruit.

- 1/4 cup red currant jelly
- 3 tablespoons red wine vinegar
- 8 cups torn fresh spinach
- 1 can (11 ounces) mandarin oranges, drained
- 1 cup sliced fresh strawberries
- 2 green onions, thinly sliced

For the dressing, in a small saucepan, cook and stir the jelly and vinegar over medium heat for 1-2 minutes or until melted and smooth. Cool completely.

Just before serving, in a large salad bowl, combine the spinach, oranges, strawberries and onions. Drizzle with dressing; toss to coat. **Yield:** 12 servings.

SEAFOOD SALAD PITAS

(Pictured below)

Linda Evancoe-Coble, Leola, Pennsylvania

You can make this lovely and interesting sandwich as a great, light lunch…it's so tasty and colorful. Or pair it with a hearty soup for a change-of-pace supper.

☑ This recipe includes Nutrition Facts and Diabetic Exchanges.

- 2 cups chopped imitation crabmeat (about 10 ounces)
- 1/2 pound cooked medium shrimp, peeled, deveined and chopped (about 1 cup)
- 2 celery ribs, chopped
- 1/2 cup thinly sliced green onions
- 3/4 cup fat-free mayonnaise
- 3/4 teaspoon seafood seasoning
- 1/4 teaspoon salt
- 1/8 teaspoon pepper
- 4 whole wheat pita breads (6 inches), halved

In a large bowl, combine the crab, shrimp, celery and onions. In a small bowl, combine mayonnaise, seafood seasoning, salt and pepper. Pour over the crab mixture; toss to coat. Cover and refrigerate for at least 2 hours. Spoon into pita halves. **Yield:** 8 servings.

Nutrition Facts: 1 filled pita half equals 162 calories, 2 g fat (trace saturated fat), 27 mg cholesterol, 755 mg sodium, 28 g carbohydrate, 3 g fiber, 10 g protein. **Diabetic Exchanges:** 2 starch, 1 very lean meat.

SWEET POTATO AND PEAR SOUP

(Pictured above)

Cristy Shank, Summersville, West Virginia

I'm a family physician who loves to try new recipes. This tasty cold-weather soup has garnered many warm compliments from my family and friends. They rave over it.

1-3/4 pounds sweet potatoes (about
    4 medium), peeled and cubed
1-3/4 cups water
   1 teaspoon salt, *divided*
1/4 teaspoon ground cinnamon
   2 large pears, peeled and sliced
   1 large onion, chopped
   2 tablespoons butter
1/2 cup white grape juice
   1 cup half-and-half cream
1/4 teaspoon white pepper

In a large saucepan, combine the sweet potatoes, water, 3/4 teaspoon salt and cinnamon. Bring to a boil. Reduce the heat; simmer, uncovered, for about 20 minutes.

Meanwhile, in another large saucepan, cook and stir the pears and onion in butter over medium heat for 5 minutes. Stir in the grape juice; bring to a boil. Reduce heat; simmer, uncovered, for 5 minutes. Stir into the sweet potato mixture. Cool slightly.

In a blender, cover and puree soup in batches; return to the pan. Stir in the cream, pepper and remaining salt; heat through (do not boil). **Yield:** 5 servings.

APPLE TUNA SANDWICHES

(Pictured below)

Ivy Eresmas, Dade City, Florida

My husband and his buddies love to pack these tasty sandwiches when they go on fishing trips. The tangy tuna salad gets fun flavor from sweet pickle relish and lots of crunch from chopped apples, celery and walnuts. The satisfying sandwiches are a complete meal in themselves.

☑ This recipe includes Nutrition Facts and Diabetic Exchanges.

1/3 cup fat-free mayonnaise
1/4 cup finely chopped celery
1/4 cup finely chopped walnuts
   2 tablespoons finely chopped onion
   1 tablespoon sweet pickle relish
   1 teaspoon sugar
1/4 teaspoon salt
   1 can (6 ounces) light water-packed
     tuna, drained
1/2 cup chopped red apple
   6 slices reduced-calorie bread, toasted
   6 lettuce leaves

In a large bowl, combine the first seven ingredients; stir in tuna and apple. Spread 1/2 cup tuna mixture on three slices of bread. Top with lettuce and remaining bread. **Yield:** 3 servings.

Nutrition Facts: 1/2 cup (calculated without bread) equals 201 calories, 9 g fat (0 saturated fat), 21 mg cholesterol, 237 mg sodium, 18 g carbohydrate, 3 g fiber, 12 g protein. **Diabetic Exchanges:** 2 starch, 2 lean meat.

AVOCADO TOMATO SALAD
(Pictured above)

Ginger Burow, Fredericksburg, Texas

This simple, colorful salad combines fresh tomatoes with avocados. It goes great with any kind of Mexican food, and it makes a wonderful appetizer when spooned on a toasted baguette.

    4 cups chopped tomatoes
  1/2 cup chopped green pepper
  1/4 cup chopped onion
  1/2 teaspoon salt
  1/8 teaspoon pepper
    2 medium ripe avocados, peeled
      and cubed
    1 tablespoon lime juice

In a large bowl, combine the tomatoes, green pepper, onion, salt and pepper. Place the avocados in another bowl; sprinkle with lime juice and toss gently to coat. Fold into tomato mixture. Serve immediately. **Yield:** 6-8 servings.

PEACH-ALMOND SPINACH SALAD

Freia Koenig, Grindrod, British Columbia

Fresh peaches and grapes, along with a citrus dressing, enliven this spinach salad. And, it goes together quickly, so you can spend more time enjoying summer.

      1 cup mayonnaise
    1/2 cup orange juice concentrate
    1/4 teaspoon ground cinnamon
      1 package (9 ounces) fresh baby spinach
      8 large fresh mushrooms, sliced
  1-1/2 cups sliced peeled peaches
      1 cup seedless red grapes, halved
      4 ounces Gruyere cheese, shredded
    1/4 cup sliced almonds, toasted

In a small bowl, whisk the mayonnaise, orange juice concentrate and cinnamon until blended. Cover and refrigerate until serving.

Arrange spinach on 12 salad plates. Top with the mushrooms, peaches, grapes, cheese and almonds. Serve with dressing. **Yield:** 12 servings.

DOUBLE-CHEESE BEEF PANINI
(Pictured below)

Lisa Huff, Clive, Iowa

Nothing beats a piping hot panini when it comes to a speedy, satisfying lunch or supper. Blue cheese and horseradish give my family-approved sandwich zip.

  1/3 cup mayonnaise
  1/4 cup crumbled blue cheese
    2 teaspoons prepared horseradish
  1/8 teaspoon pepper
    1 large sweet onion, thinly sliced
    1 tablespoon olive oil
    8 slices white bread
    8 slices provolone cheese
    8 slices deli roast beef
    2 tablespoons butter, softened

In a small bowl, combine the mayonnaise, blue cheese, horseradish and pepper; set aside. In a large skillet, saute onion in oil until tender.

Spread the mayonnaise mixture over one side of each slice of bread. On four slices, layer one piece of cheese, two slices of roast beef, sauteed onion and another piece of cheese; top with the remaining bread.

Spread butter over both sides of sandwiches. Cook on a panini maker or indoor grill for 2-3 minutes or until bread is browned and cheese is melted. **Yield:** 4 servings.

Chill-Chasing Chowders

CLASSIC CLAM CHOWDER will never go out of style, but there's more to this traditional soup than meets the eye. Here are five chowder recipes to tickle the soup-lover's fancy.

New England Clam Chowder

Rosann Mcwherter, Dublin, California

While vacationing in New England, I enjoyed a yummy clam chowder. At home, I created this shortcut.

    1 can (10-3/4 ounces) condensed New
        England clam chowder, undiluted
1-1/3 cups milk
    1 can (6-1/2 ounces) chopped clams,
        drained
    2 tablespoons sherry *or* chicken broth
    1 tablespoon butter
Shredded cheddar cheese, optional

In a large saucepan, combine the first five ingredients. Bring to a boil. Reduce heat; cover and simmer for 5 minutes. Sprinkle with the cheese if desired. **Yield:** 3 servings.

Shrimp Chowder

Michelle Conley, Evanston, Wyoming

This chowder, full of shrimp and vegetables, is hearty, but the skim milk helps to keep it light.

      1 pound red potatoes, peeled and cubed
  2-1/2 cups reduced-sodium chicken broth
      3 celery ribs, chopped
      8 green onions, chopped
    1/2 cup chopped sweet red pepper
  1-1/2 cups fat-free milk
    1/4 cup all-purpose flour
    1/2 cup fat-free evaporated milk
  1-1/2 pounds uncooked medium shrimp,
        peeled and deveined
      2 tablespoons minced fresh parsley
    1/2 teaspoon paprika
    1/2 teaspoon Worcestershire sauce

1/8 teaspoon cayenne pepper
1/8 teaspoon pepper

In a large saucepan, bring potatoes, broth, celery, onions and red pepper to a boil. Reduce heat; cover and simmer for 13-15 minutes or until the vegetables are tender. Stir in milk. Gently mash the vegetables, leaving some chunks of potatoes.

Combine flour and evaporated milk until smooth; gradually stir in potato mixture. Bring to a boil; cook and stir for 2 minutes or until thickened. Stir in the remaining ingredients. Return to a boil. Cook and stir for 2-3 minutes or until shrimp turn pink. **Yield:** 8 servings.

Wild Rice and Ham Chowder

(Pictured below)

Elma Friesen, Winnipeg, Manitoba

The warm, comforting taste of this chowder appeals to everyone who tries it. I have my younger sister to thank for sharing this recipe with me years ago.

    1/2 cup chopped onion
      2 garlic cloves, minced
    1/4 cup butter, cubed
      6 tablespoons all-purpose flour
    1/2 teaspoon salt
    1/4 teaspoon pepper
      4 cups chicken broth
  1-1/2 cups cubed peeled potatoes

1/2 cup chopped carrot
1 bay leaf
1/2 teaspoon dried thyme
1/4 teaspoon ground nutmeg
3 cups cooked wild rice
2-1/2 cups cubed fully cooked ham
2 cups half-and-half cream
1 can (15-1/4 ounces) whole kernel corn,
    drained
Minced fresh parsley

In a Dutch oven, cook onion and garlic in butter over medium heat until tender. Stir in flour, salt and pepper. Gradually add broth. Bring to a boil. Cook; stir for 2 minutes or until thickened.

Add potatoes, carrot, bay leaf, thyme and nutmeg; return to a boil. Reduce heat; cover and simmer for 30 minutes or until vegetables are tender. Stir in rice, ham, cream and corn; heat through (do not boil). Discard bay leaf. Garnish with parsley. **Yield:** 8-10 servings (2-3/4 quarts).

Reduce heat; add cheese, stirring until melted. Add chicken. Cook and stir over low heat until heated through. **Yield:** 6-8 servings.

CHEESY CHICKEN CHOWDER

Hazel Fritchie, Palestine, Illinois

Even kids like the rich flavor of this chunky chowder. I like to serve it with garlic bread and a salad.

3 cups chicken broth
2 cups diced peeled potatoes
1 cup diced carrots
1 cup diced celery
1/2 cup diced onion
1-1/2 teaspoons salt
1/4 teaspoon pepper
1/4 cup butter, cubed
1/3 cup all-purpose flour
2 cups milk
2 cups (about 8 ounces) shredded
    cheddar cheese
2 cups diced cooked chicken

In a 4-quart saucepan, bring chicken broth to a boil. Reduce heat; add the potatoes, carrots, celery, onion, salt and pepper. Cover and simmer for 12-15 minutes or until vegetables are tender.

Meanwhile, melt the butter in a medium saucepan; stir in flour until smooth. Gradually stir in milk. Bring to a boil over medium heat; cook and stir for 2 minutes or until thickened.

CORN CHOWDER WITH DUMPLINGS

(Pictured above)

Shannon Kohn, Simpsonville, South Carolina

This is a spicy version of my favorite corn chowder that my husband has declared as "awesome!"

2 large onions, chopped
2 teaspoons canola oil
4 cups chicken broth
3 cups frozen corn
2 cups cubed peeled potatoes
1 cup heavy whipping cream
1 to 3 teaspoons minced chipotle pepper
    in adobo sauce
1/2 teaspoon salt, *divided*
1/2 cup all-purpose flour
1/4 cup yellow cornmeal
1 teaspoon baking powder
1/2 cup milk
1/4 cup shredded cheddar cheese

In a large saucepan, saute onions in oil until tender. Add broth, corn, potatoes, cream, chipotle pepper and 1/2 teaspoon salt. Bring to a boil. Reduce heat; simmer, uncovered, for 3-5 minutes.

For dumplings, combine flour, cornmeal, baking powder and remaining salt. Stir in milk and cheese until moistened. Drop tablespoonfuls onto simmering chowder. Cover; simmer (do not lift lid) for 20 minutes or until a toothpick inserted into dumplings comes out clean. **Yield:** 4 servings.

CHICKEN 'N' FRUIT SALAD

(Pictured above)

Betty Hunter, Salina, Kansas

This salad has been on my menus for more than 20 years. We love it when traveling in the summer in our motor home as it so easy to fix, and we carry most of the ingredients with us. It's also a good dish for potlucks at church and other club groups. Assorted crackers and cheese are compatible accompaniments.

  1 cup cubed cooked chicken *or*
  1 can (5 ounces) chunk white
    chicken, drained
  1 cup green grapes, halved
1/2 cup sliced fresh strawberries
1/4 cup mayonnaise
  2 teaspoons lime juice
1/4 teaspoon honey
1/2 cup sliced ripe banana
  2 lettuce leaves

In a small bowl, combine the chicken, grapes and strawberries. In another bowl, combine the mayonnaise, lime juice and honey. Pour over the chicken mixture; toss to coat. Cover and refrigerate for at least 30 minutes.

Just before serving, stir in banana. Spoon onto lettuce-lined plates. **Yield:** 2 servings.

CARZALIA SWEET ONION SALAD

Connie Johnson, Columbus, New Mexico

This zippy make-ahead sweet onion salad makes a delicious change from coleslaw.

  3 pounds large sweet onions, thinly sliced
  1 cup white vinegar
1/2 cup sugar
1/2 cup water

  3 teaspoons dill weed
  2 teaspoons salt

Place onions in a 13-in. x 9-in. dish. In a small bowl, combine the remaining ingredients; stir until sugar is dissolved. Pour over the onions and toss to coat. Cover and refrigerate for 5 hours, stirring once. Serve with a slotted spoon. **Yield:** 6 cups.

BACON-TOPPED GRILLED CHEESE

(Pictured below)

Nita Crosby, St. George, Utah

Tangy sourdough bread adds a delicious twist to an all-American lunch classic. This robust version gets its heartiness from bacon and extra flavor from the onion, sour cream and oregano.

  4 slices part-skim mozzarella cheese
  8 slices sourdough bread
  2 large tomatoes, thinly sliced
  8 bacon strips, cooked
  4 tablespoons sour cream
  4 tablespoons finely chopped onion
1/4 teaspoon dried oregano
  4 slices cheddar cheese
  2 tablespoons butter, softened

Place mozzarella cheese on four bread slices; layer each with a fourth of the tomato slices, two bacon strips, 1 tablespoon sour cream, 1 tablespoon onion, a pinch of oregano, one slice of cheddar cheese. Top with remaining bread.

Butter outsides of sandwiches. In a small skillet over medium heat, toast sandwiches for 3-4 minutes on each side or until cheese is melted. **Yield:** 4 servings.

Soups, Salads & Sandwiches

1 garlic clove, peeled and halved
2 tablespoons lemon juice
2 tablespoons honey
1/8 teaspoon salt
2 medium ripe pears, thinly sliced
8 cups torn mixed salad greens
1/2 cup chopped walnuts, toasted
1/3 cup crumbled Gorgonzola cheese

Rub garlic clove over the bottom and sides of a large salad bowl; discard garlic. In the bowl, combine the lemon juice, honey and salt. Add pears; gently toss to coat. Add the greens, walnuts and cheese; toss to coat. **Yield:** 6 servings.

SIX-FRUIT SALAD
(Pictured below)

Paula Baglole, Summerside, Prince Edward Island

A refreshing medley of fruits and berries goes into this short and sweet recipe. It's a favorite dessert or side salad. If there's any left, we have it the next morning for breakfast.

2 cups fresh strawberries, quartered
1 cup cubed honeydew
1/2 cup fresh blueberries
1 large apple, chopped
1 large navel orange, peeled and chopped
1 large ripe banana, cut into 1/4-inch slices
1/2 cup orange juice

In a large bowl, combine the fruit. Drizzle with orange juice and stir gently. Serve immediately. **Yield:** 8 servings.

CREAMY ZUCCHINI SOUP
(Pictured above)

Mrs. Thomas Maust, Berlin, Pennsylvania

I serve a lot of zucchini in my home because it is so plentiful. One day I decided to try a new recipe for it, and my family really liked the results.

2 tablespoons chopped onion
3 tablespoons butter
3 tablespoons all-purpose flour
2 cups milk
1 cup water
1 teaspoon chicken bouillon granules
1/2 teaspoon salt
1/4 teaspoon pepper
1 large zucchini, shredded
1 cup (4 ounces) shredded cheddar cheese

In a large saucepan, saute onion in butter until tender. Stir in flour until blended. Gradually stir in the milk, water, bouillon, salt and pepper. Bring to a boil; cook and stir for 2 minutes or until thickened. Add zucchini. Reduce heat; simmer, uncovered, for 10 minutes or until zucchini is tender. Add cheese, stirring until melted. **Yield:** 4 servings.

WINTER SALAD

Lynn Ganser, Oakland, California

I make this salad for special dinners. Everyone loves the flavor combination and interesting textures of the pears, walnuts, greens and Gorgonzola cheese. It's nice for winter when other fruits aren't readily available.

■■■■■■■■■■■■■■

🎀 HERBED RASPBERRY-HAZELNUT SALAD

(Pictured above)

Wendy Matejek, Corpus Christi, Texas

I receive great compliments whenever I serve this salad at parties. It's refreshing and tasty.

    9 cups torn iceberg lettuce
    1 medium red onion, sliced and
      separated into rings
    1 cup chopped fresh parsley
  1/2 cup chopped fresh cilantro
  1/4 cup chopped fresh tarragon
    1 cup raspberry vinaigrette
  1/2 cup fresh raspberries
  1/2 cup chopped hazelnuts

In a large salad bowl, combine the lettuce, onion, parsley, cilantro and tarragon. Add vinaigrette and toss to coat. Top with raspberries and hazelnuts. **Yield:** 9 servings.

■■■■■■■■■■■■■■

REUBEN SANDWICHES

Kathy Jo Scott, Hemingford, Nebraska

My mouth waters just thinking of these reuben sandwiches. I adapted the recipe from one my mother found several years ago.

   12 ounces thinly sliced corned beef
    8 slices light *or* dark rye bread
    1 can (8 ounces) sauerkraut, rinsed and
      well drained
  1/2 cup Thousand Island dressing
    4 slices Swiss cheese
Butter

Arrange the corned beef on four slices of bread. Layer each with a quarter of the sauerkraut, 2 tablespoons of dressing and a slice of cheese. Top with the remaining bread slices. Butter the outsides of sandwiches.

In a large skillet over medium heat, toast the sandwiches until bread is lightly browned on both sides and cheese is melted. **Yield:** 4 servings.

GRILLED VEGGIE TORTILLA WRAPS

(Pictured below)

Marta Northcutt, Lebanon, Tennessee

You do not have to be a vegetarian to appreciate the wholesome goodness of these wraps. The tasty tortillas, stuffed with cream cheese and marinated veggies, will have everyone singing their praises.

 3 tablespoons red wine vinegar
 3 tablespoons olive oil
 1 teaspoon lemon-pepper seasoning
 1 garlic clove, minced
 1/2 teaspoon dried oregano
 1/2 teaspoon dried basil
 2 medium zucchini, cut lengthwise into
  1/4-inch slices
 1 medium yellow summer squash, cut
  lengthwise into 1/4-inch slices
 1 medium sweet red pepper, cut into
  strips
 4 ounces cream cheese, softened
 1 tablespoon prepared pesto
 4 whole wheat tortillas (8 inches),
  warmed

In a large resealable plastic bag, combine the first six ingredients; add zucchini, yellow squash and red pepper. Seal the bag and turn to coat; refrigerate overnight, turning once.

In a small bowl, combine cream cheese and pesto; set aside. Drain and discard marinade. Place vegetables in a grill basket or disposable foil pan with slits cut in the bottom. Grill, covered, over medium-high heat for 3-4 minutes on each side or until tender.

Spread the reserved pesto cream cheese over tortillas; top with vegetables. Fold sides over the filling. Serve immediately. **Yield:** 4 servings.

WILD RICE TURKEY SOUP

(Pictured above)

Barbara Schmid, Cavalier, North Dakota

Turn to this recipe when you want a tuna casserole that's a little different—the horseradish adds extra flavor. This dish is a tried-and-true favorite in our family, and it never fails.

 1 cup uncooked wild rice
 7 cups chicken broth, *divided*
 1/2 pound sliced fresh mushrooms
 1 medium onion, chopped
 1 celery rib, chopped
 1/4 cup butter, cubed
 1/2 cup all-purpose flour
 1/2 teaspoon salt
 1/2 teaspoon ground mustard
 1/2 teaspoon poultry seasoning
 1/4 teaspoon pepper
 4 cups cubed cooked turkey
 2 cups half-and-half cream

In a large saucepan, bring rice and 3 cups broth to a boil. Reduce heat; cover and simmer for 50-60 minutes or until rice is tender.

In a Dutch oven, saute the mushrooms, onion and celery in butter until tender. Stir in flour and seasonings until blended. Gradually add remaining broth. Bring to a boil; cook and stir for 2 minutes or until thickened. Reduce heat. Stir in the turkey, cream and cooked rice; heat through (do not boil). **Yield:** 8 servings (2-3/4 quarts).

ABOUT WILD RICE

A dark-hulled, aquatic grass native to North America, wild rice has a chewy texture and nutty flavor. Grains expand 3 to 4 times their original size. Be sure to rinse before cooking.

Main Dishes

GREEK SPINACH PIZZA
(Pictured at left)

Kay Young, Port Clinton, Ohio

Round out this pizza with a green salad or vegetable relish tray. Sometimes I serve a side of low-fat ranch dressing to dip the veggies and pizza crust into.

  2 cups fresh baby spinach
  3 tablespoons olive oil
  3 teaspoons Italian seasoning
  1 prebaked thin Italian bread shell crust
    (10 ounces)
  2 plum tomatoes, thinly sliced
  1 cup (4 ounces) crumbled feta cheese
1/4 cup shredded part-skim mozzarella
    cheese
1/4 cup chopped pitted Greek olives
  2 tablespoons chopped sweet onion

In a small bowl, toss the spinach, oil and Italian seasoning. Place crust on an ungreased 12-in. pizza pan. Arrange spinach mixture over crust to within 1/2 in. of edge. Place tomatoes on top; sprinkle with the cheeses, olives and onion.

Bake at 450° for 10-15 minutes or until the cheese is melted and edges are lightly browned. **Yield:** 6-8 slices.

HONEY-DIJON PORK TENDERLOIN
(Pictured at left)

Trisha Kruse, Eagle, Idaho

It's hard to believe such an elegant dish is table-ready in half an hour. To cut the prep time, use a food processor to slice the onions and mushrooms. Try mixed vegetables as a quick and easy side dish.

  1 pound pork tenderloin, cut into 1-inch
    slices
1/4 teaspoon salt
1/4 teaspoon pepper
  1 tablespoon olive oil
  1 small onion, chopped
1/2 cup sliced fresh mushrooms
  1 tablespoon butter

  2 garlic cloves, minced
1/2 cup evaporated milk
  2 tablespoons Dijon mustard
  1 tablespoon soy sauce
  1 tablespoon honey
Hot cooked noodles

Flatten pork slices to 1/2-in. thickness; sprinkle with salt and pepper. In a large skillet over medium heat, cook pork in oil in batches until meat is no longer pink. Remove and keep warm.

In the same skillet, saute the onion and mushrooms in butter until tender. Add garlic; saute 1 minute longer. Stir in the evaporated milk, mustard, soy sauce and honey. Return the pork to the pan; heat through. Serve with noodles. **Yield:** 4 servings.

EASY CHICKEN POTPIE
(Pictured at left)

Amy Briggs, Gove, Kansas

Why look for potpie in the frozen food aisle when this easy, homemade version tastes much better? Under its golden-brown crust, you'll find the ultimate comfort food for kids and adults.

  1 medium onion, chopped
  2 tablespoons canola oil
1/2 cup all-purpose flour
  1 teaspoon poultry seasoning
  1 can (14-1/2 ounces) chicken broth
3/4 cup milk
  3 cups cubed cooked chicken
  2 cups frozen mixed vegetables, thawed
  1 sheet refrigerated pie pastry

In a large saucepan, saute the onion in oil until tender. Stir in the flour and poultry seasoning until blended; gradually add the chicken broth and milk. Bring to a boil; cook and stir for 2 minutes or until thickened. Add the chicken and mixed vegetables.

Transfer to a greased 9-in. deep-dish pie plate. Top with pastry. Trim, seal and flute edges. Cut slits in pastry. Bake at 450° for 15-20 minutes or until crust is golden brown and filling is bubbly. **Yield:** 6 servings.

2 cups. Discard vegetables and bay leaves. In a large saucepan over medium heat, melt butter; stir in flour until smooth. Gradually stir in pan juices. Bring to a boil; cook and stir for 2 minutes or until thickened. Stir in lemon juice and hot pepper sauce. Serve gravy with roast. **Yield:** 14-16 servings.

Editor's Note: Ask your butcher to tie two 3-pound chuck roasts together to form a rolled chuck roast.

CARROT CAKE PANCAKES

Leane Goering, Salem, Indiana

Here's a way for fans of carrot cake to have their favorite dessert for breakfast. These delicate, decadent pancakes are drizzled with sweet, spicy maple syrup that complements the sour cream and nut topping.

        2 cups pancake mix
        1 teaspoon ground cinnamon
      1/4 teaspoon ground nutmeg
      1/8 teaspoon ground cloves
        2 eggs
        1 cup milk
        1 cup finely shredded carrots
CINNAMON SYRUP:
        1 cup maple syrup
        2 tablespoons butter
      1/4 teaspoon ground cinnamon
        1 carton (4 ounces) whipped cream
           cheese
      1/2 cup chopped pecans *or* walnuts

In a large bowl, combine the pancake mix, cinnamon, nutmeg and cloves. In a small bowl, beat eggs and milk; stir into the dry ingredients just until moistened. Stir in carrots.

Pour batter by 1/4 cupfuls onto a greased hot griddle. Turn pancakes when bubbles form on top; cook until second side is golden brown.

For syrup, in a small saucepan, combine the maple syrup, butter and cinnamon. Bring to a boil. Reduce heat; simmer for 2 minutes. Serve pancakes with cream cheese and syrup; sprinkle with nuts. **Yield:** 1 dozen (1 cup syrup).

SAVORY POT ROAST

(Pictured above)

Lee Leuschner, Calgary, Alberta

This old-fashioned pot roast with smooth pan gravy evokes memories of dinners at Mom's or Grandma's. My husband and I used to raise cattle, so I prepared a lot of beef, and this is the best.

        1 rolled boneless beef chuck roast
           (6 pounds)
        2 tablespoons canola oil
Salt and coarsely ground pepper
        1 large onion, coarsely chopped
        2 medium carrots, coarsely chopped
        1 celery rib, coarsely chopped
        2 cups water
        1 can (14-1/2 ounces) beef broth
        2 bay leaves
GRAVY:
      1/4 cup butter, cubed
      1/4 cup all-purpose flour
        1 teaspoon lemon juice
        4 to 5 drops hot pepper sauce

In a large skillet over medium-high heat, brown the roast in oil on all sides. Transfer to a large roasting pan; season with salt and pepper. Add the onion, carrots and celery.

In a large saucepan, bring the water, broth and bay leaves to a boil. Pour over the roast and vegetables. Cover and bake at 350° for 2-1/2 to 3 hours or until meat is tender, turning once.

Remove roast to a serving platter and keep warm. For gravy, strain pan juices, reserving

Main Dishes

FETTUCCINE WITH MUSHROOMS AND TOMATOES

(Pictured below)

Phyllis Schmalz, Kansas City, Kansas

To perk up a plate of fettuccine, get "saucy" with mushrooms! I can toss this dish together in 30 minutes on a busy weeknight. And it's elegant enough to serve as a vegetarian entree for guests.

    1 package (12 ounces) fettuccine
    1 pound fresh mushrooms, halved
    1 large onion, chopped
    1 large green pepper, chopped
    4 garlic cloves, minced
    1 teaspoon olive oil
    3 tablespoons all-purpose flour
    3 cups 1% milk
    1 teaspoon salt
  1/4 teaspoon pepper
  1/2 cup sun-dried tomatoes (not packed
        in oil), thinly sliced
    1 cup (4 ounces) shredded reduced-fat
        Swiss cheese
  1/4 cup grated Parmesan cheese

Cook fettuccine according to package directions. Meanwhile, in a large nonstick skillet, saute the mushrooms, onion, green pepper and garlic in oil for 4-6 minutes or until vegetables are tender.

In a small bowl, combine the flour, milk, salt and pepper until smooth; gradually stir into mushroom mixture. Add the tomatoes. Bring to a boil; cook and stir for 2 minutes or until thickened. Stir in cheeses. Drain fettuccine; toss with sauce. **Yield:** 6 servings.

MEATBALLS STROGANOFF

(Pictured above)

Nancy Carnes, Clearwater, Minnesota

This is one of my most loved, old recipes from my mother. I like to serve it over egg noodles.

    1 egg, lightly beaten
  1/2 cup soft bread crumbs
    2 tablespoons chopped onion
  1/2 teaspoon celery salt
  1/4 teaspoon dried marjoram
  1/8 teaspoon garlic salt
  1/8 teaspoon pepper
    1 pound ground beef
    2 tablespoons all-purpose flour
    1 tablespoon canola oil
    1 can (10-3/4 ounces) condensed cream
        of mushroom soup, undiluted
  3/4 cup water
  1/3 cup sour cream
Hot cooked egg noodles

In a large bowl, combine the first seven ingredients. Crumble beef over mixture and mix well. Shape into 1-1/2-in. balls. Place flour in a large resealable plastic bag; add meatballs, a few at a time, and shake to coat.

In a large skillet, brown meatballs in oil in batches. Drain; return to the pan. Combine soup and water; pour over meatballs. Bring to a boil. Reduce heat; cover and simmer for 20-25 minutes or until meat is no longer pink, stirring occasionally. Stir in sour cream; heat through (do not boil). Serve with noodles. **Yield:** 4 servings.

BEEF POTPIE
(Pictured below)

Lucile Cline, Wichita, Kansas

Filling and comforting, this meat pie is a delicious way to put leftover roast beef to use. Grated onion adds a nice flavor to the pie crust.

- 1/4 cup *each* chopped onion, green pepper and sweet red pepper
- 2 garlic cloves, minced
- 1 tablespoon canola oil
- 3 cups cubed cooked roast beef
- 2 cups frozen cubed hash brown potatoes
- 1 can (10-3/4 ounces) condensed cream of mushroom soup, undiluted
- 1 package (10 ounces) frozen corn
- 1 jar (4-1/2 ounces) sliced mushrooms, drained
- 1 teaspoon Worcestershire sauce
- 1/8 teaspoon salt
- Dash pepper

ONION PASTRY:
- 2-1/2 cups all-purpose flour
- 1-1/4 teaspoons salt
- 1 cup butter-flavored shortening
- 4 teaspoons grated onion
- 4 to 5 tablespoons cold water

In a large skillet, saute the onion, peppers and garlic in oil for 3 minutes. Stir in the beef, potatoes, soup, corn, mushrooms, Worcestershire sauce, salt and pepper. Bring to a boil. Reduce heat; cover and simmer for 10 minutes.

For pastry, combine flour and salt in a large bowl. Cut in shortening until crumbly; sprinkle with onion. Gradually add water, tossing with a fork until dough forms a ball.

Divide the dough in half so that one ball is slightly larger than the other. On a lightly floured surface, roll out larger ball to fit a 9-in. deep-dish pie plate.

Transfer pastry to plate; trim even with edge. Add filling. Roll out remaining pastry to fit top of pie; place over filling. Trim, seal and flute edges. Cut slits in top.

Bake at 375° for 45-50 minutes or until filling is bubbly and crust is golden brown. Let stand for 15 minutes before cutting. **Yield:** 8 servings.

CHICKEN WITH CHERRY SAUCE

Phyllis Knight, Ocean Park, Washington

I look forward to having fresh Bing cherries every summer. I always freeze some so I can serve this simple, tasty dish all year-round.

- 1/3 cup all-purpose flour
- 1 teaspoon salt
- 6 boneless skinless chicken breast halves (6 ounces *each*)
- 1/4 cup butter, cubed
- 3/4 cup sugar
- 3/4 cup orange juice
- 1/4 cup chopped onion
- 1 teaspoon grated orange peel
- 1/4 teaspoon ground ginger
- 1/4 teaspoon ground cinnamon
- 1-1/2 cups pitted fresh *or* frozen dark sweet cherries, thawed
- 2 teaspoons cornstarch
- 1 tablespoon water

In a large resealable plastic bag, combine flour and salt. Add chicken, one piece at a time, and shake to coat. In a large skillet over medium heat, brown chicken in butter on both sides. Remove from heat.

In a large saucepan, combine the sugar, orange juice, onion, orange peel, ginger and cinnamon. Bring to a boil; cook for 5 minutes or until slightly reduced and sugar is dissolved, stirring occasionally. Remove from the heat; stir in cherries.

Pour the sauce over chicken. Cover and cook over low heat for 30-35 minutes or until a meat thermometer reads 170°.

Remove chicken to a serving platter; keep warm. Combine cornstarch and water until smooth; stir into the sauce. Bring to a boil; cook and stir for 1-2 minutes or until thickened. Serve with chicken. **Yield:** 6 servings (2 cups sauce).

━━━━━━━━━━━━━

LEMONY VEGETABLES AND PASTA
(Pictured above)

C. Erin Renouf Mylroie, Santa Clara, Utah

This refreshing pasta dish is done in just 30 minutes. Its simplicity and flavor combinations are typical of authentic Italian cuisine. Buon appetito!

1 pound fresh asparagus, trimmed and cut into 1-inch pieces
1 medium sweet red pepper, cut into 1-inch pieces
1 medium red onion, sliced
1 tablespoon olive oil
1/2 teaspoon salt
1/4 teaspoon pepper
4-1/2 cups uncooked bow tie pasta
1 tablespoon butter
1 tablespoon all-purpose flour
3 garlic cloves, minced
1/4 teaspoon crushed red pepper flakes
1 cup vegetable broth
1 cup shredded Parmesan cheese
1/2 cup sour cream
2 tablespoons lemon juice
1 tablespoon grated lemon peel
1/2 cup chopped pistachios
1/4 cup fresh basil leaves, thinly sliced
Additional shredded Parmesan cheese

In a large bowl, combine the asparagus, red pepper, red onion, oil, salt and pepper. Transfer to a greased 15-in. x 10-in. x 1-in. baking pan. Bake at 450° for 10-15 minutes or until golden brown, stirring once.

Meanwhile, cook the pasta according to package directions. In a large saucepan, melt butter over medium heat. Stir in the flour, garlic and pepper flakes until blended. Whisk in the broth until blended. Bring to a boil over medium-high heat; cook and stir for 2 minutes or until thickened and bubbly.

Reduce heat. Stir in cheese, sour cream, lemon juice and peel; heat through. Drain pasta; place in a large bowl. Add cheese sauce and asparagus mixture; toss to coat. Sprinkle with pistachios, basil and additional cheese. **Yield:** 7 servings.

CHICKEN 'N' CORN BREAD BAKE
(Pictured above)

Ann Hillmeyer, Sandia Park, New Mexico

Here's southern comfort food at its best! This casserole is delicious made with chicken or turkey. It's often on the menu when I cook for my husband, our four children, their spouses and our 10 grandkids.

2-1/2 cups reduced-sodium chicken broth
   1 small onion, chopped
   1 celery rib, chopped
 1/8 teaspoon pepper
4-1/2 cups corn bread stuffing mix, **divided**
   4 cups cubed cooked chicken
1-1/2 cups (12 ounces) sour cream
   1 can (10-3/4 ounces) condensed cream
     of chicken soup, undiluted
   3 green onions, thinly sliced
 1/4 cup butter, cubed

In a large saucepan, combine the broth, onion, celery and pepper. Bring to a boil. Reduce heat; cover and simmer for 5-6 minutes or until the vegetables are tender. Stir in 4 cups stuffing mix.

Transfer to a greased 13-in. x 9-in. baking dish. Top with chicken. In a small bowl, combine the sour cream, soup and green onions. Spread over chicken. Sprinkle with remaining stuffing mix; dot with butter.

Bake, uncovered, for 325° for 25-30 minutes or until heated through. **Yield:** 8 servings.

BUFFALO-STUFFED BELL PEPPERS

Marlene Groves, Kiowa, Colorado

I serve these peppers, stuffed with ground buffalo meat, with an Italian salad for a complete meal.

   4 large green, sweet yellow *or* red peppers
   1 egg
1-1/2 cups meatless spaghetti sauce, *divided*
 1/4 cup chopped onion
   1 teaspoon Italian seasoning
 1/2 cup dry bread crumbs
 1/2 cup shredded Italian cheese blend,
     divided
   1 pound ground buffalo

Cut tops off peppers and remove seeds. In a large kettle, cook peppers in boiling water for 3-5 minutes. Drain and rinse in cold water; set aside.

In a large bowl, combine the egg, 1/2 cup spaghetti sauce, onion, Italian seasoning, bread crumbs and 1/4 cup cheese. Crumble buffalo over mixture and mix well. Spoon into peppers. Place in a greased 3-qt. baking dish. Top with the remaining spaghetti sauce.

Cover and bake at 350° for 55-60 minutes or until a meat thermometer reads 160°. Uncover; sprinkle with remaining cheese. Bake 5 minutes longer or until cheese is melted. **Yield:** 4 servings.

OVEN-FRIED PARMESAN CHICKEN
(Pictured below)

Bessie Suffield, Florence, Kansas

Everyone will call you a gourmet cook when you fix this nicely seasoned chicken. You don't have to tell them how easy it is to prepare!

   6 tablespoons butter, melted
   5 tablespoons dry bread crumbs
   3 tablespoons grated Parmesan cheese
   3 tablespoons cornmeal
 3/4 teaspoon salt

3/4 teaspoon dried oregano
1/4 teaspoon garlic powder
1 broiler/fryer chicken (3 to 4 pounds),
    cut up

Place butter in a shallow bowl. In another shallow bowl, combine the bread crumbs, Parmesan cheese, cornmeal, salt, oregano and garlic powder. Dip chicken in butter, then roll in crumb mixture.

Place in a greased 15-in. x 10-in. x 1-in. baking pan. Bake, uncovered, at 375° for 40-45 minutes or until juices run clear. **Yield:** 4 servings.

SAVORY ORANGE SALMON
(Pictured above)
Roseanne Turner, Denver, Indiana

Citrus sauce adds zip to this succulent salmon. You can pair it with anything from steamed broccoli to stunning yellow saffron rice.

2 garlic cloves, minced
1 teaspoon fennel seed
1 teaspoon olive oil
4 salmon fillets (1 inch thick and
    4 ounces *each*)
1/2 teaspoon salt
1 cup orange juice

In a large nonstick skillet coated with cooking spray, cook the garlic and fennel seed in oil for 2 minutes. Sprinkle salmon with salt; add to skillet. Top with orange juice. Bring to a boil. Reduce heat; cover and simmer for 8-12 minutes or until fish flakes easily with a fork.

Remove the salmon and keep warm. Simmer sauce, uncovered, for 6-9 minutes or until slightly thickened. Spoon over fillets. **Yield:** 4 servings.

OVER-THE-TOP MAC 'N' CHEESE
(Pictured below)
Connie McDowell, Greenwood, Delaware

This popular dish is the ultimate macaroni and cheese recipe. It makes a beautiful entree or even a special side. I added it to our Thanksgiving dinner, and it received rave reviews.

1 package (16 ounces) elbow macaroni
2 ounces Muenster cheese, shredded
1/2 cup *each* shredded mild cheddar, sharp
    cheddar and Monterey Jack cheese
1/2 cup plus 1 tablespoon butter, *divided*
2 cups half-and-half cream
2 eggs, lightly beaten
1 cup cubed process cheese (Velveeta)
1/4 teaspoon seasoned salt
1/8 teaspoon pepper

Cook macaroni according to package directions. Meanwhile, in a small bowl, combine the Muenster, mild cheddar, sharp cheddar and Monterey Jack cheeses; set aside.

In a large saucepan, melt 1/2 cup butter over medium heat. Stir in the cream, eggs, process cheese, seasoned salt, pepper and 1-1/2 cups of the cheese mixture. Drain pasta; add to cheese sauce and stir to coat.

Transfer to a greased 2-1/2-qt. baking dish. Sprinkle with remaining cheese mixture and dot with remaining butter. Bake, uncovered, at 350° for 40-45 minutes or until bubbly and golden brown. **Yield:** 7 servings.

Bright Breakfasts

EVEN IF the weather's cloudy, your morning menu will shine when you prepare these delightful dishes. From hearty eggs to rich pancakes, they make extra-special ways to start the day!

▪▪▪▪▪▪▪▪▪▪▪▪▪

CALICO PEPPER FRITTATA

(Pictured below)

Loretta Kelcinski, Kunkletown, Pennsylvania

My garden-fresh frittata has all-day appeal. I serve it for breakfast, brunch, lunch or dinner with crispy Italian bread. It's made in a skillet, so there's no need to heat up the oven.

☑ This recipe includes Nutrition Facts and Diabetic Exchanges.

  1 medium green pepper, chopped
  1 medium sweet red pepper, chopped
  1 jalapeno pepper, seeded and chopped
  1 medium onion, chopped
  1 garlic clove, minced
  1 tablespoon olive oil
  5 eggs
1-1/4 cups egg substitute
  1 tablespoon grated Romano cheese
1/2 teaspoon salt
1/8 teaspoon pepper

In a large nonstick skillet, saute peppers, onion and garlic in oil until crisp-tender. In a large bowl, whisk eggs and egg substitute. Pour into skillet. Sprinkle with cheese, salt and pepper.

As the eggs set, lift edges, letting uncooked portion flow underneath. Cook until eggs are completely set, about 8-10 minutes. Cut into wedges. **Yield:** 4 servings.

Editor's Note: When cutting hot peppers, disposable gloves are recommended. Avoid touching your face.

Nutrition Facts: 1 wedge equals 201 calories, 10 g fat (3 g saturated fat), 268 mg cholesterol, 559 mg sodium, 10 g carbohydrate, 2 g fiber, 17 g protein. **Diabetic Exchanges:** 2 lean meat, 2 vegetable, 1 fat.

▪▪▪▪▪▪▪▪▪▪▪▪▪

LEMON RICOTTA PANCAKES

Jackie Carberry, Centerville, Indiana

Light and lemony, these decadent pancakes are perfect sprinkled with sugar and drizzled with syrup.

  1 cup plus 2 tablespoons all-purpose flour
  1 teaspoon baking powder
1/2 teaspoon salt
1/4 teaspoon ground nutmeg
  3 eggs, lightly beaten
1-1/2 cups ricotta cheese
1/2 cup milk
1/2 cup canola oil
  3 tablespoons lemon juice
  2 teaspoons grated lemon peel
Confectioners' sugar and maple syrup

In a small bowl, combine the flour, baking powder, salt and nutmeg. In another bowl, combine the eggs, ricotta cheese, milk, oil, lemon juice and peel. Stir into the dry ingredients just until combined.

Pour batter by 1/4 cupful onto a hot griddle; turn when bubbles form on top. Cook until the second side is golden brown. Sprinkle with confectioners' sugar; serve with syrup. **Yield:** 1 dozen.

near center of quiche comes out clean. Let stand for 5 minutes before cutting. Serve warm. Refrigerate leftovers. **Yield:** 6 servings.

TOMATO AND CHEESE STRATA

(Pictured below)

Molly Seidel, Edgewood, New Mexico

This is a great make-ahead dish for any meal. It's delicious! Everyone who tries it asks for the recipe.

 10 slices white bread
  4 medium tomatoes, sliced 1/2 inch thick
  1 cup (4 ounces) shredded cheddar cheese
  4 green onions, thinly sliced
  4 eggs
  2 cups milk
 1/2 teaspoon salt

Line a greased 8-in. square baking dish with four bread slices. Layer with half of the tomatoes, cheese and onions. Top with remaining bread (slices will overlap). Layer with the remaining tomatoes, cheese and onions.

In a small bowl, whisk the eggs, milk and salt. Pour over top. Cover and refrigerate overnight.

Remove from refrigerator 30 minutes before baking. Bake, uncovered, at 350° for 45-50 minutes or until a knife inserted near the center comes out clean. Let stand for 5 minutes before cutting. **Yield:** 4-6 servings.

CRUSTLESS FOUR-CHEESE QUICHE

(Pictured above)

Susan Anderson, Park City, Utah

My husband is a real meat lover, but this luscious quiche is one meatless recipe he likes. In fact, he'll even go to the grocery store and bring home Jarlsberg cheese as a hint that he's craving it.

 1/4 cup butter
 1/4 cup all-purpose flour
 3/4 cup milk
1-1/4 cups 4% cottage cheese
 1/2 teaspoon baking powder
 1/2 teaspoon ground mustard
 1/4 teaspoon salt
  5 eggs
  2 packages (3 ounces *each*) cream cheese, cubed
 1/2 pound Jarlsberg *or* Swiss cheese, shredded
 1/4 cup grated Parmesan cheese

In a small saucepan, melt butter. Stir in flour until smooth; gradually add milk. Bring to a boil; cook and stir for 2 minutes or until thickened and bubbly. Remove from heat; cool for 15 minutes.

Meanwhile, in a small bowl, combine the cottage cheese, baking powder, mustard and salt. In a large bowl, beat eggs. Slowly beat in the cream cheese, cottage cheese mixture and white sauce until smooth. Fold in the Jarlsberg and Parmesan.

Pour into a greased 9-in. pie plate. Bake at 350° for 35-40 minutes or until a knife inserted

OMELET WEDGES WITH CHEESE SAUCE

(Pictured below)

Amy Transue, Catasauqua, Pennsylvania

Our kids can't wait for supper when these fluffy, layered omelets are on the menu. I round it out with toast or muffins and a fresh fruit salad.

    6 eggs, *separated*
    1/2 teaspoon salt
    1/4 cup cornstarch
    Dash pepper
    1/3 cup water
    SAUCE:
      1 tablespoon butter
      1 tablespoon cornstarch
      1/4 teaspoon salt
    Dash pepper
      1 cup milk
      2 cups (8 ounces) shredded cheddar cheese

In a small bowl, beat egg whites and salt until stiff peaks form. In a large bowl, beat cornstarch, egg yolks and pepper until lemon-colored. Add water; mix well. Fold in egg whites.

Pour into two greased 9-in. pie plates. Bake at 350° for 15 minutes or until a knife inserted near the center comes out clean.

Meanwhile, in a small saucepan, melt butter. Stir in the cornstarch, salt and pepper until smooth. Gradually add milk. Bring to a boil; cook and stir for 2 minutes or until thickened. Reduce heat; stir in cheese until melted.

To serve, cut each omelet into six wedges. Stack two wedges on each serving plate with cheese sauce drizzled between and on top. **Yield:** 6 servings.

CAJUN PEPPER STEAK

(Pictured above)

Ronald Treadway, Acworth, Georgia

The seasonings in this recipe turn beef into a zesty dish you'll want to enjoy again and again.

    1-1/2 pounds boneless beef top round steak, cubed
      2 tablespoons butter
      2 medium onions, halved and sliced
      2 medium green peppers, julienned
      1 medium sweet red pepper, julienned
      1 celery rib, sliced
    1-1/2 cups water
      4 teaspoons Worcestershire sauce
      1 tablespoon chili powder
      1 tablespoon soy sauce
    1/2 to 1 teaspoon Cajun seasoning
    1/4 teaspoon hot pepper sauce, optional
      2 tablespoons cornstarch
      2 tablespoons cold water
    Hot cooked egg noodles *or* rice

In a large skillet, brown beef in butter over medium heat; drain. Stir in the onions, peppers and celery; cook and stir for 2 minutes.

Add the water, Worcestershire sauce, chili powder, soy sauce, Cajun seasoning and pepper sauce if desired. Bring to a boil. Reduce heat; cover and simmer for 1 to 1-1/2 hours or until meat is tender.

Combine cornstarch and cold water until smooth; stir into meat mixture. Bring to a boil; cook and stir for 2 minutes or until thickened. Serve with noodles or rice. **Yield:** 4 servings.

Main Dishes

CALYPSO BURRITOS
(Pictured below)

Darlene Deeg, Vernon, British Columbia

When building a burrito, I use a bounty of beans, veggies, cheese and salsa. My husband doesn't notice he's not getting meat. Serve them with sour cream, chopped tomatoes and avocado...and save any leftovers as a topping for a taco salad.

    2 small zucchini, shredded
    2 medium carrots, shredded
    1 medium onion, finely chopped
    1 tablespoon canola oil
    1 can (16 ounces) kidney beans, rinsed
      and drained
    1 can (15 ounces) black beans, rinsed
      and drained
1-1/2 cups frozen corn, thawed
  3/4 cup salsa
    2 tablespoons reduced-sodium taco
      seasoning
    2 teaspoons ground cumin
    1 cup (4 ounces) shredded part-skim
      mozzarella cheese
  1/4 cup minced fresh cilantro
    8 flour tortillas (8 inches), warmed

In a large skillet over medium heat, cook and stir the zucchini, carrots and onion in oil for 3-5 minutes or until tender. Stir in the beans, corn, salsa, taco seasoning and cumin. Cook and stir for 5-7 minutes or until vegetables are tender.

Remove from the heat. Stir in cheese and cilantro. Spoon about 2/3 cup filling off center on each tortilla. Fold sides and ends over filling and roll up. **Yield:** 8 servings.

MEXICAN PORK ROAST
(Pictured above)

Chuck Allen, Dana Point, California

A friend who lives in Mexico shared this recipe with me several years ago. There they cooked the pork roast in a clay pot in a slow oven, but I found it works very well in a slow cooker, too.

    2 medium onions, sliced
    2 medium carrots, sliced
    2 jalapeno peppers, seeded and chopped
    3 garlic cloves, minced
    2 tablespoons olive oil
  1/2 cup water
  1/2 cup chicken broth
    1 teaspoon ground coriander
  1/2 teaspoon salt
  1/2 teaspoon ground cumin
  1/2 teaspoon dried oregano
  1/4 teaspoon pepper
    1 boneless pork shoulder roast
      (3 pounds)

In a large skillet, saute the onions, carrots, jalapenos and garlic in oil for 3 minutes. Transfer to a 5-qt. slow cooker; add water and broth.

In a small bowl, combine the coriander, salt, cumin, oregano and pepper; rub over the pork roast. Cut roast in half; place in the slow cooker. Cover and cook on low for 8-9 hours or until meat is tender.

Transfer the roast and vegetables to a serving platter; keep warm. Strain cooking juices and skim fat. Pour into a small saucepan. Bring to a boil; cook until liquid is reduced to about 1 cup. Serve with roast and vegetables. **Yield:** 8 servings.

Editor's Note: When cutting hot peppers, disposable gloves are recommended. Avoid touching your face.

■■■■■■■■■■■■

ROASTED PEPPER CHICKEN PENNE

(Pictured above)

Regina Cowles, Boulder, Colorado

My husband calls me an aerobic cook because I can make this Italian dish in just 30 minutes. No one will accuse you of cutting corners. It tastes like it's been simmering deliciously for hours.

> 1 pound boneless skinless chicken
>   breasts, cut into 1-inch strips
> 1/4 cup balsamic vinegar
> 1 package (16 ounces) penne pasta
> 1 medium onion, sliced
> 3 garlic cloves, sliced
> 1/4 cup olive oil
> 1 can (28 ounces) crushed tomatoes
> 1 cup roasted sweet red peppers, drained
>   and sliced
> 1 cup chicken broth
> 3 teaspoons Italian seasoning
> 1/4 teaspoon salt
> 1 cup shredded Parmesan cheese

Place chicken in a large resealable plastic bag; add vinegar. Seal bag and turn to coat; refrigerate for 15 minutes.

Cook pasta according to package directions. Meanwhile, in a large skillet, saute onion and garlic in oil for 1 minute. Drain and discard the vinegar. Add the chicken to skillet; cook for 4-5 minutes or until meat is no longer pink.

Stir in the tomatoes, red peppers, broth, Italian seasoning and salt. Bring to a boil over medium heat; cook and stir for 4-5 minutes or until heated through. Drain pasta; toss with the chicken mixture. Sprinkle with the Parmesan cheese. **Yield:** 8 servings.

■■■■■■■■■■■■

OLD-FASHIONED GLAZED HAM

(Pictured below)

Barbara Dalton, Clark, South Dakota

The fruit juices combine with the smoky ham liquid to make a sweet gravy for this impressive entree. My family looks forward to seeing it on the table every Easter and Christmas.

> 1/2 fully cooked bone-in ham
>   (6 to 7 pounds)
> 2 tablespoons whole cloves
> 1 cup packed brown sugar
> 2/3 cup orange juice
> 1/2 cup unsweetened pineapple juice
> 1/3 cup maraschino cherry juice

Place the ham on a rack in a shallow foil-lined roasting pan. Score the surface of the ham, making diamond shapes 1/2 in. deep; insert a clove into each diamond. Cover; bake at 325° for 2 hours.

Meanwhile, in a small saucepan, bring the brown sugar and juices to a boil. Reduce heat; simmer, uncovered, for 30 minutes or until glaze is reduced to 1 cup.

Baste the ham with 1/3 cup glaze. Bake, uncovered, 25-35 minutes longer or until a meat thermometer reads 140°, basting with the remaining glaze every 10 minutes. Let stand for 15 minutes before slicing. **Yield:** 8-10 servings.

KIELBASA AND PEPPER CASSEROLE

(Pictured below)

Sara Wilson, Middlebourne, West Virginia

This recipe makes for an easy and tasty home-cooked dinner. A crisp, green salad and a loaf of French bread are the perfect side dishes.

- 1/2 pound smoked kielbasa *or* Polish sausage, cut into 1/2-inch slices
- 4 small red potatoes, halved
- 1 medium onion, halved and sliced
- 1 medium sweet red pepper, cut into 1-inch pieces
- 2 tablespoons olive oil
- 1/8 teaspoon salt
- 1/8 teaspoon pepper
- 1/4 cup heavy whipping cream

Minced fresh parsley

In a small bowl, combine the sausage, potatoes, onion and red pepper. Drizzle with oil; sprinkle with salt and pepper. Toss to coat. Transfer to a greased 1-qt. baking dish.

Cover and bake at 375° for 45 minutes. Stir in cream; cover and bake 10-15 minutes longer or until the vegetables are tender and the cream has thickened. Sprinkle with the parsley. **Yield:** 2 servings.

SKILLET SEA SCALLOPS

(Pictured above)

Margaret Lowenberg, Kingman, Arizona

You'll want to keep this recipe in mind for a quick-to-fix company dish. Pasta and mixed greens nicely complement the tender, citrusy shellfish.

- 1/2 cup dry bread crumbs
- 1/2 teaspoon salt
- 1 pound sea scallops
- 2 tablespoons butter
- 1 tablespoon olive oil
- 1/4 cup white wine *or* reduced-sodium chicken broth
- 2 tablespoons lemon juice
- 1 teaspoon minced fresh parsley
- 1 garlic clove, minced

In a large resealable plastic bag, combine bread crumbs and salt. Add scallops, a few at a time, and shake to coat.

In a large skillet over medium-high heat, brown scallops in butter and oil for 1-1/2 to 2 minutes on each side or until firm and opaque. Remove and keep warm. Add the wine, lemon juice, parsley and garlic to the skillet; bring to a boil. Pour over the scallops. Serve immediately. **Yield:** 3-4 servings.

PARSLEY POINTER

Like to cook with fresh parsley? To keep it in the refrigerator for several weeks, wash the entire bunch in warm water. Then shake off all excess moisture, wrap the parsley in a paper towel and seal it in a plastic bag.

THAI TOFU LETTUCE WRAPS
(Pictured above)

Laureen Pittman, Riverside, California

This yummy, light lunch originally featured chicken, but I modified it for my vegetarian husband. Now both of us prefer the Thai-style tofu version.

  1/4 cup rice vinegar
  1/4 cup canola oil
  2 tablespoons lime juice
  2 tablespoons mayonnaise
  2 tablespoons creamy peanut butter
  1 tablespoon brown sugar
  1 tablespoon soy sauce
  2 teaspoons minced fresh gingerroot
  1 teaspoon sesame oil
  1 teaspoon Thai chili sauce
  1 garlic clove, peeled
  1/2 cup minced fresh cilantro, *divided*
  1 package (14 ounces) firm tofu, drained and cut into 1/2-inch cubes
  1/2 cup chopped green onions
  1/2 cup shredded carrots
  1 small sweet red pepper, diced
  3/4 cup dry roasted peanuts, chopped, *divided*
  8 Bibb *or* Boston lettuce leaves

For the dressing, in a blender, combine the first 11 ingredients; cover and process until smooth. Stir in 1/4 cup cilantro.

In a large bowl, combine the tofu, onions, carrots, red pepper, 1/2 cup peanuts and the remaining cilantro. Add dressing and toss to coat. Divide among the lettuce leaves; sprinkle with remaining peanuts. Fold lettuce over filling. **Yield:** 4 servings.

DIJON CHICKEN

Susie Castleberry, Poplar, Wisconsin

French-style mustard and a savory coating brings lively flavor to this tender chicken dish. Once it's been passed around our dinner table full of eight hungry kids, there's seldom any left.

  1 cup dry bread crumbs
  1 cup grated Parmesan cheese
  1/2 cup milk
  1/2 cup Dijon mustard
  1 broiler/fryer chicken (3 to 4 pounds), cut up

In a large resealable plastic bag, combine bread crumbs and Parmesan cheese. In a shallow bowl, whisk the milk and mustard until blended. Dip chicken, a few pieces at a time, into milk mixture, then place in bag and shake to coat.

Place chicken, bone side down, in a greased 13-in. x 9-in. baking dish. Bake, uncovered, at 350° for 50-55 minutes or until juices run clear. **Yield:** 4 servings.

ASPARAGUS CREAM CHEESE OMELET

Jane Cain, Junction City, Ohio

When asparagus is in season, it seems to appear at every one of my meals, from breakfast to dinner! Not only do the fresh spears go well with ordinary eggs, but they also create a very appetizing omelet.

- 4 fresh asparagus spears, trimmed
- 2 teaspoons butter
- 4 eggs
- 1/4 cup sour cream
- 2 teaspoons dried minced onion
- 1/4 teaspoon salt
- 1/4 teaspoon crushed red pepper flakes
- 2 ounces cream cheese, cut into 1/4-inch cubes

In a skillet, bring 1/2 in. of water and asparagus to a boil; cover and boil for 3 minutes. Drain and immediately place asparagus in ice water. Drain and pat dry.

In a large nonstick skillet, melt butter over medium-high heat. In a small bowl, whisk the eggs, sour cream, onion, salt and pepper flakes. Pour into skillet (mixture should set immediately at edges). As eggs set, push cooked edges toward the center, letting the uncooked portion flow underneath.

When the eggs are set, place cream cheese and asparagus over one side; fold omelet over filling. Cover and let stand for 1-1/2 minutes or until cheese is melted. Slide onto a plate; cut in half. **Yield:** 2 servings.

CHERRY CHEESE BLINTZES

(Pictured at right)

Jessica Vantrease, Anderson, Alaska

These elegant blintzes can be served as an attractive brunch entree and even as a dessert. The bright cherry sauce gives them a delightful flavor. For a change of pace, I sometimes substitute other fruits, such as raspberries, blueberries or peaches.

- 1-1/2 cups milk
- 3 eggs
- 2 tablespoons butter, melted
- 2/3 cup all-purpose flour
- 1/2 teaspoon salt

FILLING:
- 1 cup (8 ounces) 4% cottage cheese
- 1 package (3 ounces) cream cheese, softened
- 1/4 cup sugar
- 1/2 teaspoon vanilla extract

CHERRY SAUCE:
- 1 pound fresh *or* frozen pitted sweet cherries
- 2/3 cup plus 1 tablespoon water, *divided*
- 1/4 cup sugar
- 1 tablespoon cornstarch

In a small bowl, combine the milk, eggs and butter. Combine the flour and salt; add to milk mixture and mix well. Cover and refrigerate for 2 hours.

Heat a lightly greased 8-in. nonstick skillet; pour 2 tablespoons batter into the center of the skillet. Lift and tilt pan to evenly coat bottom. Cook until top appears dry; turn and cook 15-20 seconds longer. Remove to a wire rack. Repeat with remaining batter. When cool, stack crepes with waxed paper or paper towels in between. Wrap in foil; refrigerate.

For the filling, in a blender, process cottage cheese until smooth. Transfer to a small bowl; add cream cheese and beat until smooth. Add sugar and vanilla; mix well. Spread about 1 rounded tablespoonful onto each crepe. Fold opposite sides of crepe over filling, forming a little bundle.

Place seam side down in a greased 15-in. x 10-in. x 1-in. baking pan. Bake, uncovered, at 350° for 10 minutes or until heated through.

Meanwhile, in a large saucepan, bring cherries, 2/3 cup water and sugar to a boil over medium heat. Reduce heat; cover and simmer for 5 minutes or until heated through. Combine cornstarch and remaining water until smooth; stir into the cherry mixture. Bring to a boil; cook and stir for 2 minutes or until thickened. Serve with crepes. **Yield:** 9 servings.

VENISON TORTILLA LASAGNA

(Pictured above)

Debra Scutt, Mason, Michigan

I always keep a copy of this recipe around because every time someone new tries my lasagna, they want to make it, too. It freezes well and is excellent for leftovers…if there are any!

 1 pound ground venison
 1 can (14-1/2 ounces) diced tomatoes
   with mild green chilies, undrained
 1 cup salsa
 1 envelope taco seasoning
 2 eggs, lightly beaten
 2 cups (16 ounces) 4% small-curd
   cottage cheese
 1 teaspoon dried oregano
1/2 teaspoon ground cumin
 10 flour tortillas (8 inches)
1-1/2 cups (6 ounces) shredded cheddar
   cheese

In a large skillet, cook the venison over medium heat until no longer pink; drain. Add the tomatoes, salsa and taco seasoning; cook, stirring occasionally, until heated through. In a small bowl, combine eggs, cottage cheese, oregano and cumin.

Cut tortillas in half; place half of them in a greased 13-in. x 9-in. baking dish (tortillas will overlap). Top with half of the meat sauce. Spoon cottage cheese mixture over the top. Layer with remaining tortillas and meat sauce.

Cover and bake at 350° for 30 minutes or until heated through. Uncover; sprinkle with cheddar cheese. Bake 5 minutes longer or until the cheese is melted. Let stand for 10 minutes before cutting. **Yield:** 12 servings.

SPICED PORK LOIN WITH PLUMS

(Pictured below)

Ruth Kolaritsch, Towaco, New Jersey

When plums are in season, I fix this at least every other week. I originally adapted the recipe for use with chicken but discovered it was even better with pork. I prepared it for 70 people for my granddaughter's christening, and everyone wanted the recipe.

 1 tablespoon ground cumin
 1 teaspoon ground cinnamon
1/2 teaspoon salt
1/2 teaspoon ground allspice
1/4 teaspoon pepper
1/4 teaspoon ground cloves
 1 boneless whole pork loin roast
   (3 to 4 pounds)
 2 tablespoons olive oil, *divided*
 1 large onion, chopped
 2 tablespoons sugar
1/2 cup cranberry juice
 1 cup chicken broth
 4 medium fresh plums, pitted and sliced

In a small bowl, combine the first six ingredients; rub over roast. In a Dutch oven, brown roast in 1 tablespoon oil on all sides. Remove the roast and set aside.

In the same pan, cook onion in remaining oil over medium heat until tender. Add sugar; cook, stirring occasionally, 3-4 minutes longer. Add cranberry juice; bring to a boil. Cook until liquid is reduced by half.

Return roast to pan; add broth. Bring to a boil. Reduce heat; cover and simmer for 1-1/4 hours.

Add plums; cover and simmer 30-45 minutes longer or until a meat thermometer reads 160°. Thicken pan juices if desired. **Yield:** 8-10 servings.

OVEN-FRIED CHICKEN
(Pictured below)

Alice Lange, Rosser, Manitoba

I've been preparing this chicken for more than 25 years. Friends and family enjoy it, and my church has used the recipe for several of its annual dinners.

        1 cup all-purpose flour
        2 envelopes (.6 ounce *each*) individual
          serving cream of chicken soup mix
        2 envelopes Italian salad dressing mix
    1-1/2 teaspoons paprika
        1 teaspoon seasoned salt
        1 teaspoon dried thyme
        1 teaspoon rubbed sage
      1/2 teaspoon onion powder
      1/2 teaspoon curry powder, optional
        1 cup milk
        2 broiler/fryer chickens (4 pounds *each*),
          cut up
      1/4 cup butter, melted

Line two 15-in. x 10-in. x 1-in. baking pans with foil and grease the foil; set aside.

In a large resealable plastic bag, combine the flour, soup mix, dressing mix and seasonings. Place milk in a shallow dish. Dip chicken into milk, then add to flour mixture, a few pieces at a time, and shake to coat. Place in prepared pans. Drizzle with butter.

Bake at 350° for 35-50 minutes or until juices run clear. **Yield:** 8 servings.

SALMON WITH FETTUCCINE ALFREDO
(Pictured above)

Pat Patty, Spring, Texas

I used salmon, my imagination and taste buds to come up with a lightened-up twist on an Italian classic. This healthier indulgence makes a pretty dish for guests.

      4 salmon fillets (4 ounces *each*)
    1/4 teaspoon coarsely ground pepper,
        divided
      4 ounces uncooked fettuccine
      2 garlic cloves, minced
      1 tablespoon reduced-fat margarine
      1 tablespoon all-purpose flour
    1/8 teaspoon salt
      1 cup fat-free milk
      4 tablespoons grated Parmesan cheese,
        divided

Place the salmon fillets, skin side down, on a broiler rack coated with cooking spray. Sprinkle with 1/8 teaspoon pepper. Broil 4-6 in. from the heat for 10-12 minutes or until fish flakes easily with a fork. Meanwhile, cook the fettuccine according to package directions.

In a small saucepan, cook the garlic in margarine until tender. Stir in the flour, salt and remaining pepper. Gradually stir in the milk. Bring to a boil; cook and stir for 2 minutes or until thickened. Remove from the heat. Stir in 3 tablespoons cheese.

Drain fettuccine; toss with sauce. Serve with salmon. Sprinkle with remaining cheese. **Yield:** 4 servings.

Editor's Note: This recipe was tested with Parkay Light stick margarine.

Thrills from the Grill

BECOMING BORED with the same old hamburgers and hot dogs for backyard barbecues? Here's the solution! Add some excitement with the sensational specialties in this section.

▰▰▰▰▰▰▰▰▰▰▰

🎗 PINWHEEL FLANK STEAKS
(Pictured below)

Nancy Tafoya, Fort Collins, Colorado

Here's an elegant-looking main dish that's easy to make. Plus, so much prep can be done in advance.

1-1/2 **pounds beef flank steak**
1/4 **cup olive oil**
2 **tablespoons red wine vinegar**
2 **teaspoons Italian seasoning**
2 **teaspoons Worcestershire sauce**
1-1/2 **teaspoons garlic powder**
1-1/2 **teaspoons pepper,** *divided*
1 **teaspoon seasoned salt**
8 **bacon strips, cooked and crumbled**

2 **garlic cloves, minced**
1/4 **cup minced fresh parsley**
1/4 **cup finely chopped onion**
1/2 **teaspoon salt**

Flatten the steak to 1/4-in. thickness. In a large resealable plastic bag, combine the oil, vinegar, Italian seasoning, Worcestershire sauce, garlic powder, 1 teaspoon pepper and seasoned salt; add the steak. Seal the bag and turn to coat; refrigerate overnight.

Drain and discard marinade. Combine the bacon, garlic, parsley, onion, salt and remaining pepper; sprinkle over steak to within 1 in. of edges. Roll up jelly-roll style, starting with a long side; tie with kitchen string at 1-in. intervals. Cut into six 1-1/4-in. rolls.

Coat the grill rack with cooking spray before starting the grill. Grill steak rolls, uncovered, over medium heat for 10-12 minutes on each side or until meat reaches desired doneness (for medium-rare, a meat thermometer should read 145°; medium, 160°; well-done, 170°). Cut and remove string before serving. **Yield:** 6 servings.

▰▰▰▰▰▰▰▰▰▰▰

🎗 GRILLED TURKEY TENDERLOINS

Shirly Glaesman, Pelican Rapids, Minnesota

This is a recipe my son brought home from college. It's definitely become a summer favorite with my family.

1 **can (12 ounces) lemon-lime soda**
1/4 **cup soy sauce**
1/4 **cup vegetable oil**
1 **teaspoon garlic powder**
4 **turkey breast tenderloins**
   (8 ounces *each*)

In a large resealable plastic bag, combine the soda, soy sauce, oil and garlic powder; add turkey. Seal bag and turn to coat; refrigerate for 8 hours or overnight, turning occasionally.

Drain and discard marinade. Grill tenderloins, covered, over medium heat for 7-10 minutes on each side or until a meat thermometer reads 170°. Cut into 1/2-in. slices. **Yield:** 6 servings.

thickness of heavy-duty foil (about 12 in. square); sprinkle each with potatoes and carrots.

Combine soup and milk; spoon over meat and vegetables. Fold foil around mixture and seal tightly. Grill, covered, over indirect medium heat for 25-30 minutes or until meat is no longer pink and potatoes are tender. Open foil carefully to allow steam to escape. **Yield:** 4 servings.

MARINATED PORK CHOPS

(Pictured below)

Mary Hunsberger, Mechanicstown, Ohio

My sister gave me the recipe for this delicious marinade. My husband loves pork chops made this way.

    1/2 cup vegetable oil
    1/4 cup lime juice
      4 teaspoons balsamic vinegar
      2 teaspoons sugar
      2 teaspoons Worcestershire sauce
      1 teaspoon salt
      1 teaspoon paprika
      1 garlic clove, minced
      6 boneless pork loin chops (4 ounces each)

In a large resealable plastic bag, combine the first eight ingredients. Add the pork chops. Seal the bag and turn to coat; refrigerate for 8 hours or overnight.

Drain and discard marinade. Grill pork chops, covered, over medium heat for 4-5 minutes on each side or until juices run clear. **Yield:** 6 servings.

INDIVIDUAL CAMPFIRE STEW

(Pictured above)

Margaret Hanson-Maddox, Kokomo, Indiana

These individual packets of stew are perfect for grilling or whipping up over a campfire. I can get several outdoor chores done while they're cooking.

      1 egg, lightly beaten
    1/4 cup ketchup
      1 tablespoon Worcestershire sauce
    3/4 cup dry bread crumbs
      1 teaspoon seasoned salt
      1 pound lean ground beef
      2 cups frozen shredded hash brown
        potatoes, thawed
      1 cup diced carrots
      1 cup condensed cream of chicken soup,
        undiluted
    1/4 cup milk

Prepare grill for indirect heat. In a large bowl, combine the first five ingredients. Crumble beef over mixture and mix well. Shape into four patties. Place each patty on a greased double

MESS-FREE METHOD

To avoid messy hands when mixing the meat mixture for beef patties, put the ingredients in a large resealable plastic bag, then mix. Or if you do use your hands, first dampen with water, and nothing will stick to them.

STEAKS WITH SHALLOT SAUCE

(Pictured below)

Nancy Summers, Clifton, Virginia

We have big beef eaters in our family, and this recipe is always a winner. The freshly cracked pepper really brings out the flavor, and the vinegar and Worcestershire are perfect in the shallot sauce.

    2/3 cup sliced shallots *or* green onions
      2 tablespoons butter, *divided*
    1/4 cup beef broth
      1 tablespoon red wine vinegar
      2 teaspoons Worcestershire sauce
      2 beef tenderloin steaks (6 ounces *each*)
    1/2 teaspoon pepper
    1/2 teaspoon olive oil

In a small skillet, saute shallots in 1 tablespoon butter until tender. Add broth; bring to a boil. Reduce heat; simmer until liquid is reduced to about 1 tablespoon. Stir in vinegar and Worcestershire sauce; cook 1 minute longer. Remove from the heat. Stir in 1-1/2 teaspoons butter. Cover and keep warm.

Sprinkle steaks with pepper. In a large skillet, cook steaks in oil and remaining butter until meat reaches desired doneness (for medium-rare, a meat thermometer should read 145°; medium, 160°; well-done, 170°). Serve with shallot sauce. **Yield:** 2 servings.

BAKED FLOUNDER WITH TARTAR SAUCE

Phyllis Schmalz, Kansas City, Kansas

For a different take on flounder, I came up with an oven-baked, lightly breaded fillet teamed with tarragon tartar sauce. Lake perch, tilapia, sole and orange roughy work just as well in this recipe.

✓ This recipe includes Nutrition Facts and Diabetic Exchanges.

    1/3 cup dry bread crumbs
    1/4 teaspoon salt
    1/4 teaspoon pepper
      4 flounder *or* sole fillets (5 ounces *each*)
      1 tablespoon olive oil
TARRAGON TARTAR SAUCE:
    1/4 cup fat-free plain yogurt
    1/4 cup reduced-fat mayonnaise
  1-1/2 teaspoons capers, drained
      1 garlic clove, minced
    1/2 teaspoon sugar
    1/2 teaspoon lemon juice
    1/2 teaspoon dill pickle relish
    1/2 teaspoon Dijon mustard
    1/4 teaspoon dried tarragon

In a small skillet, toast the bread crumbs, salt and pepper over medium heat until lightly browned, stirring occasionally. Remove from the heat.

Brush both sides of fillets with oil; coat with toasted crumbs. Place in a 15-in. x 10-in. x 1-in. baking pan coated with cooking spray. Bake at 450° for 6-8 minutes or until fish flakes easily with a fork.

Meanwhile, in a small bowl, combine the tartar sauce ingredients. Serve sauce with the fish. **Yield:** 4 servings.

Nutrition Facts: 1 fish fillet with 2 tablespoons tartar sauce equals 241 calories, 10 g fat (2 g saturated fat), 72 mg cholesterol, 510 mg sodium, 10 g carbohydrate, trace fiber, 26 g protein. **Diabetic Exchanges:** 4 very lean meat, 1-1/2 fat, 1/2 starch.

COOKING FISH FILLETS

Overcooked fish loses its flavor and becomes tough. As a general guideline, fish is cooked 10 minutes for every inch of thickness.

For fillets, check for doneness by inserting a fork at an angle into the thickest portion of the fish and gently parting the meat. When it is opaque and easily flakes into sections with the fork, it is cooked completely.

TEX-MEX SCRAMBLE
(Pictured above)

Paula Wharton, El Paso, Texas

This homey mix of scrambled eggs, corn tortilla strips, roast beef and other savory ingredients is one of my all-time favorite dinners.

   3 corn tortillas (6 inches), cut into thin strips
   4 teaspoons olive oil, *divided*
   2 tablespoons chopped onion
   1 jalapeno pepper, seeded and chopped
   4 eggs, lightly beaten
   1 plum tomato, chopped
1/4 cup shredded cooked roast beef
1/8 teaspoon salt
1/8 teaspoon pepper
1/4 cup shredded Monterey Jack cheese

In a large nonstick skillet, cook tortilla strips in 2 teaspoons oil for 5 minutes or until lightly golden brown but not crisp. Add the onion, jalapeno pepper and the remaining oil; cook 2 minutes longer.

Add the eggs, tomato, roast beef, salt and pepper; cook and stir until eggs are completely set. Sprinkle with cheese; cover and let stand for 2-3 minutes or until the cheese is melted. **Yield:** 2 servings.

Editor's Note: When cutting hot peppers, disposable gloves are recommended. Avoid touching your face.

COUNTRY PIZZA PIE

Joyce Leigh, Grand Junction, Colorado

My children were practially raised on this hearty sausage dish. It's been a "must" in our family for over 20 years.

   1 unbaked pastry shell (9 inches)
   1 pound bulk Italian sausage
   1 small onion, chopped
   4 eggs, lightly beaten
   1 cup (4 ounces) shredded cheddar cheese
1/2 cup milk
1/2 teaspoon dried oregano
1/8 teaspoon pepper
   1 can (8 ounces) pizza sauce
   6 slices part-skim mozzarella cheese

Line unpricked pastry shell with a double thickness of heavy-duty foil. Bake at 450° for 8 minutes. Remove foil; bake 5 minutes longer. Cool on a wire rack. Reduce heat to 350°.

In a large skillet, cook sausage and onion over medium heat until meat is no longer pink; drain. Transfer to a large bowl. Stir in the eggs, cheddar cheese, milk, oregano and pepper. Pour into crust.

Bake for 30-35 minutes or until a knife inserted near the center comes out clean. Spread pizza sauce over sausage mixture; top with the mozzarella cheese. Bake 5-8 minutes longer or until cheese is melted. Let stand for 10 minutes before cutting. **Yield:** 6 servings.

▰▰▰▰▰▰▰▰▰▰▰▰▰

SOUTHWESTERN CHICKEN PACKETS

(Pictured above)

Tonya Vowels, Vine Grove, Kentucky

Black beans, corn, salsa and a sprinkling of Mexican cheese add south-of-the-border flavor to the juicy chicken in these oven-baked foil packets. Plus, this dinner's a snap to fix and clean up.

       4 boneless skinless chicken breast halves
          (4 ounces *each*)
   1/2 teaspoon salt
   1/4 teaspoon pepper
   3/4 cup salsa
       2 cups fresh *or* frozen corn, thawed
       1 can (15 ounces) black beans, rinsed
          and drained
   3/4 cup shredded Mexican cheese blend
   1/4 cup sour cream

Place each chicken breast half on a greased double thickness of heavy-duty foil (about 18 in. square). Sprinkle with salt and pepper. Top with salsa, corn, beans and cheese. Fold foil around mixture and seal tightly.

Place on a baking sheet. Bake at 425° for 25-30 minutes or until chicken juices run clear. Open foil carefully to allow steam to escape. Serve with sour cream. **Yield:** 4 servings.

FLUTING A PIE CRUST

Position your index finger on the edge of the crust, pointing out. Place the thumb and index finger of your other hand on the outside edge and pinch the dough around the index finger to form a V-shape. Continue around the edge.

▰▰▰▰▰▰▰▰▰▰▰▰▰

COUNTRY BRUNCH PIE

(Pictured below)

Karen Corn, Greenfield, Indiana

This egg pie makes a great brunch dish with fruit salad and muffins. You could also serve it for lunch with a tossed green salad and French bread.

       Pastry for single-crust pie (9 inches)
   1/2 pound bulk pork sausage
   3/4 cup shredded part-skim mozzarella
          cheese
       4 eggs
       1 cup half-and-half cream
       1 can (4 ounces) mushroom stems and
          pieces, drained
   1/4 cup chopped green pepper
   1/4 cup chopped sweet red pepper
       2 tablespoons chopped onion

Line a 9-in. deep-dish pie plate with pastry. Trim to 1/2 in. beyond edge of plate; flute edges. Line pastry shell with a double thickness of heavy-duty foil. Bake at 400° for 5 minutes. Remove foil; bake 5 minutes longer.

In a small skillet, cook sausage over medium heat until no longer pink; drain. Spoon sausage into crust; sprinkle with cheese. In a small bowl, combine the eggs, cream, mushrooms, peppers and onion; pour over cheese.

Bake at 375° for 40-45 minutes or until a knife inserted near the center of pie comes out clean. Let stand for 10 minutes before cutting. **Yield:** 6-8 servings.

TUNA 'N' PEA CASSEROLE

(Pictured above)

Jackie Smulski, Lyons, Illinois

Turn to this tasty recipe when you want a tuna casserole that's a little different. I think the addition of horseradish is the key.

    8 ounces uncooked egg noodles
    2 cans (10-3/4 ounces *each*) condensed
      cream of mushroom soup, undiluted
  1/2 cup mayonnaise
  1/2 cup milk
    2 to 3 teaspoons prepared horseradish
  1/2 teaspoon dill weed
  1/8 teaspoon pepper
    1 cup frozen peas, thawed
    1 can (4 ounces) mushroom stems and
      pieces, drained
    1 small onion, chopped
    1 jar (2 ounces) diced pimientos, drained
    2 cans (6 ounces *each*) tuna, drained
      and flaked
  1/4 cup dry bread crumbs
    1 tablespoon butter, melted

Cook the egg noodles according to the package directions. Meanwhile, in a large bowl, combine the soup, mayonnaise, milk, horseradish, dill and pepper. Stir in the peas, mushrooms, onion, pimientos and tuna.

Drain noodles; stir into soup mixture. Transfer to a greased 2-qt. baking dish. Toss bread crumbs and butter; sprinkle over the top. Bake, uncovered, at 375° for 40-45 minutes or until bubbly. **Yield:** 6 servings.

PORK TENDERLOIN MEDALLIONS

(Pictured below)

Gerry Holcomb, Fairfax, California

With tender pork and cranberry sauce, this leads my list of best recipes to serve family and guests. Pine nuts make a nice, crunchy garnish.

    2 pork tenderloins (1 pound *each*), cut
      into 1-inch slices
Salt and pepper to taste
    2 tablespoons olive oil
CRANBERRY SAUCE:
  1/3 cup finely chopped red onion
    1 garlic clove, minced
    1 can (16 ounces) whole-berry cranberry
      sauce
  2/3 cup white wine *or* chicken broth
    2 tablespoons orange juice concentrate
    2 tablespoons balsamic vinegar
    2 tablespoons Dijon mustard
    1 teaspoon reduced-sodium chicken
      bouillon granules
  1/4 teaspoon salt
  1/8 teaspoon pepper

Flatten pork slices to 1/2-in. thickness; sprinkle with salt and pepper. In a large skillet over medium heat, cook pork in oil in batches until meat is no longer pink. Remove and keep warm.

In the same skillet, saute onion in drippings until tender. Add garlic; saute 1 minute longer. Stir in the cranberry sauce, wine, orange juice concentrate, vinegar, mustard, bouillon, salt and pepper; heat through. Serve with the pork. **Yield:** 8 servings.

GARLIC CLOVE CHICKEN

(Pictured at right)

Ruth Rigoni, Hurley, Wisconsin

Dinner guests and cooks alike rave about this chicken recipe. Your company will love the tasty poultry, and you'll appreciate the stress-free slow cooker preparation. Drop the garlic cloves in boiling water for a few seconds then drain and cool. The peels should slip off easily with your fingers.

- 40 garlic cloves, peeled
- 4 celery ribs, sliced
- 1 broiler/fryer chicken (3 to 4 pounds), cut up and skin removed
- 1/2 teaspoon salt
- 1/4 teaspoon pepper
- 1 tablespoon olive oil
- 1/4 cup white wine *or* reduced-sodium chicken broth
- 3 tablespoons lemon juice
- 2 tablespoons dry vermouth
- 2 tablespoons grated lemon peel
- 2 tablespoons minced fresh parsley
- 2 teaspoons dried basil
- 1 teaspoon dried oregano

Dash crushed red pepper flakes

Place garlic and celery in a 5-qt. slow cooker. Sprinkle chicken with salt and pepper. In a large nonstick skillet, brown chicken in oil in batches; transfer to slow cooker.

In a small bowl, combine the remaining ingredients. Pour over chicken. Cover and cook on low for 3-1/2 to 4 hours or until chicken juices run clear. **Yield:** 6 servings.

FLANK STEAK FAJITAS

Twila Burkholder, Middleburg, Pennsylvania

The beef comes out tender, juicy and flavorful from the slow cooker to create these tempting fajitas. I like to serve them with a side of Spanish rice.

- 1-1/2 pounds beef flank steak
- 1 medium onion, sliced
- 1 cup tomato juice
- 1 jalapeno pepper, seeded and chopped
- 2 garlic cloves, minced
- 1 tablespoon minced fresh cilantro
- 1 teaspoon ground cumin
- 1 teaspoon chili powder
- 1/4 teaspoon salt
- 1 medium green pepper, julienned
- 1 medium sweet red pepper, julienned
- 6 flour tortillas (8 inches), warmed

Shredded cheddar cheese, sour cream and guacamole, optional

Thinly slice steak across the grain into strips; place in a 5-qt. slow cooker. Add the onion, tomato juice, jalapeno, garlic, cilantro, cumin, chili powder and salt. Cover; cook on low for 5 hours.

Add green and red peppers. Cover and cook 1 hour longer or until the meat and vegetables are tender.

Using a slotted spoon, spoon meat mixture down the center of each tortilla. Sprinkle with cheese if desired. Fold sides of tortilla over filling. Serve with sour cream and guacamole if desired. **Yield:** 6 servings.

Editor's Note: When cutting hot peppers, disposable gloves are recommended. Avoid touching your face.

FARMHOUSE CHILI DOGS

Catherine Braley, Barboursville, West Virginia

We host lots of hay rides, picnics, hot dog roasts and ice cream socials on our farm, and these chili dogs never fail to please. There's always someone who fills a paper cup with the sauce and eats it straight!

- 1 pound ground beef
- 1 medium onion, chopped
- 1 can (10-3/4 ounces) condensed tomato soup, undiluted
- 1/2 cup water
- 3 tablespoons ketchup
- 1 tablespoon sugar
- 1-1/2 teaspoons chili powder
- 8 hot dogs
- 8 hot dog buns, split

Shredded cheddar cheese, optional

In a large skillet, cook the beef and onion over medium heat until meat is no longer pink; drain. Stir in the soup, water, ketchup, sugar and chili powder; bring to a boil. Reduce heat; simmer, uncovered, for 20 minutes or until thickened.

Cook hot dogs according to package directions. Place in buns; top with meat sauce. Sprinkle with cheese if desired. **Yield:** 8 servings.

TORTILLA TREATS

Have extra flour tortillas? Turn them into a dessert to go with the fajitas at left. Brush the tortillas with butter, sprinkle on cinnamon-sugar and bake them on a cookie sheet until crisp. Serve them with vanilla ice cream.

Main Dishes

1/4 cup orange juice concentrate
1 tablespoon canola oil
1 teaspoon snipped fresh dill *or*
 1/4 teaspoon dill weed
4 red snapper *or* tilapia fillets
 (6 ounces *each*)
2 orange slices, halved
Paprika

In a large resealable plastic bag, combine the orange juice concentrate, oil and dill; add fish. Seal bag and turn to coat; refrigerate for at least 15 minutes.

Drain and discard marinade. Place the fillets in a greased 15-in. x 10-in. x 1-in. baking pan. Cover and bake at 350° for 15-20 minutes or until fish flakes easily with a fork.

Dip cut edges of orange slices in paprika; serve with fish. **Yield:** 4 servings.

CHEDDAR APPLE PIZZA
(Pictured above)

Anna Beckley, Windsor, Pennsylvania

Nuts, apples and cheddar cheese are a great combination, especially at harvesttime when this fun pizza can be made with fruit right from the tree.

Pastry for a single-crust pie (9 inches)
4 large baking apples, peeled and cut into
 1/4-inch slices (about 5 cups)
1/2 cup shredded cheddar, shredded
 part-skim mozzarella *or* shredded
 Swiss cheese
1/2 cup packed brown sugar
1/2 cup chopped walnuts
1/2 teaspoon ground cinnamon
1/2 teaspoon ground nutmeg
2 tablespoons cold butter

Roll pastry to fit a greased 12-in. pizza pan; flute edges. Bake at 400° for 10 minutes.

Arrange apples in a single layer in a circular pattern to completely cover pastry. Sprinkle with cheese. Combine the brown sugar, walnuts, cinnamon and nutmeg; sprinkle over cheese.

Cut butter into small pieces and dot top of pizza. Bake for 20 minutes longer or until apples are tender. Cut into wedges; serve warm. **Yield:** 12 servings.

HONEY-APPLE TURKEY BREAST
(Pictured below)

Rita Reinke, Wauwatosa, Wisconsin

I found this recipe in a diabetics cookbook. We really like the honey flavor. The sweetness comes through when I use the leftovers in casseroles and soups, too.

3/4 cup frozen apple juice concentrate,
 thawed
1/3 cup honey

 ## CITRUS BAKED FISH
Phyllis Allen, Vero Beach, Florida

This recipe allows me to combine two things abundant in Florida—fresh fish and orange juice. The juice gives these fillets a wonderful, tangy accent.

Main Dishes

1 tablespoon ground mustard
1 bone-in turkey breast
   (6 to 7 pounds)

In a small saucepan, combine the apple juice concentrate, honey and mustard. Cook over low heat for 2-3 minutes or just until blended, stirring occasionally.

Remove skin from turkey if desired; place on a rack in a foil-lined shallow roasting pan. Pour honey mixture over turkey.

Bake, uncovered, at 325° for 2 to 2-1/2 hours or until a meat thermometer reads 170°, basting with pan juices every 30 minutes. (Cover loosely with foil if turkey browns too quickly.) Cover and let stand for 15 minutes before carving. **Yield:** 12-14 servings.

SKILLET CABBAGE ROLLS

Versa Creek, Owensville, Indiana

This makes a hearty, one-dish meal that's easy to prepare and attractive to serve. While the rolls cook, you'll have time to whip up dessert.

1 medium head cabbage
1 pound ground beef
1 cup cooked long grain rice
1 egg, lightly beaten
1/4 cup chopped onion
1 teaspoon salt
1/4 teaspoon dried thyme
1/4 teaspoon pepper
1 can (8 ounces) tomato sauce
1 tablespoon brown sugar
1 tablespoon lemon juice

In a Dutch oven, cook cabbage in boiling water for 2-3 minutes or just until leaves fall off head. Set aside 12 large leaves for rolls (refrigerate remaining cabbage for another use). Cut out the thick vein from the bottom of each reserved leaf, making a V-shaped cut.

In a large bowl, combine the beef, rice, egg, onion, salt, thyme and pepper. Place 1/4 cup meat mixture on each cabbage leaf; overlap cut ends of leaf. Fold in sides. Beginning from the cut end, roll up completely to enclose filling.

Arrange cabbage rolls, seam side down, in a large skillet. Combine the tomato sauce, brown sugar and lemon juice; pour over rolls. Cover and cook over medium-low heat for 1 hour or until cabbage is tender and a meat thermometer reads 160°.

Uncover and cook 5 minutes longer or until the sauce reaches the desired consistency. **Yield:** 4 servings.

CASHEW CHICKEN
(Pictured below)

Oma Rollison, El Cajon, California

There are lots of recipes for cashew chicken, but my family thinks this one stands alone. We love the fresh ginger and the crunch of the water chestnuts.

2 tablespoons cornstarch
1 tablespoon brown sugar
1-1/4 cups chicken broth
2 tablespoons soy sauce
1-1/2 pounds boneless skinless chicken breasts, cubed
3 tablespoons canola oil, *divided*
1/2 pound sliced fresh mushrooms
1 small green pepper, julienned
4 green onions, sliced
1-1/2 teaspoons grated fresh gingerroot
1 can (8 ounces) sliced water chestnuts, drained
3/4 cup salted cashews
Hot cooked rice

In a small bowl, combine the cornstarch, brown sugar, broth and soy sauce until smooth; set aside. In a large skillet or wok, stir-fry the chicken in 2 tablespoons oil until no longer pink. Remove and keep warm.

In the same skillet, stir-fry the mushrooms, green pepper, onions and ginger in remaining oil until green pepper is crisp-tender, about 5 minutes. Stir in the chicken, water chestnuts and cashews; heat through.

Stir broth mixture and add to the pan. Bring to a boil; cook and stir for 1-2 minutes or until thickened. Serve with rice. **Yield:** 4-6 servings.

BRUNCH EGG BAKE
(Pictured below)

Gloria Rohlfing, York, Pennsylvania

I grew up in Pennsylvania Dutch country, where family often gathers around food. On Mother's Day, we agree brunch is the best meal to celebrate together. This colorful casserole makes things easy.

    3 cups (12 ounces) shredded cheddar cheese
    3 cups (12 ounces) shredded part-skim mozzarella cheese
    1 jar (4-1/2 ounces) sliced mushrooms, drained
  1/2 cup chopped sweet red pepper
  1/3 cup sliced green onions
    2 tablespoons butter
    2 cups diced fully cooked ham
  1/2 cup all-purpose flour
1-3/4 cups milk
    8 eggs, lightly beaten
    2 tablespoons minced fresh parsley
  1/2 teaspoon salt
  1/2 teaspoon dried basil
  1/4 teaspoon pepper

Combine the cheeses; place 3 cups in an ungreased 13-in. x 9-in. baking dish and set aside.

HOMEMADE MEATBALLS
(Pictured above)

Lucille Bilodeau, Lewiston, Maine

My family and friends are always impressed with these beef and pork meatballs, which I serve with homemade spaghetti sauce. The recipe came from an old friend of Italian descent. The mashed potatoes guarantee that the meatballs stay moist.

    2 eggs
  1/2 cup mashed potatoes (with added milk and butter)
    1 small onion, finely chopped
  1/2 teaspoon *each* salt, celery salt and pepper
    1 pound ground beef
  1/2 pound ground pork
    1 jar (26 ounces) spaghetti sauce
Hot cooked spaghetti

In a large bowl, combine the eggs, potatoes, onion, salt, celery salt and pepper. Crumble beef and pork over mixture and mix well. Shape into 1-in. balls.

Place meatballs on greased racks in shallow baking pans. Bake at 400° for 10-15 minutes or until no longer pink. Drain on paper towels.

Transfer to a large saucepan. Add spaghetti sauce; heat through. Serve with spaghetti. **Yield:** 6 servings.

In a large skillet, saute the mushrooms, red pepper and onions in butter until tender; drain. Spoon into baking dish. Sprinkle with ham and remaining cheeses.

In a large bowl, whisk flour and milk until smooth; stir in the eggs, parsley, salt, basil and pepper until blended. Slowly pour over cheeses.

Bake, uncovered, at 350° for 35-40 minutes or until a knife inserted near the center comes out clean. Let stand for 10 minutes before cutting. **Yield:** 12 servings.

LEEK AND HERB STUFFED CHICKEN

Shirley Glaab, Hattiesburg, Mississippi

Chicken breasts get a double dose of flavor thanks to the deliciously aromatic stuffing and crunchy coating in this recipe. The impressive-looking roll-ups are actually easy to make, but your family and guests will never suspect you didn't fuss!

- 3 medium leeks (white and light green portions only), cleaned and chopped
- 1 tablespoon olive oil
- 1/2 teaspoon dried rosemary, crushed
- 1/2 teaspoon dried thyme
- 1/4 teaspoon salt
- 1/4 teaspoon pepper
- 4 boneless skinless chicken breast halves (6 ounces *each*)

PECAN CRUST:
- 1/4 cup finely chopped pecans
- 1/4 cup dry bread crumbs
- 1/4 teaspoon dried rosemary, crushed
- 1/4 teaspoon dried thyme
- 1/2 teaspoon salt
- 1/4 teaspoon pepper
- 1/4 cup Dijon mustard
- 1 tablespoon olive oil

In a small skillet, saute leeks in oil until almost tender. Add the rosemary, thyme, salt and pepper; saute 1 minute longer. Remove from heat; cool.

Flatten each chicken breast half to 1/4-in. thickness; top with leek mixture. Roll up and secure with toothpicks.

In a small shallow bowl, combine the pecans, bread crumbs, rosemary, thyme, salt and pepper. Brush mustard over the chicken, then coat with the pecan mixture. Place the chicken seam side down in a greased 11-in. x 7-in. baking dish. Drizzle with oil.

Bake, uncovered, at 375° for 35-40 minutes or until a meat thermometer reads 170°. Discard toothpicks. **Yield:** 4 servings.

BLT PIZZA

(Pictured above)

Dawn Thompson, Ray, North Dakota

A friend shared the recipe for this cold pizza that gets its crispy crust from refrigerated crescent roll dough. Enjoy it as a cool, light meal on a hot summer day...or even as a snack or party appetizer.

- 1 tube (8 ounces) refrigerated crescent rolls
- 1 cup mayonnaise
- 1 tablespoon Dijon mustard
- 3 cups shredded lettuce
- 12 bacon strips, cooked and crumbled
- 1 medium tomato, seeded and chopped
- 2 green onions, thinly sliced
- 1-1/2 cups (6 ounces) shredded cheddar cheese

Separate crescent dough into eight triangles; place on a lightly greased 14-in. pizza pan with points toward the center. Press dough onto the bottom and up the sides of pan, forming a crust; seal perforations. Bake at 375° for 12-15 minutes or until golden brown. Cool completely.

In a small bowl, combine the mayonnaise and mustard; spread over the prepared crust. Sprinkle with lettuce, bacon, tomato, onions and cheese. **Yield:** 6-8 slices.

TOMATO TIP

To remove the seeds from a tomato, cut it in half horizontally and remove the stem. Holding one half over a bowl or sink, scrape out the seeds with a small spoon. Or squeeze the tomato to force out the seeds.

IT'S EASY to balance any meal with the delicious vegetable, rice and potato side dishes in this chapter. You'll be pleased with these tasty accompaniments!

FABULOUS ADDITION. Special Garden Medley (p. 75).

Side Dishes & Condiments

SPECIAL GARDEN MEDLEY
(Pictured at left)

Norma Coats, Petersburg, Tennessee

My mother used to make this in large batches to can 60 years ago. Now I make it for my freezer.

- 2 celery ribs, chopped
- 1 large onion, chopped
- 1 medium sweet yellow *or* green pepper, chopped
- 1/4 cup water
- 4 cups chopped seeded peeled tomatoes (about 9 medium)
- 4-1/2 teaspoons sugar
- 1 teaspoon salt

In a large saucepan, combine the celery, onion, yellow pepper and water. Bring to a boil. Reduce heat; cover and simmer for 20 minutes or until tender.

Stir in the tomatoes, sugar and salt; cook 6-8 minutes longer or until heated through. **Yield:** 6 servings.

ACORN SQUASH WITH CARAMEL SAUCE

Ann DeHass and Lee Ann Miller, Wilmot, Ohio

This squash recipe from one of our all-time favorite restaurants is so delicious it could be dessert. The caramel sauce is also great as a dip for apples or a topping for ice cream.

- 3 medium acorn squash
- 3/4 teaspoon ground cinnamon
- 2 tablespoons butter
- CARAMEL SAUCE:
- 2 cups packed brown sugar
- 2 cups maple pancake syrup
- 1/2 cup butter, cubed
- 1/2 cup heavy whipping cream

Cut squash in half; remove and discard seeds. Sprinkle cinnamon over squash. Place cut side down in a 15-in. x 10-in. x 1-in. baking pan; add 1/2 in. of hot water. Bake, uncovered, at 350° for 30 minutes.

Drain water from pan; turn squash cut side up and dot with butter. Bake 15-20 minutes longer or until tender.

Meanwhile, for sauce, in a large saucepan, bring brown sugar and syrup to a boil. Reduce heat to medium; cook until sugar is dissolved. Stir in butter until melted. Add cream. Remove from the heat. Serve with squash. Refrigerate the leftover sauce. **Yield:** 6 servings (4 cups sauce).

POTATO BRUNCH MEDLEY

Gerald Mathews, Omaha, Nebraska

This is a nice departure from the customary hash browns for breakfast or brunch…a colorful, tasty combination of vegetables, it's a compatible side dish to eggs prepared in anyone's favorite way.

- 1 medium potato, peeled and cubed
- 1 tablespoon butter
- 1 medium green pepper, chopped
- 1 medium onion, chopped
- 1 medium apple, peeled and cubed
- 2 tablespoons water
- 1 tablespoon brown sugar
- 1/2 teaspoon salt
- 1/8 teaspoon pepper

In a small skillet, saute potato in butter for 8 minutes. Add the green pepper, onion and apple; cook 6-8 minutes longer or until potato begins to brown.

Add the water, brown sugar, salt and pepper; cook and stir until blended and heated through. **Yield:** 2 servings.

POTATO POINTERS

When buying potatoes, look for those that are firm, well shaped and free of blemishes. Avoid ones that are wrinkled, cracked or sprouting. When stored in a cool, dark, well-ventilated place, potatoes can keep up to 2 weeks. Generally, 3 medium russets or 8-10 small potatoes equal one pound. One pound of russets equals about 3-1/2 cups chopped.

CRUNCHY SWEET POTATO BAKE

Dawn Riggestad, New Bern, North Carolina

This is one of our all-time favorites, both for holidays and everyday. The topping gives a nice nutty crunch to the smooth, sweet potatoes underneath.

    3 pounds sweet potatoes (about
        7 medium), peeled and quartered
2/3 cup sugar
1/2 cup milk
1/3 cup butter, softened
    1 tablespoon candied *or* crystallized ginger
    1 teaspoon ground cinnamon
1/4 teaspoon ground nutmeg
TOPPING:
3/4 cup cornflakes, lightly crushed
1/4 cup packed brown sugar
1/4 cup chopped pecans
1/4 cup butter, melted

Place the sweet potatoes in a large saucepan and cover with water. Bring to a boil. Reduce the heat; cover and simmer for 12-18 minutes or until tender. Drain. Mash the sweet potatoes with the sugar, milk, butter, candied ginger, cinnamon and ground nutmeg.

Transfer the potatoes to a greased 2-qt. baking dish. Cover and bake at 350° for 20 minutes or until heated through.

Combine the topping ingredients; sprinkle over potatoes. Bake, uncovered, for 5-10 minutes or until the topping is lightly browned. **Yield:** 8 servings.

CREAMED SPINACH

(Pictured above)

Jill Obreiter, Simi Valley, California

My twins wouldn't eat anything that even resembled a vegetable, but they ate seconds and sometimes thirds of this fabulous spinach. I received the recipe from a friend several years ago, and it's been part of my Thanksgiving menu ever since. I usually double or triple the recipe. My children aren't the only ones who want extra servings!

    1 large onion, finely chopped
    4 green onions, finely chopped
    4 bacon strips, diced
    1 garlic clove, minced
    2 tablespoons plus 2 teaspoons butter
1/2 cup all-purpose flour
1-1/4 teaspoons salt
1/4 teaspoon pepper
2-1/2 cups milk
    3 packages (10 ounces *each*) frozen
        chopped spinach, thawed and
        squeezed dry
1/2 cup half-and-half cream

In a large skillet, cook the onions, bacon and garlic in butter over medium heat until bacon is crisp. Stir in the flour, salt and pepper until blended. Gradually add milk. Bring to a boil; cook and stir for 2 minutes or until thickened. Stir in spinach and cream; cook 3-5 minutes longer or until spinach is heated through. **Yield:** 6 servings.

TANGY ZUCCHINI SAUTE

You don't have to go to great lengths to add zip to zucchini, as this recipe proves. Our Test Kitchen stirred up the savory solution and sauteed it in a jiffy!

    4 medium zucchini, halved lengthwise
        and sliced
    1 medium onion, chopped
    2 tablespoons olive oil
    2 garlic cloves, minced
    1 teaspoon Italian seasoning
1/2 teaspoon salt
1/4 teaspoon pepper
    1 to 2 tablespoons white balsamic vinegar

In a large skillet, saute zucchini and onion in oil until tender, about 10 minutes.

Stir in the garlic, Italian seasoning, salt and pepper; saute 1 minute longer. Add vinegar; saute for 1-2 minutes or until liquid is evaporated and zucchini is evenly coated. **Yield:** 6 servings.

Side Dishes & Condiments

▪▪▪▪▪▪▪▪▪▪▪▪▪
GREEN BEANS WITH HERBS
(Pictured above)

Jesse and Anne Foust, Bluefield, West Virginia

We both love to cook, and like to find interesting side dishes to round out our meals. After a taste, you're sure to agree that this easy-to-fix recipe takes plain green beans to a higher level.

      1 cup water
  1-1/2 pounds fresh green beans, trimmed and
         cut into 1-inch pieces
      1 medium onion, cut into thin wedges
      1 celery rib, chopped
    1/2 teaspoon dried basil
    1/4 teaspoon dried rosemary, crushed
Salt and pepper to taste

In a large saucepan, bring water to a boil. Add the beans, onion and celery. Reduce heat; cover and cook for 8-10 minutes or until crisp-tender. Drain. Sprinkle with the basil, rosemary, salt and pepper. **Yield:** 8-10 servings.

DRIED HERBS

Dried herbs don't spoil, but they do lose their flavor and potency over time. For maximum flavor in your cooking, you may want to replace herbs that are over a year old. Store dried herbs in airtight containers and keep them away from heat and light. Don't put them in the cupboard above the stove.

▪▪▪▪▪▪▪▪▪▪▪▪▪
ZUCCHINI-STUFFED ONIONS
(Pictured below)

Marguerite Shaeffer, Sewell, New Jersey

Much of my cooking is a combination of ideas, pictures and recipes. I love onions, and my theory is...if it's got onions in it, it's got to be good. I put two recipe ideas together to come up with this scrumptious, attractive dish.

      2 medium onions
      1 medium zucchini, chopped
    1/2 teaspoon olive oil
      1 garlic clove, minced
    1/2 teaspoon dried basil
      1 tablespoon seasoned bread crumbs
      1 tablespoon grated Parmesan cheese
    1/8 teaspoon salt
Dash pepper

Peel onions and cut a 1/4-in. slice from the top and bottom. Wrap onions in foil. Bake at 375° for 50 minutes or until tender. Cool slightly. Carefully remove center of onion, leaving a 1/2-in. shell; chop removed onion.

In a small skillet, saute zucchini in oil for 2 minutes. Add the chopped onion, garlic and basil; cook 1 minute longer. Remove from the heat; stir in the bread crumbs, Parmesan cheese, salt and pepper.

Stuff into onion shells. Place in a small greased baking dish. Bake, uncovered, at 375° for 10-15 minutes or until golden brown. **Yield:** 2 servings.

▚▚▚▚▚▚▚▚▚▚▚

OVEN RICE SUPREME

Barbara Hege, Chambersburg, Pennsylvania

My family was never fond of rice, until I found this recipe. They call it a winner, and it's so easy to make.

1-1/2 cups uncooked long grain rice
  2 cups chicken broth
  1 cup hot water
  2 tablespoons *each* chopped onion, celery and green pepper
  2 tablespoons minced fresh parsley
  2 tablespoons butter, melted
  1 teaspoon salt
1/2 teaspoon garlic powder
1/8 teaspoon pepper

In a greased 1-1/2-qt. baking dish, combine all ingredients. Cover and bake at 350° for 1 hour or until rice is tender. Fluff with a fork before serving. **Yield:** 6 servings.

▚▚▚▚▚▚▚▚▚▚▚

CRUMB-TOPPED ASPARAGUS CASSEROLE

(Pictured above)

Mrs. E. Allen Orem, Rochester, New York

We had plenty of fresh vegetables on the farm, so I also made this family favorite with broccoli or green beans instead of asparagus.

  2 pounds fresh asparagus, trimmed and cut into 1-inch pieces
  2 cans (10-3/4 ounces *each*) condensed cream of celery soup, undiluted
1/2 cup heavy whipping cream
1/2 cup mayonnaise
  1 tablespoon Heinz 57 steak sauce
1/4 teaspoon ground cloves
1/4 teaspoon ground nutmeg
  1 cup (4 ounces) shredded cheddar cheese
2-1/2 cups crushed seasoned stuffing
  5 tablespoons butter, melted

In a large saucepan, bring 1/2 in. of water to a boil. Add asparagus; cover and boil for 3 minutes. Drain well. Place in a greased 11-in. x 7-in. baking dish; set aside.

In a small bowl, combine the soup, cream, mayonnaise, steak sauce, cloves and nutmeg. Spread over asparagus; sprinkle with cheese.

Toss stuffing with butter; sprinkle over the casserole. Bake, uncovered, at 350° for 20-25 minutes or until bubbly. **Yield:** 8 servings.

▚▚▚▚▚▚▚▚▚▚▚

BACON MASHED POTATOES

Pat Mathison, Meadowlands, Minnesota

Featuring cheddar cheese, bacon and chives, these rich and hearty potatoes go well with anything. For a slightly different twist, add some chopped parsley.

2-1/2 cups cubed peeled potatoes (3/4 pound)
1/4 cup milk
1/4 cup mayonnaise
4-1/2 teaspoons minced chives
1/8 teaspoon garlic powder
1/8 teaspoon pepper
1/2 cup shredded cheddar cheese
  3 bacon strips, cooked and crumbled

Place potatoes in a large saucepan and cover with water. Bring to a boil. Reduce heat; cover and cook for 15-20 minutes or until tender. Drain.

Transfer to a large bowl. Add the milk, mayonnaise, chives, garlic powder and pepper; mash the potatoes. Stir in the cheese and bacon. **Yield:** 3 servings.

BETTER WAY TO COOK BACON

Here's a fast and easy way to prepare strips of bacon that requires very little cleanup. Simply line a large baking pan with aluminum foil, place the bacon strips on top of it and bake it in the oven at 400° until crisp.

ARTICHOKE STUFFING

(Pictured above)

Lorie Verkuyl, Ridgecrest, California

This dish is so good with turkey! I also halve the recipe and use it when I bake a chicken.

- 1 loaf (1 pound) sourdough bread, cut into 1-inch cubes
- 1/2 pound sliced fresh mushrooms
- 2 celery ribs, chopped
- 1 medium onion, chopped
- 3 to 4 garlic cloves, minced
- 2 tablespoons butter
- 2 jars (6-1/2 ounces *each*) marinated artichoke hearts, drained and chopped
- 1/2 cup grated Parmesan cheese
- 1 teaspoon poultry seasoning
- 1 egg
- 1 can (14-1/2 ounces) chicken broth

Place bread cubes in two ungreased 15-in. x 10-in. x 1-in. baking pans. Bake at 350° for 15 minutes or until lightly browned.

In a large skillet, saute the mushrooms, celery, onion and garlic in butter until tender. Stir in the artichokes, cheese and poultry seasoning. Transfer to a large bowl; stir in bread cubes.

In a small bowl, whisk egg and broth until blended. Pour over bread mixture and mix well.

Transfer to a greased 3-qt. baking dish (dish will be full). Cover and bake at 350° for 30 minutes. Uncover; bake 5-15 minutes longer or until a thermometer reads 160°. **Yield:** 14 cups.

BASIL POLENTA WITH BEANS 'N' PEPPERS

(Pictured below)

Kimberly Hammond, Kingwood, Texas

Basil livens up polenta and black beans in this festive and colorful meatless supper. Add a green salad to complete the nice, light meal.

- 3 cups water
- 1 teaspoon salt, *divided*
- 1 cup yellow cornmeal
- 1/2 cup chopped fresh basil
- 1 medium green pepper, cut into strips
- 1 medium sweet red pepper, cut into strips
- 1 medium onion, thinly sliced
- 3 garlic cloves, minced
- 1 tablespoon olive oil
- 1 can (15 ounces) black beans, rinsed and drained
- 1/4 teaspoon pepper

In a large saucepan, bring water to a boil; add 1/2 teaspoon salt. Gradually add the cornmeal, stirring constantly. Reduce heat to low. Stir in basil. Cook and stir for 10 minutes or until thick and creamy. Transfer to an 8-in. square dish coated with cooking spray. Cool to room temperature, about 30 minutes.

In a large skillet, saute the green and red peppers, onion and garlic in oil until tender. Stir in the beans, pepper and remaining salt; keep warm.

Cut polenta into four squares; place on an ungreased baking sheet. Broil 4 in. from the heat for 5 minutes. Turn and broil 5-6 minutes longer or until heated through. Top with the vegetable mixture. **Yield:** 4 servings.

1 medium onion, chopped
1/4 cup butter
1 medium head red cabbage, chopped
(about 8 cups)
1 teaspoon salt
1/4 teaspoon pepper
2 medium tart apples, peeled and
chopped
1/4 cup water
1/2 cup white vinegar
1/3 cup packed brown sugar

In a large saucepan, saute onion in butter until tender. Stir in the cabbage, salt and pepper. Reduce heat; cover and simmer for 10 minutes. Stir in apples and water; cover and simmer 45 minutes longer or until the cabbage and apples are tender.

Combine vinegar and brown sugar; stir into cabbage mixture. Bring to a boil. Reduce heat; simmer, uncovered, for 15 minutes or until the cabbage and apples are glazed. **Yield:** 8 servings.

※※※※※※※※※※

MASHED POTATO ROSES

Darlene Brenden, Salem, Oregon

This clever side dish turns a garden-variety meal into one that's suitable for company. To save prep time, make the roses ahead and keep them covered in the fridge. Top them with butter and paprika, then pop them into the oven shortly before eating.

4 medium baking potatoes, peeled and
quartered
1 egg
4 tablespoons butter, *divided*
2 tablespoons grated Parmesan cheese
1 teaspoon salt
1 teaspoon dried minced onion
1 teaspoon minced fresh parsley
1/8 teaspoon pepper

Place potatoes in a large saucepan and cover with water. Bring to a boil. Reduce heat; cover and cook for 15-20 minutes or until tender. Drain.

In a large bowl, mash the potatoes. Beat in the egg, 2 tablespoons butter, cheese, salt, onion, parsley and pepper.

Spoon into eight mounds, about 1/2 cup each, on a greased baking sheet. To form rose petals, hold a teaspoon or tablespoon upside down and press tip of spoon all around the bottom of each mound. Repeat, forming three or four more rows of petals.

Melt the remaining butter; drizzle over potato roses. Bake at 350° for 15-18 minutes or until heated through. **Yield:** 8 servings.

※※※※※※※※※※

COLORFUL VEGETABLE MEDLEY

(Pictured above)

Here's a tasty way to get your daily veggies. Our Test Kitchen sprinkled this crisp-tender medley with fresh parsley, lemon juice and coriander. It's a quick side dish for any meal.

✓ This recipe includes Nutrition Facts
and Diabetic Exchanges.

2 medium yellow summer squash, sliced
4 teaspoons olive oil
1-1/2 cups fresh sugar snap peas
1-1/2 cups halved cherry tomatoes
3 tablespoons minced fresh parsley
2 tablespoons lemon juice
1/2 teaspoon ground coriander
1/4 teaspoon salt
1/8 teaspoon pepper

In a large nonstick skillet, saute the squash in oil for 3 minutes. Add peas and tomatoes; saute 2-3 minutes longer or until squash is crisp-tender. Sprinkle with parsley, lemon juice, coriander, salt and pepper; toss to coat. **Yield:** 4 servings.

Nutrition Facts: 1 cup equals 101 calories, 5 g fat (1 g saturated fat), 0 cholesterol, 159 mg sodium, 12 g carbohydrate, 4 g fiber, 4 g protein.
Diabetic Exchanges: 2 vegetables, 1 fat.

※※※※※※※※※※

SWEET-AND-SOUR RED CABBAGE

Leonie Kenyon, Narragansett, Rhode Island

My grandfather was German, so my grandmother would often prepare many German dishes for him. This is the one I like best.

MUSHROOM RICE MEDLEY

(Pictured below)

Sue Mullis, Sharon, Wisconsin

We would never hear the end of it if we failed to have my grandmother's mushroom rice dish on the table for any family gathering. It's the one recipe my dad requests most often.

   3 cups water
1/2 cup uncooked brown rice
1/2 cup uncooked wild rice
   1 teaspoon chicken bouillon granules
   1 teaspoon dried oregano
1/2 pound sliced bacon, diced
1/2 pound sliced fresh mushrooms
   1 small onion, chopped
1/4 teaspoon salt, optional

In a large saucepan, combine the water, brown rice, wild rice, bouillon and oregano. Bring to a boil. Reduce heat; cover and simmer for 50-60 minutes or until rice is tender.

In a large skillet, cook the bacon over medium heat until crisp. Using a slotted spoon, remove to paper towels. Drain, reserving 2 tablespoons drippings. In the drippings, saute the mushrooms and onion until tender. Stir in the rice and bacon; heat through. Season with the salt if desired. **Yield:** 6 servings.

■■■■■■■■■■■■■

MOCK HOLLANDAISE

(Pictured above)

Millie Vickery, Lena, Illinois

Here's an easy, silky hollandaise sauce that makes any vegetable elegant. It's especially good with spring asparagus, broccoli or green beans.

3/4 cup mayonnaise
1/2 cup milk
   1 teaspoon lemon juice
   1 teaspoon grated lemon peel
1/4 teaspoon salt
Dash pepper
Cooked asparagus spears or
   vegetable of your choice

In a small heavy saucepan, whisk mayonnaise and milk until blended. Cook and stir over low heat for 3-4 minutes or until warmed. Add the lemon juice, peel, salt, and pepper; cook and stir until heated through. Serve immediately with asparagus or vegetable of your choice. Refrigerate leftovers. **Yield:** 1 cup.

BRIGHT GREEN VEGETABLES

To lock in the color of green vegetables, such as broccoli, asparagus and green beans, first steam or blanch them until crisp-tender. Immediately transfer to a bowl of ice water to stop the cooking process, allow to cool, then store in the refrigerator. Reheat when ready to serve.

ZUCCHINI POTATO PANCAKES

(Pictured below)

Jane Zielinski, Rotterdam Junction, New York

I found this recipe years ago while searching for new ways to use vegetables from our garden. My family really enjoys these delicious pancakes.

> 3 cups shredded zucchini
> (about 2 medium)
> 1 cup shredded peeled potato
> (1 medium)
> 1/2 cup seasoned bread crumbs
> 3 tablespoons all-purpose flour
> 1 teaspoon baking soda
> 1 teaspoon salt
> 1/4 teaspoon pepper
> 3 eggs, lightly beaten
> 1 small onion, finely chopped
> 2 garlic cloves, minced
> 4 tablespoons canola oil, *divided*

In a sieve or colander, drain the zucchini and potato, squeezing to remove excess liquid. Pat dry; set aside. In a large bowl, combine the bread crumbs, flour, baking soda, salt and pepper. Stir in eggs until blended. Add the onion, garlic and zucchini mixture; toss to coat.

Heat 2 tablespoons oil in a large nonstick skillet over medium heat. Drop the batter by 1/4 cupfuls into oil. Fry in batches until golden brown on both sides, using remaining oil as needed. Drain on paper towels. **Yield:** 1 dozen.

FRENCH DRESSING WITH TOMATOES

(Pictured above)

Dana Barnes, Beaufort, South Carolina

Every time I make this salad my mother-in-law gave me, it takes me back to the country. I can see myself in the garden among all of those fresh tomatoes!

> 1 can (10-3/4 ounces) condensed tomato
> soup, undiluted
> 1 cup canola oil
> 1/2 cup sugar
> 1/2 cup cider vinegar
> 1 tablespoon Worcestershire sauce
> 1 tablespoon prepared mustard
> 2 to 3 teaspoons pepper
> 1 teaspoon salt
> 1/4 teaspoon garlic powder
> Tomato wedges
> Lettuce leaves

In a blender, combine the first nine ingredients; cover and process until blended. Place tomato wedges in a bowl; add enough dressing to cover. Let stand at room temperature for 1 hour. Refrigerate remaining dressing for another use.

To serve, use a slotted spoon to place tomato wedges on lettuce leaves; drizzle with dressing left in bowl. **Yield:** 3 cups.

SPICY SPANISH RICE
(Pictured below)

Marilyn Warner, Shirley, Arkansas

This is a tasty dish to serve with a Mexican meal or to perk up any "ho-hum" dinner. We especially like it with chicken enchiladas. It's a little different to bake rice, but it's handy to not have to watch it on the stove. You can make the rice less spicy by choosing a more mild variety of canned tomatoes.

- 1 cup uncooked long grain rice
- 1 small onion, chopped
- 1 can (2-1/4 ounces) sliced ripe olives, drained
- 1 teaspoon ground cumin
- 2 cans (10 ounces *each*) diced tomatoes and green chilies, undrained
- 1 cup water
- 2 tablespoons canola oil
- 1 cup (4 ounces) shredded Monterey Jack cheese
- 2 tablespoons minced fresh cilantro, optional

In a greased 2-qt. baking dish, combine the rice, onion, olives, cumin, tomatoes, water and oil. Cover and bake at 350° for 45 minutes.

Stir in cheese. Bake, uncovered, 10-15 minutes longer or until rice is tender and liquid is absorbed. Stir in the cilantro if desired. **Yield:** 6-8 servings.

RED POTATO SKEWERS

Dawn Finch, Prosser, Washington

A seasoned mayonnaise mixture keeps these quartered red potatoes moist and heavenly. My mouths waters just thinking about how they'll taste hot off the grill.

- 2 pounds red potatoes (about 6 medium), quartered
- 1/2 cup water
- 1/2 cup mayonnaise
- 1/4 cup chicken broth
- 2 teaspoons dried oregano
- 1/2 teaspoon garlic salt
- 1/2 teaspoon onion powder

Place the potatoes and water in an ungreased microwave-safe 2-qt. dish. Cover and microwave on high for 10-12 minutes or until almost tender, stirring once; drain. In a large bowl, combine the remaining ingredients; add potatoes. Cover and refrigerate for 1 hour.

Drain, reserving mayonnaise mixture. Thread potatoes onto metal or soaked wooden skewers. Grill, uncovered, over medium heat for 4 minutes. Turn; brush with reserved mayonnaise mixture. Grill 4 minutes longer or until the potatoes are tender and golden brown. **Yield:** 6 servings.

Editor's Note: This recipe was tested in a 1,100-watt microwave.

CARROT ZUCCHINI SAUTE

Melissa Joramo, Rocklin, California

My mother and I came up with this sweet dish. It's one easy way to use up extra zucchini from the garden and get everyone to eat their veggies. With only five ingredients, it's fast and simple to make, too.

- 3 medium carrots, sliced
- 3 tablespoons butter
- 3 small zucchini, thinly sliced
- 1 medium red onion, chopped
- 2 tablespoons brown sugar

In a large skillet, saute carrots in butter for 3 minutes. Add the zucchini and onion; saute 6-8 minutes longer or until crisp-tender. Add brown sugar; cook and stir until sugar is dissolved. **Yield:** 5 servings.

2 cups (8 ounces) shredded Mexican
   cheese blend, *divided*
1 cup frozen corn, thawed
1 teaspoon ground cumin
1/2 teaspoon salt
1/4 teaspoon pepper
4 large poblano peppers, halved
   and seeded

In a small bowl, combine the sour cream, lime juice and 1/4 cup cilantro. Cover and refrigerate until serving.

In a large skillet, saute chopped onion and garlic in butter until onion is tender. Add the yellow squash, zucchini and jalapeno pepper; cook and stir over medium heat for 2 minutes. Add the chopped portobello mushroom; cook and stir for 2 minutes.

Stir in the beans, 1-1/2 cups cheese, corn, cumin, salt, pepper and remaining cilantro. Remove from the heat. Spoon into pepper halves; sprinkle with remaining cheese.

Prepare the grill for indirect heat, using a drip pan. Place peppers over pan. Grill, covered, over indirect medium heat for 10-14 minutes or until tender. Serve with the sour cream sauce. **Yield:** 4 servings.

Editor's Note: When cutting hot peppers, disposable gloves are recommended. Avoid touching your face.

GRILLED CHILES RELLENOS

(Pictured above)

Lori Nelson, Austin, Texas

Here's a healthy version of one of my favorite Mexican dishes. The grilled peppers go great with Spanish rice, gazpacho or a refreshing salad with jicama and citrus.

1 cup (8 ounces) sour cream
2 tablespoons lime juice
1/2 cup minced fresh cilantro, *divided*
1 small onion, finely chopped
1 garlic clove, minced
1 tablespoon butter
1 small yellow summer squash,
   finely chopped
1 small zucchini, finely chopped
1 jalapeno pepper, seeded and finely
   chopped
1 large portobello mushroom cap,
   finely chopped
1 can (15 ounces) black beans,
   rinsed and drained

GRILLED POTATOES

Jena Coffey, Rock Hill, Missouri

Need a simple sidekick to serve with steaks or chops? Try this potato recipe that's bursting-with-flavor. I make this recipe for picnics and potlucks. The potatoes turn out tender and well-seasoned. Plus, there's one less pot to wash.

1 tablespoon olive oil
2 garlic cloves, minced
1/2 teaspoon dried basil
1/4 teaspoon salt
1/8 teaspoon pepper
3 medium baking potatoes, peeled
   and cut into 1-inch cubes

In a large bowl, combine the olive oil, garlic, basil, salt and pepper. Add the cubed potatoes; toss to coat. Spoon onto a greased double thickness of heavy-duty foil (about 18 in. square).

Fold foil around the potato mixture and seal tightly. Grill, covered, over medium heat for 30-35 minutes or until the potatoes are tender, turning once. Open foil carefully to allow steam to escape. **Yield:** 4 servings.

Side Dishes & Condiments

♦♦♦♦♦♦♦♦♦
WHITE 'N' SWEET MASHED POTATOES
(Pictured below)

Gail Drews, Flat Rock, North Carolina

Sweet potatoes are a staple of Southern cooking here in North Carolina. Combined with russet potatoes, this recipe turns simple mashed potatoes into a very special treat.

1-1/2 pounds russet potatoes (about
    4 medium), peeled and cubed
1-1/2 pounds sweet potatoes (about
    4 medium), peeled and cubed
  1 cup milk, warmed
1/4 cup butter, cubed
  1 teaspoon salt
1/2 teaspoon ground cinnamon
1/4 teaspoon ground nutmeg

Place russet potatoes and sweet potatoes in a large saucepan and cover with water. Bring to a boil. Reduce heat; cover and simmer for 15-20 minutes or until tender. Drain.

In a large bowl, mash potatoes with the milk, butter, salt, cinnamon and nutmeg until potatoes reach desired consistency. **Yield:** 8 servings.

♦♦♦♦♦♦♦♦♦♦♦
BARBECUE GREEN BEAN BAKE
(Pictured above)

Joanne Aby, York, Pennsylvania

This recipe was given to me at a Bible study picnic by a dear lady who loved to make up her own recipes. I've shared it with many friends, including missionaries who have taken it to other countries!

  6 bacon strips, diced
  1 small onion, chopped
  1 cup ketchup
1/2 cup packed brown sugar
  1 tablespoon Worcestershire sauce
  2 packages (10 ounces *each*) frozen cut
    green beans, thawed

In a large skillet, cook diced bacon over medium heat until crisp. Remove to paper towels and drain, reserving 1 tablespoon of the drippings. Saute the chopped onion in the drippings until tender. Add the ketchup, brown sugar and Worcestershire sauce; cook and stir until the mixture comes to a boil.

Place the green beans in a greased 1-1/2-qt. baking dish; top with the onion mixture and the cooked bacon. Cover and bake at 350° for 30-35 minutes or until the green beans are tender. **Yield:** 6 servings.

HOME-BAKED *goodness is what you'll find with every recipe in this chapter. Fill your home with the enticing aroma of freshly baked breads, biscuits and muffins.*

IRRESISTIBLE. Cream-Filled Cinnamon Coffee Cake and Buttery Almond Pear Cake (both on p. 85).

Breads & Rolls

▼▲▼▲▼▲▼▲▼▲▼▲▼

BUTTERY ALMOND PEAR CAKE

(Pictured at left)

Lillian Julow, Gainesville, Florida

Pears and almonds make a mouth-watering match in this cake. It looks pretty with the sliced fruit on top. I have always wondered how something this simple can taste this wonderful!

1-1/4 cups blanched almonds
1/2 cup plus 4-1/2 teaspoons sugar, *divided*
1/3 cup all-purpose flour
1/4 teaspoon salt
5 tablespoons cold butter, *divided*
2 eggs
1/4 cup milk
1 can (15-1/4 ounces) pear halves, drained and thinly sliced

In a food processor, combine almonds and 1/2 cup sugar. Cover and process until blended; transfer to a bowl. Stir in flour and salt. In a microwave-safe bowl, melt 4 tablespoons butter; whisk in eggs and milk. Stir into almond mixture.

Pour into a greased 9-in. fluted tart pan with a removable bottom. Arrange the pear slices over batter. Sprinkle with remaining sugar; dot with remaining butter.

Place on a baking sheet. Bake at 350° for 40-45 minutes or until crust is golden brown. Serve warm or at room temperature. Refrigerate leftovers. **Yield:** 6-8 servings.

▼▲▼▲▼▲▼▲▼▲▼▲▼

CREAM-FILLED CINNAMON COFFEE CAKE

(Pictured at left)

Arlene Wengerd, Millersburg, Ohio

Repeat guests at my home phone ahead to request this cinnamony coffee cake for breakfast. You can prepare it in advance and refrigerate, or welcome company with its fresh-baked aroma.

1/2 cup butter, softened
1 cup sugar
2 eggs
1 teaspoon vanilla extract

1-1/2 cups all-purpose flour
1/2 teaspoon baking soda
1/2 teaspoon salt
1 cup (8 ounces) sour cream
TOPPING:
1/2 cup sugar
1/2 cup chopped pecans
2 teaspoons ground cinnamon
FILLING:
1 tablespoon cornstarch
3/4 cup milk
1/4 cup butter, softened
1/4 cup shortening
1/2 cup sugar
1/2 teaspoon vanilla extract

In a large bowl, cream butter and sugar until light and fluffy. Add eggs, one at a time, beating well after each addition. Beat in vanilla. Combine the flour, baking soda and salt; add to creamed mixture alternately with sour cream, beating just until combined.

Pour into two greased and waxed paper-lined 9-in. round baking pans. Combine the topping ingredients; sprinkle over batter. Lightly cut through with a knife to swirl.

Bake at 350° for 20-25 minutes or until a toothpick comes out clean. Cool for 10 minutes; remove from pans to wire racks to cool.

For the filling, in a small saucepan, mix the cornstarch and milk until smooth. Bring to a boil; cook and stir for 1-2 minutes until thickened. Cover and refrigerate until chilled. Cream the butter, shortening and sugar until light and fluffy. Add the vanilla extract and chilled milk mixture; beat on medium speed until smooth and creamy, about 10 minutes.

Place one cooled cake on a serving plate; spread with filling. Top with remaining cake. Store in the refrigerator. **Yield:** 8-10 servings.

CREAMING BUTTER

When creaming butter, it should be softened (a table knife will be able to glide through the butter). When butter is cut into a mixture, it generally should be cold from the refrigerator.

Apricot Sunshine Coffee Cake

Joyce Stewart, Vernon, British Columbia

What a great way to start a weekend morning! This coffee cake has all the right stuff to brighten anyone's day!

   2 tablespoons butter, melted
  1/4 cup packed brown sugar
   1 teaspoon ground cinnamon
   8 to 12 fresh apricots, halved *or* 2 cans
     (15-1/4 ounces *each*) apricot halves,
     drained
  1/4 cup shortening
  3/4 cup sugar
   1 egg
1-1/2 cups all-purpose flour
   2 teaspoons baking powder
  1/2 teaspoon salt
  1/2 cup milk
  16 to 24 pecan *or* walnut halves

Pour butter into a greased 8-in. square baking dish; sprinkle with brown sugar and cinnamon. Arrange the apricot halves, cut side down, in a single layer over top; set aside.

In a small bowl, beat shortening and sugar for 2 minutes or until crumbly. Beat in egg. Combine the flour, baking powder and salt; gradually add to crumb mixture alternately with milk just until combined. Spread over apricots.

Bake at 375° for 30-40 minutes or until a toothpick inserted near the center comes out clean. Cool for 10 minutes before inverting onto a serving plate. Place a pecan half in the center of each apricot half. Serve warm. **Yield:** 9-12 servings.

Mother's Rolls

(Pictured at right)

Patricia Baxter, Great Bend, Kansas

These golden cloverleaf dinner rolls were one of my mother's specialties. We always looked forward to them on holidays and special occasions.

   2 packages (1/4 ounce *each*) active
     dry yeast
   1 cup warm water (110° to 115°)
1-1/2 cups warm milk (110° to 115°)
  1/3 cup sugar
  1/3 cup shortening
   1 egg
   2 teaspoons salt
   7 to 7-1/2 cups all-purpose flour

In a large bowl, dissolve yeast in warm water. Add the milk, sugar, shortening, egg, salt and 3 cups

flour. Beat on medium speed until mixture has a spongy texture. Let stand for 10 minutes.

Stir in enough remaining flour to form a soft dough. Turn onto a lightly floured surface; knead until smooth and elastic, about 6-8 minutes. Place in a greased bowl, turning once to grease top. Cover and let rise in a warm place until doubled, about 1 hour.

Punch dough down. Turn onto a lightly floured surface; divide into three portions. Let rest for 5 minutes. Divide each portion into 36 pieces. Shape each piece into a ball; place three balls in each greased muffin cup.

Cover and let rise until almost doubled, about 30 minutes. Bake at 375° for 12-15 minutes or until golden brown. Remove from pans to wire racks. Serve warm. **Yield:** 3 dozen.

Lemon Currant Loaves

Loraine Meyer, Bend, Oregon

My grandmother made this bread often when I was growing up. I can still close my eyes and remember the tantalizing aroma of lemon as it came out of the oven.

FILLING:
   1 package (10 ounces) dried currants
  1/2 cup sugar
   2 teaspoons grated lemon peel
DOUGH:
   2 packages (1/4 ounce *each*) active
     dry yeast
  1/2 cup sugar, *divided*
  1/2 cup warm water (110° to 115°)
   2 cups warm milk (110° to 115°)
  3/4 cup butter, softened, *divided*

3 eggs, lightly beaten
5 tablespoons lemon juice
2 teaspoons grated lemon peel
1-1/2 teaspoons salt
8 to 9 cups all-purpose flour
ICING:
1 cup confectioners' sugar
1 tablespoon lemon juice

Combine the ingredients for the filling and set aside. For the dough, in a large bowl, dissolve the yeast and 1 tablespoon sugar in warm water; let stand for 5 minutes. Add milk, 1/2 cup butter, eggs, lemon juice, lemon peel, salt, remaining sugar and enough flour to form a soft dough. Turn onto a floured surface; knead until smooth and elastic, about 6-8 minutes. Place in a greased bowl, turning once to grease the top. Cover and let rise in a warm place until doubled, about 1 hour.

Punch dough down. Divide into six portions; roll each portion into a 10-in. x 4-in. rectangle. Melt the remaining butter; brush over dough. Sprinkle filling to within 1/2 in. of edges. Roll up jelly-roll style, starting with a long side, to form a rope; pinch seams to seal.

Place three ropes on a floured surface and braid; pinch ends to seal and tuck under. Transfer to a greased 9-in. x 5-in. loaf pan. Repeat with remaining ropes. Cover and let rise in a warm place until doubled, about 45 minutes.

Bake at 375° for 50-55 minutes or until golden brown, covering loosely with foil during last 15 minutes. Cool for 10 minutes before removing from pans to wire racks to cool completely.

Combine icing ingredients; drizzle over loaves. **Yield:** 2 loaves (16 slices each).

CRANBERRY SURPRISE MUFFINS
(Pictured above)

Helen Howley, Mount Laurel, New Jersey

This recipe has been in my family since 1943 and has been enjoyed during the holidays for years. The "surprise" is a dollop of cranberry sauce in the center.

2 cups all-purpose flour
2 tablespoons sugar
3 teaspoons baking powder
1/2 teaspoon salt
2 eggs
1 cup milk
1/4 cup butter, melted
1 cup jellied cranberry sauce

In large bowl, combine flour, sugar, baking powder and salt. In another bowl, whisk eggs, milk and butter. Stir into dry ingredients until moistened.

Fill 12 greased muffin cups one-fourth full. Drop a rounded tablespoonful of cranberry sauce into each cup. Top with remaining batter.

Bake at 400° for 12-15 minutes or until muffin tops spring back when lightly touched. Cool for 5 minutes before removing from pan to a wire rack. Serve warm. **Yield:** 1 dozen.

SUREFIRE BAKING POWDER

To test if baking powder is fresh, put 1 teaspoon in a cup and add 1/3 cup hot water. If it bubbles, it's okay to use. If not, buy a new can.

CINNAMON-WALNUT COFFEE CAKE

Kathy Kirkland, Maryville, Tennessee

Since this coffee cake can serve as dessert for the evening meal and a warm-up for breakfast the next day, we enjoy it often. It's just the right size for my husband and me.

    1 cup all-purpose flour
  1/2 cup sugar
1-1/2 teaspoons baking powder
  1/2 teaspoon salt
  1/2 teaspoon ground cinnamon
    1 egg
  1/2 cup milk
  1/4 cup butter, melted
  1/2 cup raisins
  1/2 cup plus 2 tablespoons chopped
      walnuts, *divided*
  1/2 teaspoon cinnamon-sugar

In a small bowl, combine the flour, sugar, baking powder, salt and cinnamon. In another bowl, whisk the egg, milk and butter; stir into the dry ingredients just until moistened. Stir in raisins and 1/2 cup walnuts.

Transfer to a greased 9-in. square baking pan. Sprinkle with cinnamon-sugar and remaining walnuts. Bake at 375° for 20-25 minutes or until golden brown and a toothpick inserted near the center comes out clean. Cool on a wire rack. **Yield:** 9 servings.

ZUCCHINI CHEDDAR BISCUITS

Jean Moore, Pliny, West Virginia

My husband grows a big garden, and our squash crop always seems to multiply! We give squash to everyone but still have plenty left over for making jelly, relish, pickles, breads, cakes and brownies.

    1 large onion, chopped
  1/4 cup butter, cubed
2-1/2 cups biscuit/baking mix
    1 tablespoon minced fresh parsley
  1/2 teaspoon dried basil
  1/2 teaspoon dried thyme
    3 eggs, lightly beaten
  1/4 cup milk
1-1/2 cups shredded zucchini
    1 cup (4 ounces) shredded cheddar cheese

In a large skillet, saute the onion in butter until tender. In a large bowl, combine the biscuit mix, parsley, basil, thyme and onion mixture. Stir in eggs and milk just until combined. Stir in the zucchini and cheese.

ORLANDO ORANGE FRITTERS
(Pictured above)

Floyce Thomas-Larson, Silver Spring, Maryland

When grandchildren came to visit my mother's house, she would make this version of Heartland fried cakes.

    2 cups all-purpose flour
  1/2 cup sugar
    2 teaspoons baking powder
  1/2 teaspoon salt
    2 eggs
  1/2 cup orange juice
    2 tablespoons butter, melted
    1 tablespoon grated orange peel
Oil for deep-fat frying
Confectioners' sugar

In a small bowl, combine the flour, sugar, baking powder and salt. Combine the eggs, orange juice, butter and orange peel; stir into dry ingredients just until moistened.

In an electric skillet or deep-fat fryer, heat oil to 375°. Drop batter by rounded tablespoonfuls, a few at a time, into hot oil. Fry until golden brown, about 1-1/2 minutes on each side. Drain on paper towels. Dust with confectioners' sugar. **Yield:** 20 fritters.

Drop by 1/4 cupfuls 2 in. apart onto greased baking sheets. Bake at 400° for 10-14 minutes or until golden brown. Serve warm. Refrigerate the leftovers. **Yield:** 16 biscuits.

LITTLE SNAIL ROLLS
(Pictured below)

Christine Panzarella, Buena Park, California

Snails aren't always slow. My daughter and I made these fun coiled rolls together in a half hour. Later, at a party we were hosting, they disappeared even faster!

  2 tubes (11 ounces *each*) refrigerated
    breadsticks
 12 pretzel sticks, broken into fourths
  1 egg yolk
  1 tablespoon water
Poppy seeds *or* sesame seeds, optional

Separate dough into 24 breadsticks. For each snail, gently roll one breadstick into an 8-in. rope. Place on an ungreased baking sheet; coil 6-1/2 in. of the rope. Slightly separate remaining portion of dough from the coil and curl upward; add two pretzel pieces for antennae.

In a small bowl, beat egg yolk and water. Brush over dough. Sprinkle with poppy or sesame seeds if desired. Bake at 375° for 10-13 minutes or until golden brown. Serve warm. **Yield:** 2 dozen.

Editor's Note: This recipe was tested with Pillsbury refrigerated breadsticks.

GREEN ONION DROP BISCUITS
(Pictured above)

Our Test Kitchen created these golden gems. Crunchy on the outside and tender inside, you'll want to save a few biscuits for mini ham sandwiches the next day. Feel free to substitute chives for green onions.

    2 cups all-purpose flour
  1/2 cup thinly sliced green onions
    2 teaspoons sugar
    2 teaspoons baking powder
  1/2 teaspoon salt
  1/4 teaspoon baking soda
    6 tablespoons cold butter
    1 egg
  3/4 cup buttermilk

In a small bowl, combine the flour, onions, sugar, baking powder, salt and baking soda. Cut in butter until mixture resembles coarse crumbs. Combine egg and buttermilk; stir into crumb mixture just until moistened.

Drop the batter by 1/4 cupfuls 2 in. apart onto a greased baking sheet. Bake at 400° for 12-15 minutes or until golden brown. Serve warm. **Yield:** 10 servings.

BUTTERMILK SUBSTITUTE

For each cup of buttermilk, use 1 tablespoon of white vinegar or lemon juice plus enough milk to measure 1 cup. Stir, then let stand for 5 minutes. You can also use 1 cup of plain yogurt or 1-3/4 teaspoons cream of tartar plus 1 cup milk.

Potluck-Pleasing Coffee Cakes

WHO DOESN'T LIKE warm, home-baked coffee cake? These recipes deliver all the yumminess of snack cake with the added convenience of being particularly potluck friendly.

ALMOND COFFEE CAKE

(Pictured below)

Mary Shivers, Ada, Oklahoma

This cake is doubly delicious due to the cream cheese and vanilla chip filling. One piece leads to another!

    1 loaf (1 pound) frozen bread dough,
      thawed
    1 package (8 ounces) cream cheese,
      softened
  1/4 cup sugar
    1 egg
  1/2 teaspoon almond extract
  3/4 cup vanilla *or* white chips
    1 tablespoon milk

GLAZE:
    1 cup confectioners' sugar
  1/4 teaspoon almond extract
    1 to 2 tablespoons milk
  1/2 cup slivered almonds, toasted

On a lightly floured surface, roll dough into a 15-in. x 9-in. rectangle. Transfer to a lightly greased baking sheet.

In a small bowl, beat cream cheese and sugar until smooth. Add egg and extract; mix well (filling will be soft). Spread down center of rectangle; sprinkle with chips. On each long side, cut 1-in.-wide strips, about 1/2 in. from filling.

Starting at one end, fold alternating strips at an angle across filling. Seal ends. Cover and let rise in a warm place until doubled, about 1 hour.

Brush the top with the milk. Bake at 350° for 20-30 minutes or until golden brown. Cool on a wire rack.

For the glaze, combine confectioners' sugar and extract. Stir in enough milk to achieve desired consistency. Drizzle over coffee cake. Sprinkle with almonds. **Yield:** 8-10 servings.

ORANGE-DATE COFFEE CAKE

Pat Walter, Pine Island, Minnesota

You'll want to eat the deliciously delicate cake a sliver at a time...just to make the enjoyment last. The splash of orange juice and chewy dates are what make this recipe extra-special.

    2 cups all-purpose flour
  1/2 cup sugar
    2 teaspoons baking powder
  1/2 teaspoon salt
    1 egg
  1/2 cup milk
  1/2 cup canola oil
  1/2 cup orange juice
    2 teaspoons grated orange peel
  1/2 cup chopped dates
  1/2 cup chopped nuts
  1/2 cup packed brown sugar
    1 teaspoon ground cinnamon
    2 tablespoons cold butter

In a large bowl, combine the flour, sugar, baking powder and salt. In another bowl, whisk the egg, milk, oil, orange juice and peel; stir into the dry ingredients just until moistened. Fold in dates.

Pour into a greased 11-in. x 7-in. baking pan. In a bowl, combine the nuts, brown sugar and cinnamon. Cut in the butter until mixture resembles coarse crumbs; sprinkle over batter.

Bake at 375° for 25-30 minutes or until a toothpick inserted near the center comes out clean. Serve warm. **Yield:** 12 servings.

CRANBERRY-SOUR CREAM COFFEE CAKE

(Pictured above right)

Carole Resnick, Cleveland, Ohio

This delicious cake is so easy to make. Plus, it has all of the flavor of an old-fashioned coffee cake, but the convenience of an easy-to-carry potluck dessert.

  3/4 cup sour cream
  1/4 cup milk
    1 cup butter, softened
  1/2 cup sugar
  1/2 cup packed brown sugar
    3 eggs
    2 teaspoons vanilla extract
2-3/4 cups all-purpose flour
    1 teaspoon baking powder
  1/2 teaspoon baking soda
  1/2 teaspoon salt
FILLING:
    3 cups chopped fresh *or* frozen cranberries, thawed
  3/4 cup sugar
    2 tablespoons orange juice
    2 teaspoons grated orange peel
    1 teaspoon ground cinnamon
  1/2 teaspoon ground cloves

In a small bowl, combine sour cream and milk; set aside. In a large bowl, cream butter and sugars until light and fluffy. Add eggs, one at a time, beating well after each addition. Beat in vanilla. Combine the flour, baking powder, baking soda and salt; add to creamed mixture alternately with sour cream mixture.

Spread two-thirds of the batter into a greased 13-in. x 9-in. baking dish. Combine the filling ingredients; sprinkle over the batter. Top with remaining batter.

Bake at 350° for 40-45 minutes or until a toothpick inserted near the center comes out clean. Cool on a wire rack. **Yield:** 12-15 servings.

★★★★★★★★★★★★
ORANGE CARROT MUFFINS
(Pictured above)

Arlyn Gagnon, Rochester, Minnesota

Nutmeg, cloves and orange peel make these carrot muffins a special anytime treat.

    1/3 cup butter-flavored shortening
    1/2 cup sugar
      2 eggs
    1/2 cup orange juice
  1-3/4 cups all-purpose flour
      3 teaspoons grated orange peel
      1 teaspoon baking soda
      1 teaspoon baking powder
    1/8 teaspoon ground nutmeg
    1/8 teaspoon ground cloves
      2 cups shredded carrots

In a large bowl, cream the shortening and sugar until light and fluffy. Beat in the eggs, then beat in orange juice. Combine the flour, orange peel, baking soda, baking powder, nutmeg and cloves; add to the creamed mixture just until combined. Fold in the carrots.

Fill greased or paper-lined muffin cups three-fourths full. Bake at 350° for 18-22 minutes or until a toothpick inserted in centers comes out clean. Cool for 5 minutes before removing from pan to a wire rack. Serve warm. **Yield:** 1 dozen.

★★★★★★★★★★★★
BROWN RICE YEAST ROLLS
(Pictured at right)

Harriet Stichter, Milford, Indiana

I've had this recipe for such a long time that I don't even remember where it came from. It's a great way to get your family to eat brown rice, which is so good for you. My family didn't even notice that the rice was in the rolls until I told them.

    6 to 7 cups all-purpose flour
    1/2 cup cornmeal
      2 packages (1/4 ounce *each*)
        active dry yeast
      1 teaspoon salt
    1/4 teaspoon baking soda
      2 cups water
    1/2 cup honey
    1/4 cup butter, cubed
      2 cups cooked brown rice

In a large bowl, combine 4 cups of the flour, cornmeal, yeast, salt and baking soda. In a small saucepan, heat the water, honey and butter to 120°-130°. Add to dry ingredients; beat until smooth. Stir in the rice and enough remaining flour to form a soft dough.

Turn the dough onto a floured surface; knead until smooth and elastic, about 6-8 minutes. Place the kneaded dough in a greased bowl, turning once to grease the top. Cover with a towel and let the dough rise in a warm place until doubled, about 1 hour.

Punch the dough down. Turn onto a lightly floured surface; divide into 30 pieces. Shape each piece into a roll. Place about 2 in. apart on greased baking sheets. Cover with a towel and let rise until doubled, about 30 minutes.

Bake at 375° for 12-15 minutes or until golden brown. Remove the rolls from pans to wire racks. **Yield:** 2-1/2 dozen.

USING RAPID-RISE YEAST

Rapid-rise yeast has two time-saving advantages over active dry yeast: It does not need to be dissolved in water before mixing, and it requires only one rise after shaping. To use, add the yeast to the flour mixture. Heat the liquid ingredients to 120°-130°. In place of the first rise, allow the dough to rest for 10 minutes before shaping. The next rise will take about half the time than a recipe that uses active dry yeast.

■■■■■■■■■■■■

CINNAMON SWIRL QUICK BREAD

(Pictured above)

Helen Richardson, Shelbyville, Michigan

While cinnamon bread is a natural for breakfast, it's great served around the clock! This is a nice twist on traditional cinnamon swirl yeast breads.

  2 cups all-purpose flour
1-1/2 cups sugar, *divided*
  1 teaspoon baking soda
1/2 teaspoon salt
  1 cup buttermilk
  1 egg
1/4 cup canola oil
  3 teaspoons ground cinnamon
GLAZE:
1/4 cup confectioners' sugar
1-1/2 to 2 teaspoons milk

In a large bowl, combine the flour, 1 cup sugar, baking soda and salt. Combine the buttermilk, egg and oil; stir into dry ingredients just until moistened. In a small bowl, combine cinnamon and remaining sugar.

Grease the bottom only of a 9-in. x 5-in. loaf pan. Pour half of the batter into the pan; sprinkle the top with half of the cinnamon-sugar mixture. Carefully spread with the remaining batter and sprinkle with the remaining cinnamon-sugar mixture; cut through the batter with a knife to form a swirl.

Bake at 350° for 45-50 minutes or until a toothpick inserted near the center comes out clean. Cool for 10 minutes before removing from the pan to a wire rack to cool completely. Combine confectioners' sugar and enough milk to reach desired consistency; drizzle over loaf. **Yield:** 1 loaf.

FLAXSEED BREAD

Jennifer Niemi, Kingston, Nova Scotia

This hearty, whole grain bread is among my all-time favorites. The flaxseed adds a nutty texture. Every slice is so satisfying.

1-1/2 cups whole wheat flour
1-1/2 to 2 cups all-purpose flour
1 package (1/4 ounce) active dry yeast
1 teaspoon salt
1-1/2 cups fat-free milk
1/4 cup packed brown sugar
2 tablespoons honey
2 tablespoons plus 1-1/2 teaspoons butter, *divided*
1/2 cup ground flaxseed
1/2 cup flaxseed

In a large bowl, combine the whole wheat flour, 1 cup all-purpose flour, dry yeast and salt. In a large saucepan, heat the milk, brown sugar, honey and 2 tablespoons butter to 120°-130°. Add to dry ingredients; beat until smooth. Stir in the ground flaxseed and whole flaxseed until smooth. Stir in enough remaining all-purpose flour to form a firm dough.

Turn onto a lightly floured surface; knead until smooth and elastic, about 6-8 minutes. Place in a large bowl coated with cooking spray, turning once to coat top. Cover and let rise in a warm place until doubled, about 1 hour.

Punch the dough down and turn onto a lightly floured surface. Shape into a loaf; place in a 9-in. x 5-in. loaf pan coated with cooking spray. Cover the dough and let rise until doubled, about 30 minutes.

Bake at 375° for 35-40 minutes or until golden brown. Remove from pan to a wire rack. Melt remaining butter; brush over bread. Cool. **Yield:** 1 loaf (16 slices).

ALMOND-FILLED BUTTERHORNS

(Pictured at right)

Loraine Meyer, Bend, Oregon

I add potato flakes to make my butterhorns moist and tender. The pillowy rolls complement any meal wonderfully with just the right sweetness. They're also great as a coffee-hour favorite. Remember to hide a few for yourself!

3-1/4 teaspoons active dry yeast
2 cups warm milk (110° to 115°)
4 eggs
1 cup mashed potato flakes
1 cup butter, softened
1/2 cup sugar
1-1/8 teaspoons salt
7 to 8 cups all-purpose flour
1 can (12-1/2 ounces) almond cake and pastry filling

In a large bowl, dissolve yeast in milk. Add the eggs, potato flakes, butter, sugar, salt and 4 cups flour. Beat on medium speed for 3 minutes. Beat until smooth. Stir in enough remaining flour to form a soft dough (dough will be sticky).

Turn dough onto a floured surface; knead until smooth and elastic, about 6-8 minutes. Place in a greased bowl, turning once to grease top. Cover and let rise in a warm place until doubled, about 1 hour.

Punch dough down. Turn onto a lightly floured surface; divide into thirds. Roll each portion into a 12-in. circle; spread each with filling. Cut each circle into 12 wedges.

Roll up wedges from the wide end and place point side down 2 in. apart on greased baking sheets. Curve ends to form a crescent. Cover and let rise until doubled, about 30 minutes.

Bake at 375° for 10-12 minutes or until lightly browned. Remove from pans to wire racks. Serve warm. **Yield:** 3 dozen.

Editor's Note: This recipe was tested with Solo brand cake and pastry filling. Look for it in the baking aisle.

PARMESAN-RANCH PAN ROLLS

(Pictured below)

Trisha Kruse, Eagle, Idaho

My mom taught me this easy roll recipe, which is great for feeding a crowd. There is never a crumb left over. Mom used her own bread dough, but using frozen dough is my shortcut. I also make a wheat bread dough version with poppy and sesame seeds that's popular, too.

- 2 loaves (1 pound *each*) frozen bread dough, thawed
- 1 cup grated Parmesan cheese
- 1/2 cup butter, melted
- 1 envelope buttermilk ranch salad dressing mix
- 1 small onion, finely chopped

On a lightly floured surface, divide the dough into 18 portions; shape each into a ball. In a small bowl, combine the cheese, butter and ranch dressing mix.

Roll balls in cheese mixture; arrange in two greased 9-in. square baking pans. Sprinkle with onion. Cover and let rise in a warm place until doubled, about 45 minutes.

Bake at 350° for 20-25 minutes or until golden brown. Remove from pans to wire racks. **Yield:** 1-1/2 dozen.

BROWN SUGAR RHUBARB MUFFINS

Frances Conklin, Cottonwood, Indiana

I make these muffins often during rhubarb season. Guests at our inn love them. For some crunch, I add our own state-grown black walnuts.

- 3 cups all-purpose flour
- 1-1/2 cups packed brown sugar
- 1 teaspoon baking soda
- 1 teaspoon salt
- 2 eggs
- 1 cup buttermilk
- 2/3 cup canola oil
- 2 teaspoons vanilla extract
- 2 cups diced fresh *or* frozen rhubarb
- 1 cup chopped walnuts

TOPPING:
- 1/4 cup packed brown sugar
- 1/4 cup chopped walnuts
- 1/2 teaspoon ground cinnamon

In a large bowl, combine the flour, brown sugar, baking soda and salt. In a small bowl, beat the eggs, buttermilk, oil and vanilla; stir into dry ingredients just until moistened. Fold in rhubarb and walnuts.

Fill greased or paper-lined muffin cups three-fourths full. Bake at 375° for 18-20 minutes or until a toothpick comes out clean. Cool for 5 minutes before removing from pans to wire racks. Serve warm. **Yield:** 20 muffins.

Editor's Note: If using frozen rhubarb, measure rhubarb while still frozen, then thaw completely. Drain in a colander, but do not press liquid out.

GOUDA MUFFINS

Margaret Schep, Thunder Bay, Ontario

These savory muffins are healthy, delicious and easy to fix. The cheese gives them an extra dose of flavor.

- 2 cups all-purpose flour
- 1/2 cup sugar
- 1 teaspoon baking powder
- 1 teaspoon salt
- 1/2 teaspoon baking soda
- 2 eggs
- 1 cup (8 ounces) plain yogurt
- 1/4 cup butter, melted
- 6 ounces Gouda cheese, shredded

In a large bowl, combine the flour, sugar, baking powder, salt and baking soda. In another bowl, whisk the eggs, yogurt and butter. Stir into dry ingredients just until moistened. Fold in cheese.

Fill well-greased muffin cups three-fourths full. Bake at 400° for 15-20 minutes or until a toothpick comes out clean. Cool for 5 minutes before removing from pan to a wire rack. Serve warm. Refrigerate leftovers. **Yield:** 1 dozen.

OLD-FASHIONED BLUEBERRY MUFFINS

(Pictured above)

June Morris, Water Mill Long Island, New York

Years ago at the end of the summer, our family often gathered to pick wild blueberries. Mother canned, and then saved them for special pie treats during the holidays. If there were any left over, she made them into these delicious blueberry muffins.

    1 cup all-purpose flour
  1/3 cup sugar
    1 teaspoon baking powder
  1/4 teaspoon salt
    1 egg
  1/4 cup milk
    2 tablespoons butter, melted
  1/2 teaspoon vanilla extract
  3/4 cup fresh *or* frozen blueberries

In a small bowl, combine the flour, sugar, baking powder and salt. In another bowl, whisk the egg, milk, butter and vanilla; stir into dry ingredients just until moistened. Fold in blueberries.

Fill greased or paper-lined muffin cups three-fourths full. Bake at 400° for 18-22 minutes or until a toothpick comes out clean. Cool for 5 minutes before removing from pan to a wire rack. Serve warm. **Yield:** 6 muffins.

Editor's Note: If using frozen blueberries, do not thaw before adding to batter.

A FEW MUFFIN TIPS

Be careful not to overmix the ingredients. Add the liquid ingredients to the dry and stir only until moistened—don't worry about small lumps. Use paper liners or grease muffin tins on the bottoms and halfway up the side of each cup. Fill the muffin cups about two-thirds full unless otherwise directed in the recipe.

SWEET TREATS *abound in this chapter that's chock-full of scrumptious chocolate goodies, oatmeal or nut-filled confections, spiced specialties and more. They're so good, you'll want to try them all!*

CHOCOLATE HEAVEN. Double Chocolate Orange Brownies (p. 99).

Cookies, Bars & Brownies

▰▰▰▰▰▰▰▰▰
DOUBLE CHOCOLATE ORANGE BROWNIES
(Pictured at left)

Elinor Townsend, North Grafton, Massachusetts

I have to give my husband credit for this idea. Since we love the combination of chocolate and orange, he suggested I come up with this recipe. They're not only his favorite, but also the whole family's. I'm always asked to bake these for family gatherings.

  3/4 cup butter, cubed
    4 squares (1 ounce *each*) unsweetened chocolate
    3 eggs
    2 cups sugar
    1 teaspoon orange extract
    1 cup all-purpose flour
    1 cup (6 ounces) semisweet chocolate chips
Confectioners' sugar

In a microwave-safe bowl, melt the butter and chocolate; stir until smooth. Cool slightly. In a large bowl, beat eggs and sugar. Stir in chocolate mixture. Beat in extract. Gradually add flour to chocolate mixture.

Pour into a greased 13-in. x 9-in. baking dish. Sprinkle with chocolate chips. Bake at 350° for 30-35 minutes or until a toothpick inserted near the center comes out clean.

Cool completely on a wire rack. Cut into squares. Just before serving, sprinkle with the confectioners' sugar. **Yield:** 2 dozen.

▰▰▰▰▰▰▰▰▰
BRENDA'S LEMON BARS

Brenda Hamilton, Nelson, British Columbia

I love to bake, and these lemon bars rank among my most often requested recipes. They have a delicious combination of sweet and tart.

2-1/4 cups all-purpose flour, *divided*
  1/2 cup plus 1 tablespoon confectioners' sugar, *divided*
    1 cup cold butter, cubed

    4 eggs
    2 cups sugar
  2/3 cup lemon juice
  1/2 teaspoon baking powder

In a large bowl, combine 2 cups flour and 1/2 cup confectioners' sugar; cut in butter until crumbly. Press into an ungreased 13-in. x 9-in. baking dish. Bake at 350° for 12-15 minutes or until lightly browned. Place on a wire rack to cool slightly.

Meanwhile, in a small bowl, beat the eggs, sugar, lemon juice, baking powder and remaining flour until frothy. Pour over the warm crust. Bake for 18-22 minutes or until lightly browned. Cool on a wire rack.

Dust with remaining confectioners' sugar. Cut into bars. Store in the refrigerator. **Yield:** 2 dozen.

▰▰▰▰▰▰▰▰▰
CHUNKY HAZELNUT OATMEAL COOKIES

Patricia Compton, Spokane, Washington

This is a great-tasting, hearty cookie. Children love them, and my husband and I like to take them with us when we go hiking.

  3/4 cup butter, softened
  1/2 cup sugar
  1/2 cup packed brown sugar
    1 egg
1-1/4 cups all-purpose flour
    1 teaspoon baking soda
1-1/2 cups old-fashioned oats
    1 cup (6 ounces) semisweet chocolate chips
  1/2 cup dried cherries
  1/2 cup chopped hazelnuts

In a large bowl, cream butter and sugars until light and fluffy. Beat in egg. Combine the flour and baking soda; gradually add to creamed mixture and mix well. Stir in the oats, chocolate chips, cherries and nuts.

Drop by tablespoonfuls 2 in. apart onto greased baking sheets. Bake at 375° for 9-12 minutes or until lightly browned. Remove to wire racks. **Yield:** 3 dozen.

CHOCOLATE-COVERED CHERRY COOKIES

(Pictured above)

Veronica Strange, Glocester, Rhode Island

I first tasted these cookies during a cookie swap at work a few years ago. They're so good, I make them every Christmas for our family get-together. People who haven't had them are always delighted by the "hidden treasure" inside.

     24 maraschino cherries
    1/2 cup butter, softened
    3/4 cup packed brown sugar
      1 tablespoon maraschino cherry juice
      1 teaspoon vanilla extract
  1-1/2 cups all-purpose flour
    1/8 teaspoon salt
      1 cup milk chocolate chips, *divided*
    1/2 teaspoon shortening

Pat cherries with paper towels to remove excess moisture; set aside. In a large bowl, cream butter and brown sugar until light and fluffy. Beat in cherry juice and vanilla. Combine flour and salt; gradually add to creamed mixture and mix well. Cover and refrigerate for 1 hour or until dough is easy to handle.

Insert a chocolate chip into each maraschino cherry. Wrap about a tablespoon of dough around each cherry. Place 1 in. apart on ungreased baking sheets.

Bake at 350° for 15-17 minutes or until set and the edges are lightly browned. Remove to wire racks to cool completely.

In a microwave, melt remaining chips and shortening; stir until smooth. Dip tops of cookies in melted chocolate; allow excess to drip off. Place on wax paper; let stand until set. Store in an airtight container. **Yield:** 2 dozen.

CEREAL COOKIE BARS

(Pictured below)

Connie Craig, Lakewood, Washington

These chewy crowd-pleasers feature all sorts of goodies, including chocolate chips, raisins, coconut and candy-coated baking bits. For a more colorful look, press the baking bits on top of the bars instead of stirring them into the cereal mixture.

      9 cups crisp rice cereal
  6-1/2 cups quick-cooking oats
      1 cup cornflakes
      1 cup flaked coconut
      2 packages (one 16 ounces, one
         10-1/2 ounces) miniature marshmallows
      1 cup butter, cubed
    1/2 cup honey
    1/2 cup chocolate chips
    1/2 cup raisins
    1/2 cup M&M's miniature baking bits

In a large bowl, combine cereal, oats, cornflakes and coconut; set aside.

In a large saucepan, cook and stir marshmallows and butter over low heat until melted and smooth. Stir in honey. Pour over cereal mixture; stir until coated. Cool for 5 minutes.

Stir in the chocolate chips, raisins and baking bits. Press into two greased 15-in. x 10-in. x 1-in. pans. Cool for 30 minutes before cutting. **Yield:** 6 dozen.

JUMBO CHOCOLATE CHIP COOKIES

(Pictured below)

Lori Sporer, Oakley, Kansas

These huge cookies are a family tradition. No one can resist their sweet chocolaty taste.

    2/3 cup shortening
    2/3 cup butter, softened
      1 cup sugar
      1 cup packed brown sugar
      2 eggs
      2 teaspoons vanilla extract
  3-1/2 cups all-purpose flour
      1 teaspoon baking soda
      1 teaspoon salt
      2 cups (12 ounces) semisweet
        chocolate chips
      1 cup chopped pecans

In a large bowl, cream the shortening, butter and sugars until light and fluffy. Beat in the eggs and vanilla. Combine the flour, baking soda and salt; add to creamed mixture and mix well. Fold in the chocolate chips and pecans. Chill for at least 1 hour.

Drop the batter by 1/4 cupfuls at least 1-1/2 in. apart onto greased baking sheets. Bake at 375° for 13-15 minutes or until golden brown. Cool for 5 minutes before removing to a wire rack. **Yield:** 2 dozen.

BLACK WALNUT BROWNIES

(Pictured above)

Catherine Berra Bleem, Walsh, Illinois

These have old-fashioned flavor because of the bold-tasting black walnuts, but they offer all the goodness of your favorite brownie. It's okay to substitute regular walnuts for the black ones.

      1 cup sugar
    1/4 cup canola oil
      2 eggs
      1 teaspoon vanilla extract
    1/2 cup all-purpose flour
      2 tablespoons baking cocoa
    1/2 teaspoon salt
    1/2 cup chopped black walnuts

In a small bowl, beat sugar and oil until blended. Beat in eggs and vanilla. Combine the flour, cocoa and salt; gradually add to sugar mixture and mix well. Stir in walnuts.

Pour batter into a greased 8-in. square baking pan. Bake at 350° for 30-35 minutes or until a toothpick comes out clean. Cool on a wire rack. **Yield:** 16 servings.

BLACK WALNUTS

English walnuts, found in the grocery store, have a light brown shell and are mild-tasting. Black walnuts have a very hard, thick black shell and a rich, intense flavor. Black walnuts are difficult to shell, so are not as widely available commercially as English walnuts.

CHOCOLATE PEANUT SQUARES
(Pictured below)

Marie Martin, Lititz, Pennsylvania

I received this recipe from a friend at our local fire hall's annual quilting bee, where ladies bring in treats to serve at break time. It was a big hit with our family.

      1 cup butter, *divided*
      6 squares (1 ounce *each*) semisweet
          chocolate, *divided*
1-1/2 cups graham cracker crumbs
  1/2 cup unsalted dry roasted peanuts,
          chopped
      2 packages (8 ounces *each*) cream
          cheese, softened
      1 cup sugar
      1 teaspoon vanilla extract

In a small microwave-safe bowl, melt 3/4 cup butter and two squares of chocolate; stir until smooth. Stir in cracker crumbs and peanuts.

Press into a greased 13-in. x 9-in. pan. Cover and refrigerate for 30 minutes or until set.

In a small bowl, beat the cream cheese, sugar and vanilla until fluffy. Spread over chocolate layer. Melt the remaining butter and chocolate; stir until smooth. Carefully spread over cream cheese layer. Cover and refrigerate until set. Cut into squares. **Yield:** 2 dozen.

GINGER CRANBERRY BARS
(Pictured above)

Lynn Newman, Gainesville, Florida

These beautiful bars were among the winners of a cranberry festival bake-off. They're tangy, crunchy and subtly sweet.

      1 cup butter, softened
  1/2 cup sugar
      2 teaspoons almond extract, *divided*
      2 cups all-purpose flour
      2 cans (16 ounces *each*) whole-berry
          cranberry sauce
      2 tablespoons candied *or* crystallized
          ginger, chopped
      3 egg whites
  1/2 cup confectioners' sugar
  1/2 cup sliced almonds

In a large bowl, cream butter and sugar until light and fluffy. Stir in 1-1/2 teaspoons almond extract. Beat in flour until crumbly. Press into a greased 13-in. x 9-in. baking dish. Bake at 350° for 25-28 minutes or until golden brown.

Meanwhile, in a small saucepan, heat the cranberry sauce and ginger. In a small bowl, beat the egg whites on medium speed until soft peaks form. Gradually beat in the confectioners' sugar, 1 tablespoon at a time, and remaining almond extract on high until stiff glossy peaks form. Spread the cranberry mixture over crust. Spread the meringue over the cranberry layer; sprinkle with almonds.

Increase heat to 400°. Bake for 14-15 minutes or until lightly browned. Cool completely before cutting the bars. Refrigerate the leftovers. **Yield:** 2 dozen.

HONEY MAPLE COOKIES
(Pictured below)

Barbara Kuder, Tribune, Kansas

Honey and maple syrup turn these chocolate chip cookies into something special. The maple flavor is light and subtle.

- 1 cup shortening
- 3/4 cup honey
- 3/4 cup maple syrup
- 2 eggs
- 1 teaspoon vanilla extract
- 2-1/2 cups all-purpose flour
- 1 teaspoon baking soda
- 1 teaspoon salt
- 2 cups (12 ounces) semisweet chocolate chips
- 1 cup chopped pecans

In a large bowl, beat shortening until light and fluffy. Add honey and syrup, a little at a time, beating well after each addition. Add eggs, one at a time, beating well after each addition (mixture will appear curdled). Beat in vanilla. Combine the flour, baking soda and salt. Gradually add to honey mixture and mix just until moistened. Stir in the chocolate chips and pecans.

Drop by rounded tablespoonfuls onto greased baking sheets. Bake at 350° for 8-10 minutes or until golden brown. Remove to wire racks. **Yield:** 5 dozen.

CHIPPY BLOND BROWNIES
(Pictured above)

Anna Allen, Owings Mills, Maryland

If you love chocolate and butterscotch, you won't be able to resist these chewy brownies. I often include this recipe with a baking dish as a wedding present. Everyone, young and old, enjoys these sweet treats.

- 6 tablespoons butter, softened
- 1 cup packed brown sugar
- 2 eggs
- 1 teaspoon vanilla extract
- 1-1/4 cups all-purpose flour
- 1 teaspoon baking powder
- 1/2 teaspoon salt
- 1 cup (6 ounces) semisweet chocolate chips
- 1/2 cup chopped pecans

In a large bowl, cream butter and brown sugar until light and fluffy. Add the eggs, one at a time, beating well after each addition. Beat in vanilla. Combine the flour, baking powder and salt; gradually add to creamed mixture. Stir in the chocolate chips and pecans.

Spread into a greased 11-in. x 7-in. baking pan. Bake at 350° for 25-30 minutes or until a toothpick inserted near the center comes out clean. Cool on a wire rack. **Yield:** 2 dozen.

Contest Winning Bars

EVERY BAR in this special section has won an award because of its exceptional flavor. If you're looking for tasty treats that are surefire winners, look no further.

RASPBERRY PATCH CRUMB BARS
(Pictured below)

Leanna Thorne, Lakewood, Colorado

To give these fresh, fruity bars even more crunch, add a sprinkling of nuts to the yummy crumb topping. Everyone will want to indulge.

        3 cups all-purpose flour
  1-1/2 cups sugar, *divided*
        1 teaspoon baking powder
      1/4 teaspoon salt
      1/4 teaspoon ground cinnamon
        1 cup shortening
        2 eggs, lightly beaten
        1 teaspoon almond extract
        1 tablespoon cornstarch
        4 cups fresh *or* frozen raspberries

In a large bowl, combine the flour, 1 cup sugar, baking powder, salt and cinnamon. Cut in the shortening until mixture resembles coarse crumbs. Stir in eggs and extract. Press two-thirds of the mixture into a greased 13-in. x 9-in. baking dish.

In a large bowl, combine the cornstarch and remaining sugar; add the berries and gently toss. Spoon over the crust. Sprinkle with the remaining crumb mixture.

Bake at 375° for 35-45 minutes or until bubbly and golden brown. Cool on a wire rack. Cut into bars. Store in the refrigerator. **Yield:** 3 dozen.

Editor's Note: If using frozen berries, do not thaw before tossing with cornstarch mixture.

CHEWY DATE NUT BARS

Linda Hutmacher, Teutopolis, Illinois

You'll need just six ingredients, including a convenient boxed cake mix, to bake up these chewy bars chock-full of walnuts and dates. They are my husband's favorite snack, and he loves to take them to work. I often whip up a batch for bake sales or to share with my co-workers.

        1 package (18-1/4 ounces) yellow
          cake mix
      3/4 cup packed brown sugar
      3/4 cup butter, melted
        2 eggs
        2 cups chopped dates
        2 cups chopped walnuts

In a large bowl, combine dry cake mix and brown sugar. Add butter and eggs; beat on medium speed for 2 minutes. Combine dates and walnuts; stir into batter (batter will be stiff).

Spread into a greased 13-in. x 9-in. baking pan. Bake at 350° for 35-45 minutes or until edges are golden brown. Cool on a wire rack for 10 minutes. Run a knife around sides of pan to loosen; cool completely before cutting. **Yield:** 3 dozen.

APPLE PIE BARS

Janet English, Pittsburgh, Pennsylvania

This is only one of the many wonderful recipes that my mother handed down to me. These delicious bars, with their flaky crust and scrumptious fruit filling, are the perfect way to serve apple pie to a crowd.

 4 cups all-purpose flour
 1 teaspoon salt
 1 teaspoon baking powder
 1 cup shortening
 4 egg yolks
 2 tablespoons lemon juice
 8 to 10 tablespoons cold water
FILLING:
 7 cups finely chopped peeled apples
 2 cups sugar
 1/4 cup all-purpose flour
 2 teaspoons ground cinnamon
Dash ground nutmeg
GLAZE:
 1 cup confectioners' sugar
 1 tablespoon milk
 1 tablespoon lemon juice

In a large bowl, combine flour, salt and baking powder. Cut in the shortening until the mixture resembles coarse crumbs. In a small bowl, whisk egg yolks, lemon juice and cold water; gradually add to the flour mixture, tossing with a fork until the dough forms a ball. Divide the dough in half. Chill for 30 minutes.

Roll out one portion of the dough between two large sheets of waxed paper into a 17-in. x 12-in. rectangle. Transfer to an ungreased 15-in. x 10-in. x 1-in. baking pan. Press pastry onto the bottom and up the sides of pan; trim pastry even with top edge.

For the filling, in a large bowl, toss the chopped apples, sugar, flour, cinnamon and nutmeg; spread over crust. Roll out the remaining pastry to fit top of pan; place over filling. Trim edges; brush edges between pastry with water or milk; pinch to seal. Cut slits in top.

Bake the bars at 375° for 45-50 minutes or until golden brown. Cool on a wire rack. Combine the ingredients for the glaze until smooth; drizzle over the bars before cutting them. **Yield:** about 2 dozen.

PEANUT BUTTER BROWNIE BARS
(Pictured above)

Radelle Knappenberger, Oviedo, Florida

A brownie mix makes this a simple treat that appeals to adults and children alike. Creamy peanut butter, nuts and crisp cereal make the bars fun to bite into.

 1 package fudge brownie mix
   (13-inch x 9-inch pan size)
 12 peanut butter cups, chopped
 1/2 cup salted peanuts, chopped
 2 cups (12 ounces) semisweet
   chocolate chips
 1-1/4 cups creamy peanut butter
 1 tablespoon butter
 1/8 teaspoon salt
 1-1/2 cups crisp rice cereal
 1 teaspoon vanilla extract

Prepare brownie batter according to package directions. Spread into a greased 13-in. x 9-in. baking pan. Bake at 350° for 20-25 minutes or until a toothpick comes out with moist crumbs.

Sprinkle with peanut butter cups and peanuts. Bake 4-6 minutes longer or until chocolate is melted. Cool on a wire rack.

Meanwhile, in a large saucepan, combine the chocolate chips, peanut butter, butter and salt. Cook and stir until chips are melted and mixture is smooth. Remove from the heat; stir in cereal and vanilla. Carefully spread over brownies. Cover and refrigerate for at least 2 hours before cutting. **Yield:** 3 dozen.

CARAMEL PECAN BARS
(Pictured below)

Emma Manning, Crossett, Arkansas

This recipe won first place at a cookie contest held where I work. These rich bars really capture the flavor of pecan pie.

> 1 cup butter, cubed
> 2-1/4 cups packed brown sugar
> 2 eggs
> 2 teaspoons vanilla extract
> 1-1/2 cups all-purpose flour
> 2 teaspoons baking powder
> 2 cups chopped pecans
> Confectioners' sugar, optional

In a large saucepan, heat butter and brown sugar over medium heat until sugar is dissolved. In a small bowl, beat the eggs, vanilla and butter mixture. Combine the flour and baking powder; gradually add to the butter mixture and mix well. Stir in pecans.

Spread into a greased 13-in. x 9-in. baking pan. Bake at 350° for 20-25 minutes or until a toothpick inserted near the center comes out with moist crumbs and edges are crisp. Cool on a wire rack. Dust with confectioners' sugar if desired. Cut into bars. **Yield:** 4 dozen.

GERMAN CHOCOLATE TOFFEE COOKIES
(Pictured above)

Joyce Robb, Dillon, Montana

When I first shared these crisp cookies with folks at the hospital where I work as a cook, everyone's palate was pleased! German sweet chocolate gives them a unique and delicious twist.

> 1 cup butter, softened
> 1 cup shortening
> 2-1/2 cups sugar
> 1/2 cup packed brown sugar
> 1 package (4 ounces) German sweet chocolate, melted
> 4 eggs
> 2 teaspoons water
> 2 teaspoons vanilla extract
> 6-1/2 cups all-purpose flour
> 2 teaspoons baking soda
> 1-1/2 teaspoons salt
> 1-1/2 cups English toffee bits *or* almond brickle chips
> 1-1/2 cups chopped walnuts

In a large bowl, cream butter, shortening and sugar until light and fluffy. Beat in chocolate. Add eggs, one at a time, beating well after each addition. Beat in water and vanilla. Combine the flour, baking soda and salt; gradually add to the creamed mixture and mix well. Stir in toffee bits and walnuts.

Drop by tablespoonfuls 2 in. apart onto greased baking sheets. Bake at 350° for 12-15 minutes or until golden brown. Remove to wire racks to cool. **Yield:** 13 dozen.

Cookies, Bars & Brownies

APPLE SPICE DROPS

(Pictured below)

Blanche Whytsell, Arnoldsburg, Wyoming

It's a snap to stir up these soft frosted cookies. With their big apple flavor and abundance of nuts, you'll have a hard time eating just one.

- 1/2 cup butter, softened
- 2/3 cup sugar
- 2/3 cup packed brown sugar
- 1 egg
- 1/4 cup apple juice
- 2 cups all-purpose flour
- 1 teaspoon ground cinnamon
- 1/2 teaspoon baking soda
- 1/2 teaspoon ground nutmeg
- 1 cup finely chopped peeled tart apple
- 1 cup chopped walnuts

FROSTING:
- 1/4 cup butter, softened
- 3 cups confectioners' sugar
- 1 teaspoon vanilla extract
- 3 to 4 tablespoons apple juice

In a large bowl, cream butter and sugars until light and fluffy. Beat in egg and apple juice. Combine dry ingredients; gradually add to the creamed mixture and mix well. Stir in apple and walnuts.

Drop the batter by teaspoonfuls 2 in. apart onto greased baking sheets. Bake at 375° for 12-14 minutes or until golden brown. Remove to wire racks to cool.

For frosting, cream the butter, sugar, vanilla and enough apple juice to achieve spreading consistency. Frost the cooled cookies. **Yield:** about 3-1/2 dozen.

GRADUATION CAPS

(Pictured above)

Margy Stief, Essington, Pennsylvania

Nothing says "graduation" like a mortarboard with tassels. I made these cute treats for my daughter's graduation. They really topped off the party fun!

- 24 miniature peanut butter cups
- 1 tube (6 ounces) decorating frosting in color of your choice
- 24 After Eight thin mints
- 24 milk chocolate M&M's in color of your choice *or* 24 semisweet chocolate chips

Remove paper liners from peanut butter cups; place upside down on waxed paper. Place a small amount of frosting on each peanut butter cup; center a mint on each. Using frosting, make a loop for each cap's tassel. Place an M&M on top of each loop. **Yield:** 2 dozen.

GRADUATION PARTY

When hosting a graduation party, buffets are the way to go. There's no serving involved, which allows you to mingle while keeping an eye on the table for refills. Look for recipes that can be prepared ahead, and avoid serving foods with lots of last-minute preparation.

Shield corners of dish with triangles of foil. Place the dish on an inverted microwave-safe saucer. Cook, uncovered, at 70% power for 8-10 minutes or until a toothpick comes out clean. Cook on high for 1 minute longer. Remove to a wire rack to cool completely. Store in the refrigerator. **Yield:** 1 dozen.

Editor's Note: Shielding with small pieces of foil prevents overcooking of food in the corners of a square or rectangular dish. Secure the foil firmly to the dish and do not allow it to touch the inside of oven.

Editor's Note: This recipe was tested in a 1,100-watt microwave.

MARBLE BROWNIES
(Pictured above)

Diana Coppernoll, Linden, North Carolina

I love to bake and enjoy trying new recipes. The cream cheese topping in these delights made them a fast favorite in my house.

     5 **tablespoons butter**
     2 **squares (1 ounce *each*) unsweetened chocolate**
   2/3 **cup sugar**
     2 **eggs**
     1 **teaspoon vanilla extract**
   2/3 **cup all-purpose flour**
   1/2 **teaspoon baking powder**
CHEESECAKE LAYER:
     1 **package (8 ounces) cream cheese**
   1/2 **cup sugar**
     1 **egg**
     1 **teaspoon vanilla extract**
     1 **cup (6 ounces) semisweet chocolate chips**

In a large microwave-safe bowl, combine butter and chocolate. Cover and microwave on high for 30-60 seconds; stir until smooth. Beat in sugar, eggs and vanilla. Combine flour and baking powder; gradually add to chocolate mixture until blended. Spread into a greased microwave-safe 8-in. square dish; set aside.

For cheesecake layer, in a large microwave-safe bowl, microwave cream cheese on high for 30-45 seconds or until softened; stir until smooth. Beat in sugar, egg and vanilla. Spoon over brownie batter; cut through batter with a knife to swirl. Sprinkle with chocolate chips.

BABY PACIFIER FAVORS
(Pictured below)

Lori Hertzog, Allentown, Pennsylvania

What a simple way to create adorable party favors for your friends and family who are expecting. They're perfect for a baby shower.

    12 **pieces red shoestring licorice *or* licorice whips**
    24 **small red gumdrops (1/2 inch)**
    24 **cutout butter cookies**

Cut the licorice into twenty-four 4-1/2-in. pieces. Make a small slit in the bottom of a gumdrop near one edge; insert one licorice piece end into the gumdrop. Make another slit in the opposite side of the gumdrop; insert the other end of the licorice.

Carefully push the small end of gumdrop up through the hole of a butter cookie. Repeat with remaining gumdrops, licorice and cookies. **Yield:** 2 dozen.

LADYBUG COOKIES

(Pictured above)

Kendra Barclay, De Kalb, Illinois

These bright, sweet "ladybugs" bring me luck when it comes to pleasing guests. I frost chocolate-covered marshmallow cookies to make the whimsical treats. They're pretty enough to be a centerpiece.

    1 cup vanilla frosting
  1/2 cup vanilla *or* white chips
Red liquid *or* paste food coloring
    1 package (12 ounces) chocolate and
      marshmallow cookies
    3 strips black shoestring licorice, cut into
      1-inch pieces
   12 large black gumdrops

In a microwave-safe bowl, melt the vanilla frosting and chips at 70% power; stir until smooth. Stir in the food coloring. Spread over the rounded tops of the cookies; place on a waxed paper-lined baking sheet.

For head, insert two pieces of licorice into gumdrops for antennae. With a toothpick, attach a gumdrop onto the side of each cookie.

Use a toothpick or knife to draw a line from the head down the center of each cookie. For legs, insert six pieces of licorice into frosting of each ladybug. Chop remaining licorice into small pieces; place on top for spots. **Yield:** 1 dozen.

FREEZING BAKED COOKIES

To freeze baked cookies for up to 3 months, wrap the cookies in plastic, stack in an airtight container, seal and freeze. Thaw wrapped cookies at room temperature before serving.

DOUBLE BUTTERSCOTCH COOKIES

(Pictured below)

Beverly Duncan, Lakeville, Ohio

I've made this old-fashioned recipe for years. It can also be made with miniature chocolate chips or coconut in place of the toffee bits.

  1/2 cup butter, softened
  1/2 cup shortening
    4 cups packed brown sugar
    4 eggs
    1 tablespoon vanilla extract
    6 cups all-purpose flour
    3 teaspoons baking soda
    3 teaspoons cream of tartar
    1 teaspoon salt
    1 package English toffee bits (10 ounces) *or*
      almond brickle chips (7-1/2 ounces)
    1 cup finely chopped pecans

In a large bowl, cream the butter, shortening and brown sugar until light and fluffy. Add the eggs, one at a time, beating well after each addition. Beat in the vanilla. Combine the flour, baking soda, cream of tartar and salt; gradually add to the creamed mixture and mix well. Stir in the toffee bits and pecans.

Shape the dough into three 14-in. rolls; wrap each in plastic wrap. Refrigerate for 4 hours or until firm.

Unwrap the dough and cut into 1/2-in. slices. Place 2 in. apart on greased baking sheets. Bake at 375° for 9-11 minutes or until lightly browned. Cool for 1-2 minutes before removing from pans to wire racks to cool completely. **Yield:** about 7 dozen.

DECADENT DESSERTS *grace the pages of this chapter for those with a serious sweet tooth. You won't be disappointed with the dozens of dinner finales.*

TEMPT YOUR TASTE BUDS. Chocolate Peanut Butter Dessert (p. 111).

Dazzling Desserts

CHOCOLATE PEANUT BUTTER DESSERT

(Pictured at left)

Christine Montalvo, Windsor Heights, Iowa

When I want to splurge on a rich dessert, I whip up this chocolate-glazed, frozen peanut butter mousse. It's so luscious, even a thin slice will satisfy. It tastes like a peanut butter cup.

1-1/4 cups packed dark brown sugar
  1 cup heavy whipping cream, *divided*
  3 egg yolks
1-1/4 cups creamy peanut butter
  6 tablespoons butter, softened
GLAZE:
1-1/2 cups heavy whipping cream
  2 tablespoons butter
  4 teaspoons dark corn syrup
 12 squares (1 ounce *each*) bittersweet
     chocolate, chopped
1/4 cup coarsely chopped dry roasted
     peanuts

In a small saucepan, combine brown sugar, 1/2 cup cream and yolks. Cook and stir over medium heat until mixture reaches 160° and is thick enough to coat the back of a metal spoon. Cover and refrigerate for 3 hours or until thickened.

Line an 8-in. x 4-in. loaf pan with plastic wrap; set aside. In a large bowl, cream peanut butter and butter until light and fluffy. Add brown sugar mixture; beat until smooth. In small bowl, beat remaining cream until stiff peaks form. Fold into peanut butter mixture. Spoon into prepared pan. Cover and refrigerate.

For glaze, in a large heavy saucepan, bring the cream, butter and corn syrup to a boil, stirring frequently. Remove from the heat. Add the chocolate; whisk until smooth. Set aside 1/3 cup glaze until cool. Place the remaining glaze in a microwave-safe bowl; cover and refrigerate overnight. Spread cooled glaze over loaf; cover and freeze overnight.

Using plastic wrap, lift loaf out of pan. Place chocolate side down in a 15-in. x 10-in. x 1-in. pan; place on a wire rack. Discard plastic wrap.

In microwave, warm refrigerated glaze; stir until smooth. Pour over loaf; spread with a metal spatula to completely cover top and sides. Sprinkle with peanuts. Freeze for 1 hour or until glaze is set. **Yield:** 10-12 servings.

BLUE-RIBBON BUTTER CAKE

Joan Gertz, Palmetto, Florida

I found this recipe in an old cookbook I bought at a garage sale. I knew it had been someone's favorite because of the stained and well-worn page.

  1 cup butter, softened
  2 cups sugar
  4 eggs
  2 teaspoons vanilla extract
  3 cups all-purpose flour
  1 teaspoon baking powder
1/2 teaspoon baking soda
1/2 teaspoon salt
  1 cup buttermilk
BUTTER SAUCE:
  1 cup sugar
1/2 cup butter, cubed
1/4 cup water
1-1/2 teaspoons almond extract
1-1/2 teaspoons vanilla extract

In a large bowl, cream butter and sugar until light and fluffy. Add eggs, one at a time, beating well after each addition. Beat in vanilla. Combine the flour, baking powder, baking soda and salt; add to creamed mixture alternately with buttermilk, beating well after each addition.

Pour into a greased and floured 10-in. tube pan. Bake at 350° for 65-70 minutes or until a toothpick inserted near the center comes out clean. Cool for 10 minutes. Run a knife around edge and center tube of pan. Invert cake onto a wire rack over waxed paper.

For sauce, combine the sugar, butter and water in a small saucepan. Cook over medium heat just until butter is melted and sugar is dissolved. Remove from the heat; stir in extracts.

Poke holes in the top of the warm cake; spoon 1/4 cup sauce over cake. Let stand until sauce is absorbed. Repeat twice. Poke holes into sides of cake; brush remaining sauce over sides. Cool completely. **Yield:** 12-16 servings.

JAM-TOPPED MINI CHEESECAKES

(Pictured above)

Presto! Our Test Kitchen turned cheesecake into finger food in just 15 minutes with this simple recipe. For fun, experiment with a variety of jams and preserves, such as strawberry or apricot.

    1 **cup graham cracker crumbs**
    3 **tablespoons butter, melted**
    1 **package (8 ounces) cream cheese, softened**
1/3 **cup sugar**
    1 **egg, lightly beaten**
    1 **teaspoon vanilla extract**
Assorted jams, warmed

In a small bowl, combine the graham cracker crumbs and butter. Press gently onto the bottom of 12 paper-lined muffin cups. In another small bowl, beat cream cheese, sugar, egg and vanilla until smooth. Spoon over crusts.

Bake at 350° for 15-16 minutes or until center is set. Cool for 10 minutes before removing from pan to a wire rack to cool completely. Refrigerate for at least 1 hour.

Remove paper liners; top each cheesecake with 1 teaspoon jam. **Yield:** 1 dozen.

FLAVOR BOOST FOR CRUSTS

Next time you're making a graham cracker crust, give it a touch of flair. It's easy to add 1/4 teaspoon cinnamon to the crumbs. Or, simply subsitute 1/4 cup of the graham cracker crumbs with chopped nuts or flaked coconut for extra texture and flavor.

APPLE PIE

(Pictured below)

Maggie Greene, Granite Falls, Washington

I remember coming home sullen one day because we'd lost a softball game. Grandma, in her wisdom, suggested, "Maybe a slice of hot apple pie will make you feel better." One bite…and Grandma was right.

1/2 **cup sugar**
1/2 **cup packed brown sugar**
    3 **tablespoons all-purpose flour**
    1 **teaspoon ground cinnamon**
1/4 **teaspoon ground ginger**
1/4 **teaspoon ground nutmeg**
    6 **to 7 cups thinly sliced peeled tart apples**
    1 **tablespoon lemon juice**
Pastry for double-crust pie (9 inches)
    1 **tablespoon butter**
    1 **egg white**
Additional sugar

In a small bowl, combine the sugars, flour and spices; set aside. In a large bowl, toss apples with lemon juice. Add sugar mixture; toss to coat.

Line a 9-in. pie plate with bottom crust; trim pastry even with edge. Fill with apple mixture; dot with butter. Roll out remaining pastry to fit top of pie. Place over filling. Trim, seal and flute edge. Cut slits in pastry.

Beat egg white until foamy; brush over pastry. Sprinkle with sugar. Cover edge loosely with foil.

Bake at 375° for 25 minutes. Remove foil and bake 20-25 minutes longer or until crust is golden brown and filling is bubbly. Cool on a wire rack. **Yield:** 8 servings.

STRAWBERRY RHUBARB TART

(Pictured above)

Kristy Martin, Circle Pine, Minnesota

Your family and friends will love this seasonal sweet-tart treat. The flavor of late spring fills every forkful. And oats make the from-scratch crust plain, old-fashioned good!

- 1/2 cup old-fashioned oats, toasted
- 2/3 cup all-purpose flour
- 1/4 cup sugar
- 1 teaspoon grated lemon peel
- 3/4 teaspoon baking powder
- 1/4 teaspoon salt
- 2 tablespoons canola oil
- 3 tablespoons milk
- 1/2 teaspoon vanilla extract

FILLING:
- 3-1/2 cups sliced fresh strawberries, *divided*
- 2 cups sliced fresh *or* frozen rhubarb
- 1/4 cup sugar
- 1/2 teaspoon grated lemon peel
- 5 teaspoons cornstarch
- 1 tablespoon cold water
- 4 teaspoons currant jelly, melted

Process oats in a food processor until finely ground. Place in a large bowl; add the flour, sugar, lemon peel, baking powder and salt. Slowly add oil, stirring until mixture resembles coarse crumbs. Combine milk and vanilla; stir into flour mixture, a tablespoon at a time, until mixture forms a ball.

Turn onto a floured surface; knead 7-8 times. Place pastry between sheets of waxed paper; roll out to fit a 9-in. fluted tart pan with removable bottom. Grease tart pan; gently press pastry into pan. Line pastry shell with a double thickness of heavy-duty foil. Bake at 350° for 12 minutes. Remove foil; bake 8-12 minutes longer or until lightly browned. Cool on a wire rack.

For filling, combine 1 cup strawberries, rhubarb, sugar and lemon peel in a large saucepan. Let stand for 30 minutes.

Cook and stir over medium-low heat for 8-10 minutes or until rhubarb is tender but retains shape. Combine cornstarch and water until smooth; stir into fruit mixture. Bring to a boil; cook and stir for 2 minutes or until thickened. Pour into a bowl; cover surface with waxed paper. Refrigerate for 1-2 hours.

Just before serving, spread filling into crust. Arrange remaining strawberries on top. Brush with jelly. **Yield:** 12 servings.

Editor's Note: If using frozen rhubarb, measure while still frozen, then thaw completely. Drain in a colander, but do not press liquid out.

BLUEBERRY LEMON CAKE

(Pictured below)

Leona Luecking, West Burlington, Iowa

I always set aside some of my fresh-picked blueberries to make this quick and easy dessert. Lemon flavor sparks the fruit layer and tender cake.

- 1/4 cup butter, cubed
- 1/2 cup sugar
- 2 teaspoons grated lemon peel, *divided*
- 2 cups fresh *or* frozen blueberries
- 1 package (9 ounces) yellow cake mix

Whipped cream, optional

In a small saucepan, melt the butter; stir in the sugar until dissolved. Add 1 teaspoon lemon peel. Pour into a greased 8-in. square baking dish. Arrange the blueberries in a single layer over top; set aside.

Prepare cake batter according to package directions. Stir in the remaining lemon peel. Carefully pour over blueberries.

Bake at 350° for 30-35 minutes or until a toothpick inserted near the center of cake comes out clean. Cool on a wire rack. Serve with whipped cream if desired. **Yield:** 9 servings.

BANANA ICE CREAM

(Pictured below)

Donna Robbins, Skiatook, Oklahoma

My son-in-law says this is the best ice cream he's ever had. It's always requested at family gatherings.

  4 cups half-and-half cream
2-1/2 cups sugar
Dash salt
  4 eggs, lightly beaten
  4 cups heavy whipping cream
  1 can (5 ounces) evaporated milk
  1 tablespoon vanilla extract
  2 cups mashed ripe bananas
    (4 to 5 medium)

In a large heavy saucepan, heat half-and-half to 175°; stir in sugar and salt until dissolved. Whisk a small amount of hot mixture into eggs. Return all to the pan, whisking constantly. Cook and stir over low heat until mixture reaches 160° and coats the back of a metal spoon.

Remove from heat. Cool quickly by placing pan in a bowl of ice water; stir for 2 minutes. Stir in the whipping cream, milk and vanilla. Press plastic wrap onto surface of custard. Refrigerate for several hours or overnight.

Stir in the bananas. Fill cylinder of ice cream freezer two-thirds full; freeze according to the manufacturer's directions. Refrigerate remaining mixture until ready to freeze. When ice cream is frozen, transfer to a freezer container; freeze for 2-4 hours before serving. **Yield:** 3 quarts.

CHERRY WALNUT CAKE

(Pictured above)

Jan Johnson, Naches, Washington

This recipe has been in our family for four generations. Even people who normally shy away from sour cherries welcome this special dessert.

  1 can (14-1/2 ounces) pitted tart cherries
1/3 cup shortening
1-1/4 cups sugar
  2 eggs
2-1/2 cups all-purpose flour
1-1/2 teaspoons baking powder
1/2 teaspoon baking soda
  1 cup milk
  1 cup chopped walnuts
CHERRY GLAZE:
1/2 cup sugar
  3 tablespoons cornstarch
Pinch salt
  1 cup water
1/4 teaspoon almond extract
  1 to 2 drops red food coloring, optional

Drain cherries, reserving 3/4 cup juice; set aside. In a large bowl, cream shortening and sugar until light and fluffy. Add eggs, one at a time, beating well after each addition. Combine the flour, baking powder and baking soda; add to creamed mixture alternately with milk and mix well. Stir in walnuts and reserved cherries.

Transfer to a greased 13-in. x 9-in. baking dish. Bake at 350° for 30-35 minutes or until a toothpick inserted near the center comes out clean. Cool completely on a wire rack.

For glaze, combine the sugar, cornstarch and

salt in a small saucepan. Stir in the water and reserved cherry juice until smooth. Cook and stir over medium heat until mixture comes to a boil. Cook and stir 1-2 minutes longer or until thickened. Remove from the heat; stir in the almond extract and food coloring if desired. Cool for 15 minutes. Spread over cake; let stand until set. **Yield:** 12-15 servings.

PUMPKIN ICE CREAM PIE

Marion Stoll, Dent, Minnesota

The holidays are the perfect time to try this quick twist on a traditional pumpkin pie. I often make it ahead, so it effortlessly goes from freezer to feast!

   1 quart vanilla ice cream, softened
3/4 cup canned pumpkin
1/4 cup honey
1/2 teaspoon ground cinnamon
1/4 teaspoon salt
1/4 teaspoon ground ginger
Dash ground nutmeg
Dash ground cloves
   1 graham cracker crust (9 inches)
Whipped topping and pecan halves, optional

In a large bowl, combine the first eight ingredients; beat until smooth. Spoon into crust. Cover and freeze for 2 hours or until firm.

Remove from the freezer 15 minutes before serving. Garnish with whipped topping and pecans if desired. **Yield:** 6-8 servings.

CHERRIES OVER CREAMY FLUFF

Barb Cooan, Birchwood, Wisconsin

This sweet, no-bake dish is a definite keeper. The classic, cherry dessert recipe has been in our family for over 40 years.

   1 package (8 ounces) cream cheese, softened
1/2 cup sugar
   1 teaspoon vanilla extract
   2 cups heavy whipping cream, whipped
   2 cups miniature marshmallows
   1 can (21 ounces) cherry pie filling

In a large bowl, beat the cream cheese, sugar and vanilla until fluffy. Fold in whipped cream and marshmallows. Cover and refrigerate for at least 30 minutes.

Spoon into dessert bowls. Top with the pie filling. **Yield:** 7-8 servings.

POPPY SEED CHIFFON CAKE

(Pictured above)

Barbara Sonsteby, Mesa, Arizona

This terrific cake recipe was given to me by my grandchild. I hope you enjoy it as much as we do.

   7 eggs, *separated*
1/2 cup poppy seeds
   1 cup hot water
   2 cups all-purpose flour
1-1/2 cups sugar
   3 teaspoons baking powder
   1 teaspoon salt
1/4 teaspoon baking soda
   1 cup canola oil
   2 teaspoons vanilla extract
1/2 teaspoon cream of tartar

Let eggs stand at room temperature for 30 minutes. In a small bowl, soak poppy seeds in hot water for 15 minutes.

In a large bowl, combine the flour, sugar, baking powder, salt and baking soda. In a bowl, whisk the egg yolks, oil, vanilla and poppy seeds with water. Add to dry ingredients; beat until well blended. In another large bowl, beat egg whites and cream of tartar until stiff peaks form. Fold into batter.

Pour into an ungreased 10-in. tube pan. Cut through batter with a knife to remove the air pockets. Bake at 350° for 50-55 minutes or until cake springs back when lightly touched.

Immediately invert pan; cool completely, about 1 hour. Run a knife around side and center tube of pan. Remove cake to a serving plate. **Yield:** 12-16 servings.

Classic Cupcakes

THOSE FABULOUS flavors you loved as a kid are featured in these little cakes. Bite into the old-fashioned taste of either root beer, red velvet cake or bananas with chocolate and peanut butter.

ROOT BEER CUPCAKES

(Pictured above)

Dot Kraemer, Cape May Court House, New Jersey

Root beer barrel candies and a spice cake-like batter give these cupcakes a down-home flavor. Kids especially will love them!

- 1/2 cup butter, softened
- 1 cup packed brown sugar
- 2 eggs
- 2 cups all-purpose flour
- 1 teaspoon baking powder
- 1/8 teaspoon baking soda
- 1/8 teaspoon ground cinnamon
- 1/8 teaspoon ground allspice
- 1 cup root beer
- 1-1/2 cups whipped topping
- 12 root beer barrel candies, crushed

In a large bowl, cream butter and brown sugar until light and fluffy. Add eggs, one at a time, beating well after each addition. Combine the flour, baking powder, baking soda, cinnamon and allspice; gradually add to creamed mixture alternately with root beer, beating well after each addition.

Fill paper-lined muffin cups two-thirds full. Bake at 350° for 18-22 minutes or until a toothpick comes out clean. Cool for 10 minutes. Remove from pan to a wire rack; cool completely.

Just before serving, combine whipped topping and crushed candies; frost cupcakes. Refrigerate leftovers. **Yield:** 1 dozen.

SURPRISE RED CUPCAKES

(Pictured below)

Betty Claycomb, Alverton, Pennsylvania

Catch your honey red-handed this Valentine's Day with a batch of these confections. Our family loves these filled cakes and makes them disappear in a day.

- 2 cups sugar, *divided*
- 3 tablespoons plus 2 cups all-purpose flour, *divided*
- 1/2 cup milk
- 1/2 cup plus 1/3 cup shortening, *divided*
- 2 eggs
- 1 bottle (1 ounce) red food coloring
- 1 tablespoon white vinegar
- 2 teaspoons vanilla extract, *divided*
- 3 tablespoons baking cocoa

1 teaspoon baking soda
1 cup buttermilk
1/2 cup butter, softened
3 tablespoons confectioners' sugar
FROSTING:
1 cup (6 ounces) semisweet chocolate
chips
1/3 cup plus 1 to 3 teaspoons evaporated
milk, *divided*
1-1/2 cups confectioners' sugar

In a heavy saucepan, combine 1/2 cup sugar, 3 tablespoons flour and milk until smooth. Bring to a boil; cook and stir for 1-2 minutes or until thickened. Remove from the heat; cool.

In a large bowl, cream 1/2 cup shortening and remaining sugar. Add eggs, one at a time, beating well after each addition. Beat in the food coloring, vinegar and 1 teaspoon vanilla extract. Combine the cocoa, baking soda and remaining flour; gradually add to creamed mixture alternately with the buttermilk.

Fill paper-lined muffin cups two-thirds full. Bake at 350° for 20-25 minutes or until a toothpick comes out clean. Cool for 10 minutes before removing cupcakes from pans to wire racks to cool completely.

In a small bowl, beat butter and remaining shortening. Beat in the confectioners' sugar, cooled sugar mixture and remaining vanilla until light and fluffy, about 3 minutes. Insert a large round tip into a pastry or plastic bag; fill with filling. Insert the tip halfway into the center of each cupcake and fill with a small amount of filling.

For frosting, in a heavy saucepan, melt chips with 1/3 cup evaporated milk over low heat; stir until smooth. Remove from the heat. Beat in confectioners' sugar. Add enough remaining milk to achieve spreading consistency. Frost cupcakes. **Yield:** 2 dozen.

▰▰▰▰▰▰▰▰▰▰▰

ELVIS CUPCAKES
(Pictured above right)

The spirit of Elvis lives on in this festive cupcake! Our Test Kitchen took the King of Rock's favorite flavors and rolled them into a banana cupcake frosted with peanut butter and kissed by chocolate.

2 cups all-purpose flour
3/4 cup sugar
1 teaspoon baking soda
1/2 teaspoon salt
1 cup mayonnaise
1-1/3 cups mashed ripe bananas
(about 3 medium)
1 teaspoon vanilla extract
18 milk chocolate kisses
PEANUT BUTTER FROSTING:
1/3 cup creamy peanut butter
2 cups confectioners' sugar
1 teaspoon vanilla extract
3 to 4 tablespoons milk
Milk chocolate chips, optional

In a large bowl, combine the flour, sugar, baking soda and salt. In another bowl, combine the mayonnaise, bananas and vanilla; stir into dry ingredients just until combined.

Spoon 1 tablespoon of batter into each paper-lined muffin cup. Top each with a chocolate kiss, pointed side down. Fill cups two-thirds full with remaining batter.

Bake at 350° for 20-25 minutes or until a toothpick comes out clean. Cool for 10 minutes before removing from pans to wire racks to cool completely.

For frosting, in a large bowl, combine the peanut butter, confectioners' sugar, vanilla and enough milk to achieve spreading consistency. Frost the cupcakes. Garnish with the chocolate chips if desired. **Yield:** 1-1/2 dozen.

MANGO DELIGHT GELATIN MOLD
(Pictured below)

Candy McMenamin, Lexington, South Carolina

My son and I found this South American recipe while doing some research for a school project about Colombia. We made the gelatin as a visual aid for his project, and it was a hit!

    5 medium ripe mangoes, peeled and pitted
    1 cup evaporated milk
3/4 cup sugar
    1 cup orange juice
    3 envelopes unflavored gelatin
    2 cups whipped topping

Cut the mangoes into large chunks; place in a food processor. Cover and process until smooth; transfer to a large bowl. Stir in milk and sugar; set aside.

Place the orange juice in a small saucepan; sprinkle the gelatin over juice. Let stand for 2 minutes. Heat over low heat, stirring until gelatin is completely dissolved. Stir into mango mixture. Fold in whipped topping.

Transfer to an 8-cup mold coated with cooking spray. Cover and refrigerate for 2 hours or until firm. Just before serving, unmold onto a serving platter. **Yield:** 10 servings.

LEMONADE DESSERT
(Pictured above)

Margaret Linder, Quincy, Washington

Here's a wonderfully refreshing way to finish off your summer barbecue. Adults and kids will be standing in line for this easy-to-make treat.

1-1/2 cups all-purpose flour
    3/4 cup packed brown sugar
    3/4 cup cold butter
    3/4 cup chopped pecans
    1/2 gallon vanilla ice cream, softened
    1 can (12 ounces) frozen pink lemonade
       concentrate, thawed

In a small bowl, combine flour and brown sugar; cut in butter until crumbly. Stir in pecans. Spread in a single layer into a greased 15-in. x 10-in. x 1-in. baking pan. Bake at 375° for 9-12 minutes or until golden brown, stirring once. Cool on a wire rack for 10 minutes.

In a large bowl, beat ice cream and lemonade until blended. Sprinkle half of the crumbles into a greased 13-in. x 9-in. dish. Spread with ice cream mixture; sprinkle with the remaining crumbles. Cover and freeze overnight. Remove from the freezer 15 minutes before serving. **Yield:** 12-15 servings.

SOFTENING ICE CREAM

To easily soften ice cream for a recipe, transfer it from the freezer to the refrigerator 20-30 minutes before using. Or, let it stand at room temperature for 10-15 minutes. Hard ice cream can also be softened in the microwave at 30% power for about 30 seconds.

CHOCOLATE MACADAMIA MACAROONS
(Pictured below)

Darlene Brenden, Salem, Oregon

I love coconut, chocolate and macadamia nuts, so in my effort to come up with the taste of my favorite candy bar, Almond Joy, I created this recipe. To make them more like a candy bar, I dipped the bottoms into chocolate. This has become my family's signature Christmas cookie.

> 2 cups flaked coconut
> 1/2 cup finely chopped macadamia nuts
> 1/3 cup sugar
> 3 tablespoons baking cocoa
> 2 tablespoons all-purpose flour
> Pinch salt
> 2 egg whites, beaten
> 1 tablespoon light corn syrup
> 1 teaspoon vanilla extract
> 4 squares (1 ounce *each*) semisweet chocolate

In a large bowl, combine the coconut, macadamia nuts, sugar, cocoa, flour and salt. Add the egg whites, corn syrup and vanilla and mix well.

Drop by rounded tablespoonfuls onto greased baking sheets. Bake at 325° for 15-20 minutes or until set and dry to the touch. Cool for 5 minutes before removing from pans to wire racks to cool completely.

In a microwave, melt the chocolate squares; stir until smooth. Dip the bottom of each cookie in the melted chocolate; allow the excess to drip off. Place on waxed paper; let stand until set. **Yield:** 1-1/2 dozen.

PEANUT BUTTER ICE CREAM SANDWICHES
(Pictured above)

Teresa Gaetzke, North Freedom, Wisconsin

Store-bought ice cream treats can't hold a candle to homemade ones. This frozen dessert is fantastic.

> 1/2 cup shortening
> 1/2 cup creamy peanut butter
> 3/4 cup sugar, *divided*
> 1/2 cup packed brown sugar
> 1 egg
> 1/2 teaspoon vanilla extract
> 1-1/2 cups all-purpose flour
> 1 teaspoon baking soda
> 1/2 teaspoon salt
> 12 ounces dark chocolate candy coating, chopped
> 1 quart vanilla ice cream, softened

In a large bowl, cream the shortening, peanut butter, 1/2 cup sugar and brown sugar until light and fluffy. Beat in egg and vanilla. Combine the flour, baking soda and salt; gradually add to creamed mixture and mix well.

Roll into 1-in. balls; roll in remaining sugar. Place 1 in. apart on ungreased baking sheets. Flatten with a fork, forming a crisscross pattern.

Bake at 350° for 9-11 minutes or until set (do not overbake). Remove to wire racks to cool completely.

In a microwave, melt candy coating; stir until smooth. Spread a heaping teaspoonful on the bottom of each cookie; place chocolate side up on waxed paper until set.

To make sandwiches, place 1/4 cup ice cream on the bottom of half of the cookies; top with remaining cookies. Wrap in plastic wrap; freeze. **Yield:** 16 servings.

▚▚▚▚▚▚▚▚▚▚

PEAR PRALINE PIE
(Pictured above)

Diane Halferty, Corpus Christi, Texas

This home-spun pie is good served warm or at room temperature. We like it with scoops of vanilla ice cream or thick whipped cream on top and served with a cup of coffee or glass of milk.

    1/4 cup all-purpose flour
    1/2 teaspoon grated lemon peel
    1/2 teaspoon ground ginger
      4 medium pears, peeled and sliced
Pastry for double-crust pie (9 inches)
      1 cup packed brown sugar
    1/2 cup chopped pecans, toasted
    1/4 cup butter, melted

In a large bowl, combine the flour, lemon peel and ginger. Add pears; toss gently to coat.

Line a 9-in. pie plate with bottom pastry; trim even with edge of plate. Add pear mixture. Combine the brown sugar, pecans and butter; sprinkle over pears.

Roll out remaining pastry to fit top of pie; cut a decorative design in the center if desired. Place over filling; trim, seal and flute edges. (If using whole pastry on top without a decorative design, cut slits in pastry.)

Bake the pie at 400° for 35-45 minutes or until filling is bubbly and pears are tender (cover the edges of the pie crust with foil during the last 15 minutes to prevent overbrowning if necessary). Cool completely on a wire rack. Store in the refrigerator. **Yield:** 6-8 servings.

▚▚▚▚▚▚▚▚▚▚

BANANA FRITTERS

Heidi Duquette, Morrisonville, New York

This is my family's favorite twist on a banana split. It's delicious on a warm summer night and appeals to kids and adults alike.

      1 cup self-rising flour
      1 egg
    3/4 cup lemon-lime soda
Oil for deep-fat frying
      4 large firm bananas, cut into quarters
      1 jar (12-1/4 ounces) caramel ice cream
        topping
Vanilla ice cream, whipped cream and chopped
    pecans, optional

Place flour in a small bowl. Combine egg and soda; stir into flour just until moistened.

In an electric skillet, heat 1/4 in. of oil to 375°. Coat banana pieces with batter. Fry bananas, a few at a time, for 1 minute on each side or until golden brown. Drain on paper towels.

Drizzle with caramel topping. Serve with ice cream, whipped cream and pecans if desired. **Yield:** 4 servings.

Editor's Note: As a substitute for 1 cup of self-rising flour, place 1-1/2 teaspoons baking powder and 1/2 teaspoon salt in a measuring cup. Add all-purpose flour to measure 1 cup.

▰▰▰▰▰▰▰▰▰▰

CHOCOLATE MOUSSE

Lewy Olfson, Madison, Wisconsin

When time is of the essence, I mix up this tried-and-tested mousse. The smooth blend of chocolate and mocha flavors satisfies any sweet tooth.

- 2 squares (1 ounce *each*) semisweet chocolate
- 1 square (1 ounce) unsweetened chocolate
- 3 tablespoons strong brewed coffee
- 2 eggs
- 1/3 cup sugar
- 1/8 teaspoon salt
- 2/3 cup heavy whipping cream

Place a small bowl in a larger bowl filled with ice cubes; set aside. In a microwave-safe bowl, heat chocolate and coffee until chocolate is melted; stir until smooth and set aside.

In a small heavy saucepan over low heat, whisk the eggs, sugar and salt until mixture reaches 160°, about 2 minutes. Remove from the heat; whisk in chocolate mixture.

Pour into prepared bowl. Let stand for 5 minutes or until cooled, stirring occasionally. Add the cream. With a hand mixer, beat until soft peaks form. Spoon into dishes; refrigerate until serving. **Yield:** 4 servings.

▰▰▰▰▰▰▰▰▰▰

PEANUT ICE CREAM DELIGHT
(Pictured at right)

Barb Rader, Brock, Nebraska

This dessert, with a cookie crust topped with ice cream, peanuts and homemade caramel and chocolate sauce, was a hit at my daughter-in-law's bridal shower.

- 1 package (14 ounces) cream-filled chocolate sandwich cookies, crushed
- 1/3 cup butter, melted
- 1/2 gallon vanilla ice cream, softened
- 1-1/2 cups salted peanuts

CARAMEL SAUCE:
- 1 cup packed brown sugar
- 1 cup heavy whipping cream
- 1/2 cup butter, cubed
- 1 teaspoon vanilla extract

CHOCOLATE SAUCE:
- 1 can (12 ounces) evaporated milk
- 1 cup (6 ounces) semisweet chocolate chips
- 1/2 cup butter, cubed
- 2 cups confectioners' sugar
- 1 teaspoon vanilla extract

In a bowl, combine cookie crumbs and butter; press onto the bottom and up the sides of an ungreased 13-in. x 9-in. dish. Spread ice cream over crust; sprinkle with peanuts. Cover and freeze for at least 1 hour.

For the caramel sauce, in a small saucepan, combine the brown sugar, cream and butter. Bring to a boil; cook and stir for 1 minute. Remove from the heat; stir in the vanilla. Cool. Drizzle over peanuts. Cover and freeze for at least 1 hour.

For the chocolate sauce, in a large saucepan, combine the evaporated milk, chocolate chips and butter. Cook and stir over low heat until melted and smooth. Stir in the confectioners' sugar. Bring to a boil. Reduce the heat; simmer, uncovered, for 8-10 minutes or until thickened, stirring frequently. Remove from the heat; stir in vanilla. Cool.

Drizzle over the dessert. Cover and freeze for 2 hours or until firm. **Yield:** 12-15 servings.

in the towel jelly-roll style, starting with a short side. Cool completely on a wire rack.

For frosting, in microwave-safe bowl, melt the chocolate and butter; stir until smooth. Gradually beat in confectioners' sugar and enough milk to achieve desired consistency.

Unroll cake; spread ice cream evenly over cake to within 1/2 in. of edges. Roll up again. Place seam side down on a serving platter. Spread with frosting. Cover and freeze overnight. **Yield: 14 servings.**

CHOCOLATE CHERRY LINCOLN LOG
(Pictured above)

Marilyn Jensen, Cody, Wyoming

The first time I made this festive cake roll was for Lincoln's birthday, but it's an impressive dessert for any holiday or special meal. Feel free to change the ice cream flavor.

   3 eggs
   1 cup sugar
1/3 cup water
   1 teaspoon vanilla extract
   1 cup all-purpose flour
1/3 cup baking cocoa
   1 teaspoon baking powder
1/4 teaspoon salt
Confectioners' sugar
   1 quart cherry ice cream, softened
FROSTING:
   1 square (1 ounce) unsweetened chocolate
   1 tablespoon butter
1-1/4 cups confectioners' sugar
   2 to 3 tablespoons milk

Line a greased 15-in. x 10-in. x 1-in. baking pan with waxed paper; grease the paper and set aside. In a large bowl, beat eggs for 3 minutes. Gradually add the sugar; beat for 2 minutes or until the mixture becomes thick and lemon-colored. Stir in water and vanilla. Combine the flour, cocoa, baking powder and salt; fold into egg mixture (batter will be thin).

Spread evenly into prepared pan. Bake at 375° for 10-13 minutes or until cake springs back when lightly touched. Cool for 5 minutes. Invert onto a kitchen towel dusted with confectioners' sugar. Gently peel off waxed paper. Roll up cake

STRAWBERRY MALLOW POPS
(Pictured below)

Arlene Pickard, Redvers, Saskatchewan

These strawberry pops are popular with our family on hot summer days. It's fun biting into the yummy bits of fruit and marshmallow.

   1 package (8 ounces) cream cheese, softened
1/4 cup honey
   1 package (16 ounces) frozen sweetened sliced strawberries, thawed
   3 cups miniature marshmallows
   1 cup heavy whipping cream, whipped

In a small bowl, beat the cream cheese and honey until smooth. Add the strawberries with juice; beat until blended. Fold in marshmallows and whipped cream.

Pour 1/4 cupfuls into 24 plastic molds or 3-oz. paper cups; top with holders or insert Popsicle sticks into cups. Freeze until firm. **Yield: 2 dozen.**

■■■■■■■■■■■■

FLUFFY PUMPKIN PIE

(Pictured above)

Phyllis Renfro, White Bear Lake, Minnesota

Children love this pie—marshmallows make the filling light and fluffy. It's a quick and easy recipe that I've shared many times over the years. Since it doesn't need to bake, the pie comes in handy at Thanksgiving and Christmas when your oven is in demand.

24 large marshmallows
1 can (15 ounces) solid-pack pumpkin
1/2 teaspoon ground cinnamon
1/2 teaspoon ground allspice
1/4 teaspoon salt
1 carton (8 ounces) frozen whipped topping, thawed
1 pastry shell (9 inches), baked
Additional whipped topping and ground cinnamon, optional

In a small heavy saucepan, melt marshmallows over low heat. Remove from the heat. Stir in the pumpkin, cinnamon, allspice and salt; cool to room temperature.

Fold in whipped topping. Spoon into pastry shell. Refrigerate for at least 4 hours before serving. Garnish with additional whipped topping and cinnamon if desired. **Yield:** 6-8 servings.

COOKING PUMPKIN SQUASH

"Pie pumpkins" are the best variety for use in baking. To cook, wash, peel, remove seeds and cut into chunks. Steam until soft. Puree in a food mill or processor. Cool and pack into freezer bags or containers in set amounts. Use cup-for-cup in place of canned pumpkin.

■■■■■■■■■■■■

BILTMORE'S BREAD PUDDING

(Pictured below)

Here's a great way to turn stale bread into a luxurious dessert. The caramel sauce truly carries this sweet treat over the top! It comes from the Inn on Biltmore Estate in Asheville, North Carolina.

8 cups cubed day-old bread
9 eggs
2-1/4 cups milk
1-3/4 cups heavy whipping cream
1 cup sugar
3/4 cup butter, melted
3 teaspoons vanilla extract
1-1/2 teaspoons ground cinnamon
CARAMEL SAUCE:
1 cup sugar
1/4 cup water
1 tablespoon lemon juice
2 tablespoons butter
1 cup heavy whipping cream

Place bread cubes in a greased 13-in. x 9-in. baking dish. In a large bowl, whisk eggs, milk, cream, sugar, butter, vanilla and cinnamon. Pour evenly over bread.

Bake, uncovered, at 350° for 40-45 minutes or until a knife inserted near the center comes out clean. Let stand for 5 minutes before cutting.

Meanwhile, for the sauce, in a small saucepan, bring the sugar, water and lemon juice to a boil. Reduce heat to medium; cook until the sugar is dissolved and mixture turns a golden amber color. Stir in butter until melted. Add cream. Remove from the heat. Serve with the bread pudding. **Yield:** 12 servings.

CREAM CHEESE ICE CREAM

(Pictured below)

Johnnie McLeod, Bastrop, Louisiana

This is hands-down the best homemade ice cream I've ever eaten. It tastes like cheesecake with a zesty hint of lemon.

2-1/2 cups half-and-half cream
    1 cup milk
1-1/4 cups sugar
    2 eggs, lightly beaten
  12 ounces cream cheese, cubed
    1 tablespoon lemon juice
    1 teaspoon vanilla extract

In a large saucepan, heat the cream and milk to 175°; stir in sugar until dissolved. Whisk a small amount of hot mixture into the eggs. Return all to the pan, whisking constantly. Cook and stir over low heat until mixture reaches at least 160° and coats the back of a metal spoon.

Remove from the heat. Whisk in the cream cheese until smooth. Cool quickly by placing pan in a bowl of ice water; stir for 2 minutes. Stir in lemon juice and vanilla. Press plastic wrap onto surface of the custard. Refrigerate for several hours or overnight.

Fill cylinder of ice cream freezer two-thirds full; freeze according to manufacturer's directions. Refrigerate remaining mixture until ready to freeze. Transfer to a freezer container; freeze for 2-4 hours before serving. **Yield:** 1-1/2 quarts.

SOUR CREAM CHOCOLATE CAKE

(Pictured above)

Marsha Lawson, Pflugerville, Texas

Popular in the past, this classic layer cake is still hard to beat for a Sunday dinner or birthday celebration. It's impressive to look at but easy to make.

    1 cup baking cocoa
    1 cup boiling water
    1 cup butter, softened
2-1/2 cups sugar
    4 eggs
    2 teaspoons vanilla extract
    3 cups cake flour
    2 teaspoons baking soda
 1/2 teaspoon baking powder
 1/2 teaspoon salt
    1 cup (8 ounces) sour cream
FROSTING:
    2 cups (12 ounces) semisweet chocolate chips
 1/2 cup butter, cubed
    1 cup (8 ounces) sour cream
    1 teaspoon vanilla extract
4-1/2 to 5 cups confectioners' sugar

Dissolve the cocoa in boiling water; cool. In a large bowl, cream the butter and sugar until light and fluffy. Add eggs, one at a time, beating well after each. Beat in vanilla. Combine the flour, baking soda, baking powder and salt; gradually add to creamed mixture alternately with sour cream, beating well after each addition. Add the cocoa mixture and mix well.

Pour into three greased and floured 9-in. round baking pans. Bake at 350° for 30-35 minutes or

until a toothpick inserted near the center comes out clean. Cool for 10 minutes before removing from pans to wire racks to cool completely.

In a microwave, melt chocolate chips and butter over low heat; stir until smooth. Cool for 5 minutes. Transfer to a large bowl. Add sour cream and vanilla; beat until blended. Add confectioners' sugar; beat until light and fluffy. Spread between layers and over top and sides of cake. Store in the refrigerator. **Yield:** 16 servings.

🟥🟥🟥🟥🟥🟥🟥🟥🟥🟥

CINNAMON POACHED APPLES
(Pictured below)

Libby Orendorff, Uniontown, Arkansas

For a lighter holiday dessert, consider these spicy and sweet apples. They're refreshing when chilled, but my family also likes them served warm.

- 2 cups sugar
- 2 cups water
- 1/4 cup red-hot candies
- 6 small tart apples, cored and peeled

In a large saucepan, bring the sugar, water and red-hots to a boil. Cook and stir until red-hots are dissolved, about 5 minutes. Reduce heat; carefully add apples. Cover and simmer for 15 minutes or just until apples are tender, turning once.

With a slotted spoon, remove apples to a large bowl. Bring syrup to a boil; cook, uncovered, until reduced to about 1-1/2 cups. Cool. Pour the syrup over apples; cover and refrigerate until serving. **Yield:** 6 servings.

🟥🟥🟥🟥🟥🟥🟥🟥🟥🟥

FRESH BLACKBERRY PIE
(Pictured above)

Gladys Gibbs, Brush Creek, Tennessee

I grew up on a farm, and in early summer we always picked blackberries and used them to make pies.

- 1 cup sugar
- 1/3 cup quick-cooking tapioca
- 1/4 teaspoon salt
- 4 cups fresh blackberries, *divided*
- 2 tablespoons butter

Pastry for double-crust pie (9 inches)

In a large saucepan, combine the sugar, tapioca and salt. Add 1 cup blackberries; toss to coat. Let stand for 15 minutes. Cook and stir over medium heat until berries burst and mixture comes to a gentle boil. Remove from the heat; gently stir in remaining berries.

Line a 9-in. pie plate with bottom pastry; trim pastry even with edge of plate. Add filling; dot with butter. Roll out remaining pastry to fit top of pie; place over filling. Trim, seal and flute edges. Cut slits in top.

Bake at 400° for 35-40 minutes or until crust is golden brown and filling is bubbly. Cool on a wire rack. **Yield:** 6-8 servings.

PIE CRUST PROTECTOR

If the edge of your pie crust is becoming too brown while baking, cover it with foil. On a 12-inch disposable foil pizza pan, draw a 7-inch-diameter circle in the center. Cut out the circle and discard. Then simply center the foil over the pie to cover the crust.

'Crafty' Sweets

THERE'S MORE than meets the eye with these copycat desserts that are great for kids' parties, bake sales and more!

▰▰▰▰▰▰▰▰▰▰▰

BURGER 'N' HOT DOG CAKE
(Pictured below)

Joan Ehrstein, Valparaiso, Indiana

Contestants in our Cub Scout pack's annual Father-Son Cake Bake came up with this clever entry. I like to let kids pile the cakes high with candy condiments.

   1 package (18-1/4 ounces) white cake mix
1/2 cup butter, softened
3/4 cup sugar
   4 eggs
   2 cups all-purpose flour
   6 teaspoons baking powder
   2 tablespoons semisweet chocolate chips, melted
1/4 teaspoon vanilla extract
   3 teaspoons lemon extract
   1 teaspoon sesame seeds
   3 cans (16 ounces *each*) vanilla frosting
Red, green, yellow, orange, brown and black paste food coloring

   4 individual cream-filled sponge cakes, *divided*
   2 flexible straws

Prepare the cake batter according to the package directions. Pour into a greased and floured 13-in. x 9-in. baking pan. Bake at 350° for 25-30 minutes or until a toothpick comes out clean. Cool for 10 minutes. Remove from pan to a wire rack to cool.

In a large bowl, cream butter and sugar until light and fluffy. Add eggs, one at a time, beating well after each. Combine the flour and baking powder; stir into creamed mixture. Set aside 1/4 cup batter; stir in melted chocolate and vanilla. Stir lemon extract into remaining batter.

Line a baking sheet with parchment paper. Draw two 2-3/4-in. circles, two 1-1/2-in. circles and two 3-1/4-in. x 1-1/2-in. ovals on the paper. Spread 1-1/2-in. circles with chocolate batter. On each oval and each remaining circle, spread 2 tablespoons lemon batter; sprinkle circles with sesame seeds. Bake at 400° for 10-12 minutes or until edges are golden brown. Remove to wire racks to cool completely.

Drop remaining batter by tablespoonfuls 3 in. apart onto greased baking sheets. Bake for 8 minutes or until edges are golden brown. Remove to wire racks to cool completely.

Place cake on a tray or 14-in. x 10-in. tray or covered board. Tint two cans of frosting pink with red food coloring; frost top and sides of cake. With star tip #16 and white frosting, pipe a rope border around top and bottom of cake.

Use white frosting to form two 4-in. circles on cake for plates. Place a round lemon cookie, sesame side down, on one plate for burger bun. Tint 3 tablespoons frosting green; spread half over bun for lettuce. Top with a chocolate cookie. For cheese, tint 2 tablespoons frosting with yellow and orange food coloring; spread 1 tablespoon over burger. For ketchup, tint 2 tablespoons frosting red; drizzle 2 teaspoons over cheese. For mustard, tint 2 tablespoons frosting yellow; drizzle 2 teaspoons over ketchup.

Top with another chocolate cookie burger; repeat layers of cheese, ketchup and mustard. Set remaining ketchup and mustard aside for hot dog.

For hamburger bun top, spread remaining green frosting over bottom of remaining round lemon cookie; place over mustard.

For hot dog bun, place an oval cookie, top side down, on second plate. Cut one sponge cake in half lengthwise and shape into a hot dog (save remaining half for another use). Tint 1/4 cup frosting brownish-red; spread over hot dog. Place on bun. Drizzle with reserved ketchup and mustard. Place remaining oval cookie on top for bun top.

For soda can, cut one end off each of the remaining sponge cakes. Cut two sponge cakes in half lengthwise. Stand third sponge cake, cut side down, on cake. Arrange remaining halves around sponge cake, cut side in. Tint 3/4 cup frosting red; frost sides of can. Tint 3 tablespoons frosting gray with black food coloring; frost top and make a rim around can bottom. Insert straws into center of can. Pipe "cola" and designs on can with white frosting. **Yield:** 12-15 servings plus 20 cookies.

Editor's Note: A coupler ring will allow you to easily change pastry tips for different designs.

BASKETBALL CAKE

Lonna Liccini, Clifton, Virginia

Dimpled orange frosting and licorice laces make this basketball cake look deliciously realistic. It's as much fun to make as it is to eat.

  1 package (18-1/4 ounces) chocolate
    cake mix
1-1/2 cups vanilla frosting
Orange paste food coloring
  4 pieces black shoestring licorice

Prepare cake batter according to package directions. Pour into a greased and floured 2-1/2-qt. ovenproof bowl.

Bake at 350° for 60-70 minutes or until a toothpick inserted near the center comes out clean. Cool for 10 minutes before removing from bowl to a wire rack to cool completely.

In a small bowl, combine the frosting and the food coloring. Place the cake on a serving plate. Spread with frosting. Gently press a meat mallet into the frosting so texture resembles a basketball. For the seams, gently press licorice into frosting. **Yield:** 12-16 servings.

COOKIE PUDDING POTS
(Pictured above)

Christine Panzarella, Buena Park, California

You can change what you "plant" in the cookie pudding for different seasons. For autumn or Halloween, use mini candy pumpkins or gummy worms.

  6 new terra-cotta flowerpots
    (3-1/2-inch diameter)
  4 cups cold milk
  2 packages (3.9 ounces *each*) instant
    chocolate fudge pudding mix
  7 cream-filled chocolate sandwich
    cookies, crushed, *divided*
  6 medium fresh strawberries
12 mint sprigs

Line flowerpots with plastic wrap; set aside. In a large bowl, whisk milk and pudding mixes for 2 minutes. Let stand for 2 minutes or until soft-set.

Sprinkle 2 teaspoons of cookie crumbs into each flowerpot. Top each with 2/3 cup pudding; sprinkle with remaining crumbs. Cut each strawberry to resemble a rose.

Garnish each pot with a strawberry rose and mint sprigs. Chill until serving. **Yield:** 6 servings.

🏵 FROSTY RASPBERRY PARFAITS
(Pictured above)

Clare Hafferman, Kalispell, Montana

My layered dessert looks so elegant and pretty. It gets compliments every time I serve it. Parfaits are a traditional part of our Fourth of July buffet.

- 4 cups fresh *or* frozen raspberries, thawed, *divided*
- 4 egg yolks, lightly beaten
- 1/2 cup sugar
- 1 teaspoon vanilla extract
- 1 cup heavy whipping cream, whipped

Additional fresh raspberries, optional

Place 2 cups raspberries in a food processor; cover and process until blended. Press through a fine mesh strainer; discard seeds and pulp.

In a small saucepan, combine egg yolks and sugar; stir in raspberry puree until smooth. Cook and stir over medium heat until mixture reaches at least 160° and coats the back of a metal spoon. Remove from the heat; stir in vanilla. Transfer to a bowl. Refrigerate until chilled.

Fold in whipped cream. Coarsely mash remaining raspberries. In six freezer-proof parfait glasses, layer 1 tablespoon mashed berries and 1/4 cup cream mixture. Repeat layers. Cover and freeze for 6 hours or overnight. Garnish with the additional raspberries if desired. **Yield:** 6 servings.

🏵 APPLE HARVEST CAKE
(Pictured below)

E. Bartuschat, Abington, Massachusetts

Tender apple slices and subtle flavors make this old-fashioned cake one of our favorites.

- 2-1/4 cups sugar, *divided*
- 1 cup canola oil
- 4 eggs
- 1/4 cup orange juice
- 2-1/2 teaspoons vanilla extract
- 3 cups all-purpose flour
- 3 teaspoons baking powder
- 1/2 teaspoon salt
- 4 medium tart apples, peeled and cubed
- 2 teaspoons ground cinnamon

Whipped cream and additional cinnamon, optional

In a large bowl, beat 2 cups sugar, oil, eggs, orange juice and vanilla until well blended. Combine the flour, baking powder and salt; gradually beat into sugar mixture until blended. Stir in apples.

Spread half of the batter into a greased 13-in. x 9-in. baking dish. Combine cinnamon and remaining sugar; sprinkle over batter. Carefully spread remaining batter over the top.

Bake at 350° for 40-50 minutes or until a toothpick inserted near the center comes out clean. Cool on a wire rack. Garnish with whipped cream and additional cinnamon if desired. **Yield:** 12-15 servings.

CHOCOLATE PECAN KISSES

Josephine Beals, Zionsville, Indiana

A good friend gave me this recipe and I, in turn, have shared it with many others. The cookies are quite easy to prepare, and the recipe has a generous yield. I call these "forgotten" cookies because they don't need to come out of the oven until the next morning.

> 1 egg white
> 1/3 cup sugar
> 1/2 cup miniature semisweet chocolate chips
> 1/2 cup chopped pecans

Place the egg white in a small bowl; let stand at room temperature for 30 minutes. Beat on medium speed until soft peaks form. Gradually beat in sugar, 1 tablespoon at a time, on high until stiff peaks form. Fold in chocolate chips and pecans.

Drop by rounded teaspoonfuls 2 in. apart onto parchment paper-lined baking sheets. Bake at 250° for 40-45 minutes or until firm to the touch. Turn oven off and let cookies dry in the oven for 1-1/2 hours.

Carefully remove the cookies from the parchment paper. Store in an airtight container. **Yield:** 1-1/2 dozen.

COCONUT-CRANBERRY APPLE CRISP

Geri Williamson, Fallbrook, California

I pick apples right off the trees on my property for this tasty fruit crisp. It's one of my most-used recipes.

> 5 medium apples, peeled and sliced
> 1/2 cup fresh *or* frozen cranberries, halved
> 1/4 cup sugar
> 3/4 cup old-fashioned oats
> 1/2 cup packed brown sugar
> 1/4 cup all-purpose flour
> 1/4 teaspoon *each* ground cinnamon, nutmeg and ginger
> 1/2 cup cold butter
> 1/2 cup chopped nuts
> 1/4 cup flaked coconut
> Vanilla ice cream

In a large bowl, combine apples and cranberries. Add sugar; toss to coat. Transfer to a greased 11-in. x 7-in. baking dish.

In a small bowl, combine the oats, brown sugar, flour and spices; cut in butter until crumbly. Stir in nuts and coconut; sprinkle over fruit.

Bake at 375° for 30-35 minutes or until topping is golden brown and filling is bubbly. Serve warm with ice cream. **Yield:** 8 servings.

CHOCOLATE RASPBERRY TEA CAKES

(Pictured above)

Deborah Fagan, Lancaster, Pennsylvania

With a family of six children, it seems I'm always on the lookout for variety in menus and special treats as surprises. This recipe was given to me by a co-worker. The combination of raspberry jam and chocolate chips is very pleasing.

> 3/4 cup all-purpose flour
> 2 tablespoons sugar
> 2 tablespoons brown sugar
> 1 teaspoon baking powder
> 1/8 teaspoon salt
> 1 egg white
> 1/4 cup milk
> 1/4 cup butter, melted
> 1/2 cup milk chocolate chips
> 6 teaspoons seedless raspberry jam

In a small bowl, combine the flour, sugar, brown sugar, baking powder and salt. In another bowl, whisk the egg white, milk and butter; stir into dry ingredients just until moistened. Fold in chocolate chips.

Fill each of six greased or paper-lined muffin cups with 1 tablespoon batter. Drop 1 teaspoon of jam into each cup; top with remaining batter.

Bake at 350° for 20-25 minutes or until a toothpick comes out clean. Cool for 10 minutes before removing from pan to a wire rack to cool completely. **Yield:** 1/2 dozen.

MEASURING MELTED BUTTER

When melted butter is called for in a recipe, the solid butter is measured first, then melted. The convenient markings on the side of the wrappers make it easy to slice off the amount you need and melt it.

BANANA CHEESECAKE
(Pictured below)

Sera Smith, West Palm Beach, Florida

We have banana trees in our backyard that bear fruit all year. After making banana bread, muffins and cookies, I still had some of our bountiful crop left, so I decided to try this recipe. It's decadent!

      3/4 cup all-purpose flour
      3/4 cup finely chopped pecans
        3 tablespoons sugar
        2 tablespoons brown sugar
    1-1/2 teaspoons vanilla extract
        6 tablespoons butter, melted
FILLING:
        1 cup mashed ripe bananas
        2 tablespoons lemon juice
        2 packages (8 ounces *each*) cream
          cheese, softened
    1-1/4 cups sugar
        2 tablespoons cornstarch
      1/8 teaspoon salt
        3 eggs, lightly beaten
        1 cup (8 ounces) sour cream
    1-1/4 teaspoons vanilla extract
TOPPING:
        1 cup (8 ounces) sour cream
      1/4 cup sugar
      1/4 teaspoon vanilla extract
        1 cup assorted fresh fruit

Combine the first five ingredients; stir in butter. Press onto the bottom of a greased 9-in. spring-form pan; place on a baking sheet. Bake at 350° for 10 minutes or until lightly browned. Cool on a wire rack.

For the filling, combine bananas and lemon juice; set aside. In a large bowl, beat the cream cheese, sugar, cornstarch and salt until smooth. Add eggs; beat on low speed just until combined. Stir in the sour cream, vanilla and banana mixture. Pour into the crust. Place pan on a baking sheet.

Bake at 350° for 50-60 minutes or until center is almost set. Let stand for 5 minutes. For the topping, combine sour cream, sugar and vanilla; spread over the top of cheesecake. Bake 5 minutes longer.

Cool on a wire rack for 10 minutes. Carefully run a knife around edge of pan; cool 1 hour longer. Refrigerate overnight. Remove sides of pan; garnish with fruit. **Yield:** 12-14 servings.

MAINE BLUEBERRY CAKE

Diane Vachon, Berwick, Maine

Maine produces the very best blueberries—although small, they're oh-so-sweet. When I was a little girl, my mother always made this cake in blueberry season. Served with real whipped cream, it's wonderful!

      1/3 cup butter, softened
        1 cup plus 1 tablespoon sugar, *divided*
        2 eggs
        2 cups all-purpose flour
        1 teaspoon salt
        1 teaspoon baking powder
      1/4 teaspoon baking soda
      1/4 teaspoon ground nutmeg
      1/2 cup buttermilk
    1-1/2 cups fresh *or* frozen blueberries

In a large bowl, cream butter and 1 cup sugar until light and fluffy. Add eggs, one at a time, beating well after each addition. Combine the flour, salt, baking powder, baking soda and nutmeg; gradually add to creamed mixture alternately with buttermilk, beating well after each addition. Gently fold in blueberries.

Transfer to a greased 9-in. square baking pan; sprinkle with remaining sugar. Bake at 350° for 40-45 minutes or until cake springs back when lightly touched. Cool on a wire rack. **Yield:** 9 servings.

Editor's Note: If using frozen blueberries, do not thaw before adding to batter.

ORANGE COCONUT MERINGUE PIE

(Pictured above)

Daisy Duncan, Stillwater, Oklahoma

I have won first place in two cream pie competitions with this recipe. It's one of my absolute favorites.

- 1 cup sugar
- 3 tablespoons cornstarch
- 3 tablespoons all-purpose flour
- 1/4 teaspoon salt
- 1-1/2 cups water
- 3/4 cup orange juice
- 3 egg yolks, lightly beaten
- 3/4 cup flaked coconut
- 2 tablespoons butter
- 1 tablespoon grated orange peel
- 2 tablespoons lemon juice
- 1 pastry shell (9 inches), baked

MERINGUE:

- 3 egg whites
- 1/2 teaspoon vanilla extract
- 1/4 teaspoon cream of tartar
- 6 tablespoons sugar

In a large saucepan, combine the sugar, cornstarch, flour and salt. Gradually stir in water and orange juice until smooth. Cook and stir over medium-high heat until thickened and bubbly.

Reduce heat; cook and stir 2 minutes longer. Remove from the heat.

Stir a small amount of hot filling into egg yolks; return all to the pan, stirring constantly. Bring to a gentle boil; cook and stir 2 minutes longer. Remove from the heat. Stir in the coconut, butter and orange peel. Gently stir in lemon juice. Pour into pastry shell.

In a small bowl, beat the egg whites, vanilla and cream of tartar on medium speed until soft peaks form. Gradually beat in sugar, 1 tablespoon at a time, on high until stiff glossy peaks form and sugar is dissolved. Spread evenly over hot filling, sealing edges to crust.

Bake at 350° for 12-15 minutes or until meringue is golden brown. Cool on a wire rack for 1 hour. Refrigerate for at least 3 hours before serving. Refrigerate leftovers. **Yield:** 6-8 servings.

PERFECT MERINGUE PIE

Spread meringue over hot filling to minimize "weeping" (the watery layer between the meringue and filling) and seal to the edges of the pastry. After baking, cool the pie away from drafts on a wire rack for 1 hour. Refrigerate for at least 3 hours before cutting and serving.

RHUBARB DESSERT CAKE
(Pictured above)

Loraine Meyer, Bend, Oregon

I have shared this popular recipe with many people ever since it was given to me by a relative. I freeze rhubarb when it's in season so I can make the yummy cake throughout the year.

            2 tablespoons butter, melted
            1 cup packed brown sugar
            4 cups sliced fresh *or* frozen rhubarb
      1-1/2 cups sugar
      1-1/2 cups all-purpose flour
      1-1/2 teaspoons baking powder
         1/8 teaspoon salt
            3 eggs
         1/2 cup water
            1 teaspoon vanilla extract
Whipped cream *or* vanilla ice cream

In a greased 13-in. x 9-in. baking dish, combine butter and brown sugar. Top with rhubarb.

In a large bowl, combine the sugar, flour, baking powder and salt. In another bowl, whisk the eggs, water and vanilla; stir into dry ingredients just until moistened. Pour over rhubarb.

Bake at 350° for 30-35 minutes or until cake springs back when lightly touched. Cool for 10 minutes on a wire rack. Serve warm or at room temperature with whipped cream or ice cream.
Yield: 12 servings.

   Editor's Note: If using frozen rhubarb, measure while still frozen, then thaw completely. Drain in a colander, but do not press liquid out.

CALIFORNIA LEMON POUND CAKE
(Pictured below)

Richard Killeaney, Spring Valley, California

This favorite pound cake recipe, which I received from my mother, uses fresh fruit from my backyard lemon trees. Its delicate texture is enhanced by the zesty, citrus-rich glaze.

            1 cup butter, softened
         1/2 cup shortening
            3 cups sugar
            5 eggs
            1 tablespoon grated lemon peel
            1 tablespoon lemon extract
            3 cups all-purpose flour
            1 teaspoon salt
         1/2 teaspoon baking powder
            1 cup milk
FROSTING:
         1/4 cup butter, softened
      1-3/4 cups confectioners' sugar
            2 tablespoons lemon juice
            1 teaspoon grated lemon peel

In a large bowl, cream the butter, shortening and sugar until light and fluffy, about 5 minutes. Add the eggs, one at a time, beating well after each addition. Stir in lemon peel and extract. Combine the flour, salt and baking powder; gradually add to creamed mixture alternately with milk. Beat just until combined.

   Pour into a greased 10-in. fluted tube pan. Bake at 350° for 70 minutes or until a toothpick inserted near the center comes out clean. Cool for 10 minutes before removing from pan to a wire rack to cool completely.

   In a small bowl, combine the frosting ingredients; beat until smooth. Spread over top of cake.
Yield: 12-16 servings.

heat. Transfer to a bowl; cover and refrigerate until mixture reaches spreading consistency, stirring occasionally.

In a small bowl, combine cracker crumbs and remaining sugar. Using a melon baller, scoop out 1-in. balls of cheesecake; place on parchment paper-lined baking sheets. Top each with a heaping teaspoonful of chocolate mixture. Sprinkle crumb mixture over half of the balls and toffee bits over remaining balls. Cover and freeze for 2 hours or until firm. **Yield:** 5-1/2 dozen.

MAPLE PEARS
(Pictured below)

Amelia Ginett, Sodus, New York

These buttery baked pears enjoy round-the-clock popularity. They bring ease and elegance to dessert or breakfast.

 3 medium pears, peeled and cubed
1/4 cup sliced almonds
 2 tablespoons toasted wheat germ
 2 tablespoons maple syrup
 1 tablespoon butter, melted
1/2 teaspoon vanilla extract
TOPPING:
1-1/2 cups (12 ounces) vanilla yogurt
4-1/2 teaspoons maple syrup

In a large bowl, combine the first six ingredients. Transfer to a greased 1-qt. baking dish. Bake, uncovered, at 350° for 30-35 minutes or until pears are tender.

In a small bowl, combine the topping ingredients. Serve with warm pears. **Yield:** 4 servings.

FROZEN CHEESECAKE BITES
(Pictured above)

Frank Millard, Janesville, Wisconsin

It only takes one of these delicious nibbles to cure your cheesecake cravings. But the bites are so good, your guests are sure to ask for more.

 3 packages (8 ounces *each*) cream cheese, softened
1-1/4 cups sugar, *divided*
1-1/2 teaspoons vanilla extract
1/2 teaspoon salt
 4 eggs, lightly beaten
 9 squares (1 ounce *each*) semisweet chocolate, chopped
3/4 cup heavy whipping cream
1/2 cup graham cracker crumbs
1/2 cup English toffee bits *or* almond brickle chips, crushed

Line the bottom of a 9-in. springform pan with parchment paper; coat paper and sides of pan with cooking spray. Set aside. In a large bowl, beat the cream cheese, 1 cup sugar, vanilla and salt until smooth. Add eggs; beat on low speed just until combined. Pour into prepared pan.

Place on a baking sheet. Bake at 325° for 40-45 minutes or until center is almost set. Cool on a wire rack for 10 minutes. Carefully run a knife around edge of pan to loosen; cool 1 hour longer. Cover and freeze overnight.

Remove from the freezer and let stand for 30 minutes or until easy to handle. Meanwhile, in a small saucepan over low heat, melt chocolate with cream; stir until blended. Remove from the

FRUITY CHOCOLATE TORTILLA CUPS

(Pictured above)

Marion Karlin, Waterloo, Iowa

These sweet treats, with south-of-the-border flair, are meal-ending favorites. You'll love the presentation of strawberries, apricots, peaches and plums in chocolate-drizzled tortilla cups.

> 1 to 2 tablespoons butter, softened
> 8 flour tortillas (6 inches), warmed
> 3/4 cup semisweet chocolate chips
> 1 teaspoon shortening

FILLING:

> 1 pound fresh apricots, halved
> 2 tablespoons honey
> 1-1/2 cups halved fresh strawberries
> 3 small plums, sliced
> 2 medium peaches, sliced
> 1/2 cup heavy whipping cream
> 2 tablespoons confectioners' sugar

Spread butter over one side of each tortilla. Press tortillas, butter side down, into ungreased 8-oz. custard cups. Place on a 15-in. x 10-in. x 1-in. baking pan. Bake at 400° for 10-12 minutes or until golden brown. Remove tortilla cups from custard cups; cool on wire racks.

In a microwave, melt chocolate chips and shortening; stir until smooth. Drizzle over the insides of tortilla cups; refrigerate for 3-4 minutes or until set.

For the filling, in a food processor, combine the apricots and honey; cover and process until smooth. In a large bowl, combine the strawberries, plums and peaches; add the apricot mixture and gently toss to coat. Spoon 1/2 cup into each tortilla cup.

In a small bowl, beat cream until it begins to thicken. Add confectioners' sugar; beat until stiff peaks form. Dollop onto fruit. **Yield:** 8 servings.

STRAWBERRY CHEESECAKE PIE

(Pictured above)

Debbi Oeltjen, Sublimity, Oregon

There's a "berried" treasure at the bottom of this creamy concoction. You'll not find a fresher finale to a summertime meal.

> 4 ounces cream cheese, softened
> 1/4 cup sugar
> 1/2 cup sour cream
> 1 teaspoon vanilla extract
> 1-3/4 cups whipped topping
> 1 cup strawberry glaze

1 graham cracker crust (9 inches)
2 pints fresh strawberries, thinly sliced
Fresh mint and additional strawberries,
   optional

In a small bowl, beat cream cheese and sugar until smooth. Stir in sour cream and vanilla until blended. Fold in whipped topping.

Spread half of the glaze over bottom of crust; layer with strawberries. Top with the remaining glaze. Spoon cream cheese mixture over the top. Refrigerate for 2-4 hours or until set. Garnish with the mint and additional berries if desired. **Yield:** 6-8 servings.

ALL-AMERICAN BANANA SPLIT

Melissa Blystone, Latrobe, Pennsylvania

In 1904, the first banana split was made in Latrobe, Pennsylvania by David Strickler, an eager apprentice pharmacist at a local drug store. At Valley Dairy Inc., we still use his original formula when we make splits in our restaurants.

1 medium banana, peeled and split
   lengthwise
1 scoop *each* vanilla, chocolate and
   strawberry ice cream
2 tablespoons sliced fresh strawberries *or*
   1 tablespoon strawberry topping
2 tablespoons pineapple chunks *or*
   1 tablespoon pineapple topping
2 tablespoons whipped cream
1 tablespoon chopped peanuts
1 tablespoon chocolate syrup
2 maraschino cherries with stems

Place banana in a dessert dish; place scoops of ice cream between banana. Top with remaining ingredients. Serve immediately. **Yield:** 1 serving.

MAPLE CREAM MERINGUE PIE
(Pictured at right)

Nicole Hardy, St. Albans, Vermont

This dessert won first place in the pie category at the annual Vermont Maple Festival. It's simple to make and uses more maple syrup than most other maple cream pies.

3 egg whites
2 tablespoons cornstarch
1/4 cup water
1 cup maple syrup

1 cup heavy whipping cream
2 egg yolks, lightly beaten
3 tablespoons butter
1 pastry shell (9 inches), baked
1/2 teaspoon vanilla extract
1/4 teaspoon cream of tartar
6 tablespoons sugar

Place egg whites in a small bowl; let stand at room temperature for 30 minutes.

In a small saucepan, combine cornstarch and water until smooth. Stir in syrup and cream. Cook and stir over medium-high heat until thickened and bubbly. Reduce heat to medium; cook, stirring constantly, 2 minutes longer. Remove from the heat.

Stir a small amount of hot filling into egg yolks; return all to the pan, stirring constantly. Bring to a gentle boil; cook and stir 2 minutes longer. Remove from the heat. Stir in butter. Pour into pastry shell.

Add vanilla and cream of tartar to egg whites; beat on medium speed until soft peaks form. Gradually beat in sugar, 1 tablespoon at a time, on high until stiff glossy peaks form and sugar is dissolved. Spread evenly over hot filling, sealing the edges to crust.

Bake at 350° for 12-15 minutes or until the meringue is golden brown. Cool on a wire rack for 1 hour. Refrigerate for at least 3 hours before serving. **Yield:** 6-8 servings.

THE PERFECT PORTION *for two is easy with the trimmed-back fare found in this chapter. These delicious dishes are sure to satisfy any hearty appetite.*

DINNER FOR A DUO. Clockwise from top left: Apple Pie Dessert (p. 137), Hot Cocoa (p. 139), Turkey Dijon Melts (p. 137) and Mushroom Barley Soup (p. 137).

Cooking for Two

TURKEY DIJON MELTS

Sarah Marshall, Creedmoor, North Carolina

I enjoy making this when I am craving comfort food but don't have the time or energy for a big meal. It works well with deli or leftover turkey.

- 4 slices whole wheat bread
- 4 teaspoons mayonnaise
- 1/4 pound thinly sliced cooked turkey
- 4 slices Monterey Jack cheese
- 1/4 cup thinly sliced onion
- Dash salt and pepper
- 1 tablespoon honey Dijon salad dressing
- 1 tablespoon butter, softened

Spread two slices of bread with the mayonnaise. Layer with turkey, cheese and onion; sprinkle with salt and pepper. Spread remaining slices of bread with salad dressing; place over onion. Butter the outsides of sandwiches.

In a small skillet over medium heat, toast the sandwiches for 4-5 minutes on each side or until bread is lightly browned and cheese is melted. **Yield:** 2 servings.

MUSHROOM BARLEY SOUP

Aimee Lawrence, Wimberley, Texas

This soup is one of my favorite meals. It's quick, easy to prepare and the perfect amount for two. The mushrooms, carrots and barley create a good combination of flavors and colors.

- 1 cup sliced fresh mushrooms
- 2 garlic cloves, minced
- 1 tablespoon butter
- 2 cans (14-1/2 ounces *each*) chicken broth
- 1/3 cup medium pearl barley
- 1 tablespoon soy sauce
- 1 medium carrot, sliced
- 1/2 teaspoon dill weed
- Salt and pepper to taste

In a small saucepan, saute mushrooms and garlic in butter for 3 minutes. Stir in the broth, barley and soy sauce. Bring to a boil. Reduce heat; cover and simmer for 20 minutes.

Add the carrot, dill, salt and pepper. Cover and simmer for 15 minutes or until barley and carrot are tender. **Yield:** 3 cups.

APPLE PIE DESSERT

Jeanie Krimm, West Hills, California

My aunt gave me this small-yield recipe, and it is a wonderful fall dessert. It tastes like apple pie yet is less time-consuming to prepare. With the special touch of the homemade butter sauce, it always receives raves.

- 1/4 cup butter, softened
- 1/3 cup sugar
- 1 egg
- 1/2 cup all-purpose flour
- 1/4 teaspoon baking soda
- 1/8 teaspoon salt
- 1/8 teaspoon ground cinnamon
- 1/8 teaspoon ground nutmeg
- 1 cup chopped tart apple
- 1/4 cup chopped walnuts
- BUTTER SAUCE:
- 1/4 cup sugar
- 1-1/2 teaspoons cornstarch
- 1/8 teaspoon salt
- 1/2 cup water
- 1 tablespoon butter
- 1/2 teaspoon vanilla extract

In a small bowl, cream the butter and sugar until light and fluffy. Beat in egg. Combine the flour, baking soda, salt, cinnamon and nutmeg; add to the creamed mixture and mix well. Stir in the apple and walnuts.

Transfer to a greased 7-in. pie plate. Bake at 350° for 25-35 minutes or until a toothpick inserted near the center comes out clean.

For the butter sauce, in a small saucepan, combine the sugar, cornstarch and salt. Gradually stir in the water until smooth. Bring to a boil; cook and stir for 2 minutes or until thickened. Remove from the heat; stir in the butter and vanilla. Serve the butter sauce warm with the apple dessert. **Yield:** 2 servings.

HEARTY CHEESE SOUP
(Pictured below)

Suzanna Snader, Fredericksburg, Pennsylvania

Thick and creamy, this soup is chock-full of cheese flavor. I came home with the filling recipe after an exchange at my church several years ago, and I have shared it with many people since.

      1-1/2 cups cubed peeled potatoes
      1/2 cup water
      1/4 cup sliced celery
      1/4 cup sliced fresh carrots
        2 tablespoons chopped onion
      1/2 teaspoon chicken bouillon granules
      1/2 teaspoon dried parsley flakes
      1/4 teaspoon salt
    Dash pepper
    1-1/2 teaspoons all-purpose flour
      3/4 cup milk
      1/4 pound process cheese (Velveeta), cubed

In a small saucepan, combine the first nine ingredients. Bring to a boil. Reduce heat; cover and simmer for 10-12 minutes or until potatoes are tender.

In a small bowl, combine flour and milk until smooth. Stir into the vegetable mixture. Bring to a boil; cook and stir for 2 minutes or until thickened. Reduce heat to low; stir in cheese until melted. **Yield:** 2 servings.

BLUE CHEESE PEAR SALAD
(Pictured above)

Anne Bennett, Delmar, Maryland

Featuring a homemade dressing, this pretty and flavorful salad has an excellent contrast of textures. It's delicious, versatile and a nice accompaniment to a variety of entrees. Plus, the recipe can easily be increased to serve many more.

        3 cups torn leaf lettuce
        1 can (8-1/2 ounces) pear halves, drained
        2 thin slices red onion, separated into rings
        3 tablespoons crumbled blue cheese
        3 tablespoons chopped walnuts
      1/4 cup olive oil
        2 tablespoons raspberry vinegar
        2 teaspoons maple syrup
      1/4 teaspoon Dijon mustard
      1/8 teaspoon garlic powder
      1/8 teaspoon onion powder

Divide lettuce between two salad plates. Top with the pears, onion, blue cheese and walnuts. In a small bowl, whisk the oil, vinegar, syrup, mustard, garlic powder and onion powder until blended. Drizzle over salads. **Yield:** 2 servings.

HOT COCOA

(Pictured on page 136)

Ruth Wimmer, Bland, Virginia

With the first chill in the air, I begin thinking of hot cocoa. This simple version, which can be stirred up in no time, is rich-tasting and just enough for two.

- 2 tablespoons sugar
- 1 tablespoon baking cocoa
- 2 cups water, *divided*
- 2/3 cup nonfat dry milk powder
- 1/4 teaspoon vanilla extract

In a small saucepan, combine the sugar and cocoa; stir in 2/3 cup water. Bring to a boil. Reduce heat; cook and stir for 5 minutes. Remove from the heat.

Stir in the milk powder and remaining water. Return to the heat; cook and stir until heated through. Stir in vanilla. **Yield:** 2 servings.

CHOCOLATE BANANA SMOOTHIES

Want to add low-fat dairy to your diet? Consider these frothy, chocolaty smoothies whipped up with both milk and yogurt. It's a sweet treat kids and adults will request morning, noon and night.

- 1 cup chocolate milk
- 1/2 cup plain yogurt
- 1 medium banana, peeled, cut into chunks and frozen
- 1 teaspoon honey
- 1/2 teaspoon vanilla extract
- 1 cup ice cubes

In a blender, combine the milk, yogurt, banana, honey and vanilla; cover and process until smooth. Add ice cubes; cover and process until blended. Pour into chilled glasses; serve immediately. **Yield:** 2 servings.

CLEANING A BLENDER

If you aren't using your blender because it's too hard to clean, then here's the perfect tip for you! To thoroughly clean a blender, after using it, fill the jar halfway with hot water, then add a drop of dishwashing liquid. Cover it and blend on high for 10-15 seconds. Rinse the blender jar well with hot water and allow to air-dry in a dish rack overnight.

STRAWBERRY RHUBARB CREAM

(Pictured below)

Norma DesRoches, Warwick, Rhode Island

A friend gave me this recipe a long time ago. It is decadent and creamy yet refreshing. I make it often in early summer when rhubarb is readily available.

- 1/2 cup chopped fresh *or* frozen rhubarb
- 2 tablespoons plus 1-1/2 teaspoons sugar, *divided*
- 1-1/2 teaspoons water
- 1/2 cup sliced fresh strawberries
- 1/3 cup heavy whipping cream, whipped
- **Additional sliced fresh strawberries, optional**

In a small saucepan, combine the rhubarb, 2 tablespoons sugar and water. Bring to a boil, stirring constantly. Reduce heat; simmer, uncovered, for 10 minutes or until tender. Transfer to a small bowl; cool to room temperature.

Place strawberries and remaining sugar in a food processor; cover and process until pureed. Stir into rhubarb mixture. Fold in whipped cream. Spoon into two parfait glasses or dessert dishes. Cover and refrigerate until chilled. Garnish with additional berries if desired. **Yield:** 2 servings.

Editor's Note: If using frozen rhubarb, measure rhubarb while still frozen, then thaw completely. Drain in a colander, but do not press liquid out.

1/2 cup *each* fresh raspberries, blueberries, blackberries and sliced strawberries
2 teaspoons chopped walnuts, toasted

For the dressing, in a jar with a tight-fitting lid, combine the first 10 ingredients; shake well. Combine the spinach and berries in a small salad bowl. Drizzle with dressing and sprinkle with walnuts; toss to coat. **Yield:** 2 servings.

PARMESAN RICE PILAF

Kellie Mulleavy, Lambertville, Michigan

My mom discovered this recipe in a local newspaper years ago, and it has been one of our favorite side dishes for a long time. The original recipe was a little bland, so I jazzed it up a bit to improve the taste. Sometimes I make more than I need for one meal so I can enjoy the leftovers.

　1 small onion, chopped
　2 tablespoons plus 1-1/2 teaspoons butter
　1 cup uncooked instant rice
　1 cup water
　1 teaspoon beef bouillon granules
1/4 teaspoon garlic powder
1/4 teaspoon pepper
　2 tablespoons grated Parmesan cheese
Fresh marjoram sprig and shaved Parmesan cheese, optional

In a small saucepan, saute onion in butter until tender. Stir in the rice, water, bouillon, garlic powder and pepper; bring to a boil.

Remove the saucepan from the heat; cover and let stand for 5 minutes. Stir in the grated Parmesan cheese. Garnish with a fresh sprig of marjoram and shaved Parmesan cheese if desired. **Yield:** 2 servings.

FOUR-BERRY SPINACH SALAD
(Pictured above)

Betty Lise Anderson, Gahanna, Ohio

Nature's "candy" abounds in this berry-filled spinach salad. Its slightly tart dressing contrasts deliciously with sweet in-season fruit.

　1 tablespoon canola oil
　1 tablespoon orange juice
　1 tablespoon red wine vinegar
　1 tablespoon balsamic vinegar
　1 tablespoon water
　2 teaspoons lemon juice
1/2 teaspoon sugar
1/2 teaspoon poppy seeds
1/8 teaspoon ground allspice
Dash ground cinnamon
　4 cups fresh baby spinach

A BIT ABOUT BERRIES

Fresh berries should be stored covered in your refrigerator, washed just before using and used within 10 days of purchase. To wash, place berries a few at a time in a colander in the sink. Gently spray with water, then spread out on paper towels to pat dry.

SUMMER SQUASH MEDLEY

Heather Irwin, Clarksville, Tennessee

This garden-fresh, colorful side dish would go well with any entree, and it's quick and easy to prepare. I came up with the recipe on my own about a year ago and really liked the combination of flavors.

　1 medium yellow summer squash, thinly sliced
　1 small zucchini, thinly sliced
1/3 cup chopped onion
　1 tablespoon butter
　1 tablespoon brown sugar

1/4 teaspoon minced garlic
1/8 teaspoon lemon juice
1/8 teaspoon salt

In a small skillet, saute yellow squash, zucchini and onion in butter until crisp-tender; add the remaining ingredients. Cook and stir until vegetables are tender. **Yield:** 2 servings.

CHICKEN DINNER PACKETS
(Pictured below)

Jeanne Barney, Saratoga Springs, New York

This is a quick yet satisfying all-in-one meal. The foil-wrapped chicken stays nice and moist during baking. I especially like the fact that this recipe saves so much time on both preparation and cleanup.

  1/2 **pound boneless skinless chicken breasts, cut into strips**
   2   **small red potatoes, thinly sliced**
  3/4 **cup shredded cheddar cheese**
  1/2 **small sweet red pepper, julienned**
  1/2 **small green pepper, julienned**
   2   **tablespoons barbecue sauce**
   1   **green onion, chopped**
  1/4 **teaspoon salt**
  1/8 **teaspoon pepper**

Divide the chicken strips between two pieces of heavy-duty foil (about 12 in. square). In a small bowl, combine the remaining ingredients; spoon over the chicken. Fold foil around the mixture and seal tightly.

Place packets on a baking sheet. Bake at 375° for 25-30 minutes or until chicken is no longer pink and potatoes are tender. Open foil carefully to allow steam to escape. **Yield:** 2 servings.

MUSTARD-CRUSTED SALMON
(Pictured above)

Judy Wilson, Sun City West, Arizona

Our daughter sent us whole salmon for Christmas one year, so I searched the Web and found this recipe. I serve it with a wild rice pilaf and a green vegetable.

  3-1/2 **teaspoons cider vinegar**
    1   **tablespoon sugar**
    1   **tablespoon Dijon mustard**
   3/4   **teaspoon ground mustard**
    2   **tablespoons canola oil**
    2   **salmon fillets (6 ounces *each*)**
   1/4   **teaspoon dried thyme**
   1/4   **teaspoon salt**
   1/8   **teaspoon pepper**
   1/2   **cup soft bread crumbs**

In a blender, combine the vinegar, sugar and mustards; cover and process until smooth. While processing, gradually add oil in a steady stream.

Place salmon, skin side down, in a greased 8-in. square baking dish. Sprinkle with thyme, salt and pepper.

Spread mustard mixture over fillets; gently press bread crumbs on top. Bake, uncovered, at 375° for 20-25 minutes or until fish flakes easily with a fork. **Yield:** 2 servings.

SPICED PEAR DESSERT

(Pictured above)

JoAnne Badger, Oakland, Maine

At our bed and breakfast, we always serve some kind of fruit. This is an easy and delicious way to present fresh pears, and our guests love it.

> 1 large pear, peeled and sliced
> 1 tablespoon butter, softened
> 1 tablespoon brown sugar
> **Dash ground cinnamon**
> **Dash ground nutmeg**

Arrange the pear slices in a single layer in a microwave-safe dish. In a small bowl, combine the butter, brown sugar, cinnamon and nutmeg; spread over pears.

Microwave, uncovered, at 50% power for 1-1/2 to 2 minutes or until tender. Serve warm. **Yield:** 2 servings.

Editor's Note: This recipe was tested in a 1,100-watt microwave.

FROSTED CAULIFLOWER

Thelma Brown, Fulton, Illinois

I found this recipe in a small cookbook I bought just before I was married in 1950. I adjusted the recipe a little by cutting the cauliflower into chunks. Try this vegetable dish with a main course of pork or beef.

> 2 cups fresh cauliflowerets
> 1 tablespoon water
> 2 tablespoons mayonnaise
> 1 teaspoon Dijon mustard
> 1/8 teaspoon salt
> **Chopped fresh parsley, optional**

Place cauliflower and water in a small microwave-safe bowl. Cover and microwave on high for 4-5 minutes or until crisp-tender, stirring once.

In a small bowl, combine the mayonnaise, mustard and salt. Drain cauliflower and place in a serving bowl. Top with mayonnaise mixture. Sprinkle with parsley if desired. **Yield:** 2 servings.

Editor's Note: This recipe was tested in a 1,100-watt microwave.

STRING BEAN SALAD

(Pictured below)

Jean Grade, Sheboygan, Wisconsin

This tasty salad was served at our condo potlucks, and our office staff distributed the recipe. The combination of crisp beans and tender potatoes coated with a light vinaigrette is very refreshing.

> 1 small red potato, halved and cut into
>   1/4-inch slices
> 1/3 pound fresh green beans, trimmed
> 2 tablespoons olive oil
> 1 tablespoon chopped red onion
> 1 garlic clove, minced
> **Salt and pepper to taste**

Place potato slices in a steamer basket; place in a small saucepan over 1 in. of water. Bring to a boil; cover and steam for 5 minutes. Add beans; steam 8-10 minutes longer or until vegetables are tender.

In a jar with a tight-fitting lid, combine the oil, onion and garlic; shake well. Transfer vegetables to a bowl; add dressing and toss to coat. Season with salt and pepper. Cover and refrigerate for at least 1 hour. Yield: 2 servings.

BREAD PUDDING WITH BUTTER SAUCE

(Pictured above)

Norma Burggraf, Marshfield, Ohio

When we went out to eat, bread pudding was my dessert choice. I eventually found out how it was made and have enjoyed eating and serving it ever since.

> 2 slices white bread, cubed
> 2 tablespoons raisins
> 1 egg
> 1/2 cup evaporated milk
> 3 tablespoons water
> 2 tablespoons sugar
> 1/4 teaspoon ground cinnamon
> 1/4 teaspoon ground nutmeg

BUTTER SAUCE:

> 2 tablespoons butter
> 2 tablespoons sugar
> 1 egg yolk, beaten
> 1 tablespoon water
> 1 tablespoon bourbon, optional

Divide the bread cubes and raisins between two greased 8-oz. ramekins or custard cups. In a small bowl, whisk the egg, milk, water, sugar, cinnamon and nutmeg. Pour over bread mixture.

Bake, uncovered, at 350° for 35-40 minutes or until a knife inserted near the center comes out clean. Cool for 15 minutes.

Meanwhile, for the sauce, in a small saucepan, melt butter. Stir in the sugar, egg yolk and water. Cook and stir over medium-low heat for 4 minutes or until sugar is dissolved and mixture comes to a boil. Remove from the heat; stir in bourbon if desired. Serve warm with bread pudding. **Yield:** 2 servings.

CAN-DO CLUE

When you have leftover evaporated milk and would like to save it, transfer the milk from the can to another container for storage. If stored in a covered container in the refrigerator, evaporated milk can be used safely within 3 days.

OVEN SWISS STEAK

Carol Brown, Midway, Ontario

Here's my version of this diner classic. It isn't difficult to make and tastes so delicious, especially when I'm craving down-home cooking.

- 1/2 pound boneless beef top round steak
- 2 tablespoons all-purpose flour
- 1/2 teaspoon salt
- 1 tablespoon canola oil
- 1/4 cup chopped celery
- 1/4 cup chopped carrot
- 1 tablespoon chopped onion
- 1 can (14-1/2 ounces) stewed tomatoes, undrained
- 1/4 teaspoon Worcestershire sauce
- 2 tablespoons shredded sharp cheddar cheese

Trim beef; cut into two portions and flatten to 1/4-in. thickness. In a large resealable plastic bag, combine flour and salt; add beef and shake to coat. In a small ovenproof skillet, brown beef in oil on both sides. Remove and keep warm.

In the drippings, saute the celery, carrot and onion for 3-4 minutes or until crisp-tender. Add tomatoes and Worcestershire sauce, stirring to loosen browned bits from pan. Bring to a boil. Reduce heat; simmer, uncovered, for 5 minutes. Return the beef to the pan; spoon some of the vegetable mixture over the top.

Cover; bake at 325° for 1 hour or until meat is tender. Uncover; sprinkle with cheese. Bake 5 minutes longer to melt cheese. **Yield:** 2 servings.

BROCCOLI AND NOODLES

Dorothy Haskenhoff, E. Carondelet, Illinois

This simple dish is so comforting on a chilly day. It's quick to fix and very satisfying. I rely on it when I'm super busy and have very little time to make dinner.

- 1 cup uncooked egg noodles
- 1-1/2 cups fresh broccoli florets
- 1 small onion, chopped
- 1 tablespoon butter
- 1 cup sliced fresh mushrooms
- 1/4 to 1/2 teaspoon salt
- 1/4 teaspoon garlic powder
- 1/4 teaspoon pepper

Cook noodles according to package directions. Meanwhile, in a large skillet, saute the broccoli and onion in the butter for 2 minutes. Add the mushrooms, salt, garlic powder and pepper; saute 2-3 minutes longer or until tender.

Drain the noodles and add to the vegetables in the skillet; cook and stir until heated through. **Yield:** 2 servings.

CREAMY PINEAPPLE COLESLAW

Carol Baggett, Englewood, Florida

Give coleslaw a tangy burst of citrus with this picnic-perfect recipe. It requires just five ingredients.

- 2-1/2 cups shredded cabbage
- 1 can (8 ounces) unsweetened crushed pineapple, drained
- 1/4 cup mayonnaise
- 1/4 teaspoon salt
- 1/4 teaspoon pepper

In a small bowl, combine all of the ingredients. Cover and refrigerate for at least 2 hours before serving. **Yield:** 2 servings.

CHOCOLATE CHIP CHEESECAKE DESSERT

Cheri Oswell, Fort Carson, Colorado

These easy-to-serve cheesecake bars are always popular at potlucks and social functions. They travel well and are a chocolate-lover's delight!

- 1/2 cup graham cracker crumbs
- 2 tablespoons sugar
- 4 teaspoons baking cocoa
- 3 tablespoons butter, melted
- 2/3 cup miniature semisweet chocolate chips, *divided*
- 1 package (8 ounces) cream cheese, softened
- 2/3 cup sweetened condensed milk
- 1 egg, lightly beaten
- 3/4 teaspoon vanilla extract

In a small bowl, combine the crumbs, sugar and cocoa; stir in butter. Press onto the bottom of a greased 8-in. square baking dish. Bake at 325° for 10-12 minutes or until golden brown. Cool on a wire rack.

In a microwave, melt 1/3 cup chocolate chips; stir until smooth. Set aside. In a small bowl, beat cream cheese until fluffy; gradually beat in milk and melted chips. Add egg and vanilla; beat on low speed just until combined. Pour over the crust; sprinkle with remaining chips.

Bake at 325° for 15-20 minutes or until set. Cool on a wire rack for 1 hour. Cover and refrigerate for 2 hours or until chilled. Cut into squares. Refrigerate leftovers. **Yield:** 9 servings.

SAUSAGE RICE CASSEROLE

(Pictured below)

Eleanor Deaver, Fresno, California

The key to the distinctive flavor in this casserole is the use of Italian sausage. The nice balance of ingredients gives it an old-fashioned taste.

- 1/2 pound bulk Italian sausage
- 1/4 cup chopped onion
- 1/4 cup chopped sweet red pepper
- 1/2 cup uncooked instant rice
- 1/4 teaspoon dried basil
- 1 can (10-3/4 ounces) condensed tomato soup, undiluted
- 1/4 cup water
- 1/4 cup plus 2 tablespoons shredded part-skim mozzarella cheese, *divided*

In a small skillet, cook the sausage, onion and red pepper over medium heat until sausage is no longer pink; drain. Remove from the heat. Stir in the rice, basil, soup, water and 1/4 cup cheese.

Transfer to an ungreased 3-cup baking dish. Cover and bake at 350° for 25-30 minutes or until rice is tender. Uncover; sprinkle with remaining cheese. Bake 5 minutes longer or until cheese is melted. **Yield:** 2 servings.

BEEF BURGUNDY STEW

Blanche Rattigan, Glen Burnie, Maryland

I was drawn to this recipe because it makes a perfect portion for two. I made it often because my mother, who was an excellent cook, loved it and specifically asked me to prepare it!

- 1/4 cup all-purpose flour
- 1/4 teaspoon salt
- 1/4 teaspoon pepper
- 3/4 pound boneless beef sirloin steak, cut into thin strips
- 2 tablespoons canola oil, *divided*
- 1 medium onion, thinly sliced
- 1 garlic clove, minced
- 2/3 cup beef broth
- 2/3 cup burgundy wine *or* additional beef broth
- 1/2 teaspoon dried basil

Hot cooked egg noodles

In a large resealable plastic bag, combine flour, salt and pepper; add beef in batches and shake to coat.

In a small skillet, brown beef in 1 tablespoon oil on all sides; remove and set aside. In the same skillet, saute the onion and garlic in the remaining oil until tender.

THAI TILAPIA
(Pictured below)

You can take a taste trip to Asia even on a hectic weeknight with this no-fuss fish dish. The sauce adds a mellow, peanutty flavor and a bit of a kick.

    1-1/2 cups cooked rice
      1/3 cup chopped green onions
      1/3 cup chopped sweet red pepper
        1 tablespoon minced fresh basil
        2 tilapia fillets (6 ounces *each*)
        1 cup fresh snow peas
      1/3 to 1/2 cup Thai peanut sauce

Prepare grill for indirect heat. Combine the rice, onions, red pepper and basil; place on a greased double thickness of heavy-duty foil (about 15 in. square). Top with the tilapia fillets, snow peas and peanut sauce. Fold foil around mixture and seal tightly.

Grill, covered, over indirect medium-hot heat for 8-10 minutes or until fish flakes easily with a fork. Open foil carefully to allow steam to escape. **Yield:** 2 servings.

Return beef to the pan; stir in the broth, wine and basil. Bring to a boil. Reduce heat; cover and simmer for 25-30 minutes or until meat is tender. Serve with egg noodles. **Yield:** 2 servings.

PEACHES 'N' CREAM
(Pictured above)

Jane Arentzen, Philadelphia, Pennsylvania

I enjoy cooking for family and friends, and this is the recipe that is most often requested. A surprisingly simple and fresh summer dessert, it is heavenly warm from the oven with its sweet and tender peaches.

    1/3 cup sugar
      2 tablespoons water
    1/2 teaspoon vanilla extract
      2 cups sliced peeled peaches
           (about 3 medium)
    1/3 cup heavy whipping cream

In a small saucepan, bring the sugar and water to a boil. Reduce the heat; cover and simmer for 5 minutes. Remove the saucepan from the heat; stir in the vanilla extract.

Place peaches in two small baking dishes. Add syrup; stir gently to coat. Bake, uncovered, at 350° for 30-35 minutes or until peaches are tender. Serve warm or chilled with cream. **Yield:** 2 servings.

■■■■■■■■■■■■■■■

CHICKEN ASPARAGUS BUNDLES
(Pictured above)

Marie Delffs, Normandy, Tennessee

This is such a dressy way to serve chicken breasts, and it is surprisingly easy to prepare. I like to present this on holidays and other special occasions.

> 8 **fresh asparagus spears, trimmed**
> 2 **boneless skinless chicken breast halves**
>   **(6 ounces *each*)**
> 1/4 **teaspoon Italian seasoning**
> 1/8 **teaspoon garlic salt**
> 1/8 **teaspoon pepper**
> 2 **sweet red pepper rings (1/2 inch thick)**
> 1-1/2 **teaspoons olive oil**

In a skillet, bring 1/2 in. of water to a boil. Add asparagus; cover and boil for 3 minutes. Drain and immediately place asparagus in ice water. Drain and pat dry.

Flatten chicken to 1/4-in. thickness. Combine the Italian seasoning, garlic salt and pepper; sprinkle half over chicken. Top with asparagus; roll up into a bundle. Secure with a pepper ring.

Brush bundles with oil; sprinkle with remaining seasoning mixture. Place in a small greased baking pan. Bake, uncovered, at 375° for 30-35 minutes or until a meat thermometer reads 170°. **Yield:** 2 servings.

■■■■■■■■■■■■■■■

CREAMY CHEESE RICE
(Pictured above)

Ashley Scherf, Dousman, Wisconsin

The best part about this dish is that it's great hot or cold. Because it travels well, I like to increase the recipe and take it to picnics and barbecues.

> 1 **cup water**
> 1/2 **cup uncooked long grain rice**
> 1/4 **teaspoon salt**
> 1/4 **cup cubed process cheese (Velveeta)**
> 1 **tablespoon minced fresh parsley,**
>   **optional**

In a small saucepan, bring water, rice and salt to a boil. Reduce heat; cover and simmer for 20 minutes or until liquid is absorbed and rice is tender.

Remove from heat; stir in cheese and parsley if desired. Cover and let stand for 2 minutes or until cheese is melted. Stir until blended. **Yield:** 2 servings.

STUFFED ARTICHOKES

Dolores Tottino, Castroville, California

When it comes to impressing dinner guests, I often rely on this delicious side dish. It really isn't difficult to make, and it always goes over big. The Gouda cheese and Canadian bacon give the baked artichokes an extra-rich touch.

- 2 large artichokes
- 1/2 cup soft bread crumbs, toasted
- 2 ounces smoked Gouda cheese, shredded (about 1/2 cup)
- 4 slices Canadian bacon, chopped
- 1/2 teaspoon pepper
- 1 tablespoon olive oil

Using a sharp knife, level the bottom of each artichoke and cut 1 in. from the top. Using kitchen scissors, snip off the tips of the outer leaves. Place in a steamer basket; place in a large saucepan over 1 in. of water. Bring to a boil; cover and steam for 20-25 minutes or until leaves near the center pull out easily.

With a spoon, carefully scrape out the fuzzy center portions of artichokes and discard.

In a small bowl, combine the bread crumbs, cheese, bacon and pepper. Add oil; mix well. Gently spread artichoke leaves apart; fill with bread crumb mixture.

Place the stuffed artichokes in a greased 8-in. square baking dish. Bake, uncovered, at 350° for 10-15 minutes or until the filling is lightly browned. **Yield:** 2-4 servings.

STRAWBERRY FLAX SMOOTHIES

Esther Hylden, Park River, North Dakota

In an effort to promote flax, which we grow on our farm, my husband and I came up with this recipe while driving to the annual Pride of Dakota Show to sell our flax products. We made our first Strawberry Flax Smoothie at the show, and it was a hit! The smoothie can be prepared without flax as well.

- 1 cup refrigerated strawberry breeze juice blend
- 2 cups ice cubes
- 1-1/2 cups frozen unsweetened strawberries
- 1/2 medium banana
- 2 tablespoons ground flaxseed

In a blender, combine the juice blend, ice cubes, fruit and flaxseed; cover and process until smooth. Pour into chilled glasses; serve immediately. **Yield:** 2 servings.

ZIPPY TOMATO-TOPPED SNAPPER
(Pictured below)

Mary Anne Zimmerman, Silver Springs, Florida

Seafood lovers will be more than satisfied by this pleasantly zesty entree for two. Serve the red snapper fillets with a crisp, green salad and baked potato, and you'll have a complete meal.

✓ This recipe includes Nutrition Facts and Diabetic Exchanges.

- 3/4 teaspoon lemon-pepper seasoning
- 1/8 teaspoon salt
- 1 red snapper fillet (3/4 pound), cut in half
- 1/2 cup canned diced tomatoes with green chilies
- 2 tablespoons chopped onion
- 2 tablespoons chopped celery
- 1 tablespoon minced fresh parsley
- 1/8 teaspoon celery seed

Combine the lemon-pepper and salt; sprinkle over both sides of fish. Place in an 11-in. x 7-in. baking dish coated with cooking spray.

In a small bowl, combine the tomatoes, onion, celery, parsley and celery seed; spoon over the snapper. Cover and bake at 350° for 25-30 minutes or until fish flakes easily with a fork. **Yield:** 2 servings.

Nutrition Facts: 1 serving equals 179 calories, 2 g fat (trace saturated fat), 60 mg cholesterol, 643 mg sodium, 4 g carbohydrate, 1 g fiber, 34 g protein. **Diabetic Exchanges:** 4-1/2 lean meat, 1 vegetable.

SIZZLING COUNTRY STEAK

Peggy Cihlar, Mosinee, Wisconsin

I have used this recipe ever since I was a newlywed. Through the years, I have increased the amount it makes because it has always been a favorite with my husband, and then it became popular with our three boys. A touch of rosemary makes the flavor unique.

> 2 boneless beef sirloin steaks
>   (3/4 inch thick and 6 ounces *each*)
> 1/3 cup dry bread crumbs
> 1/4 cup minced fresh parsley
> 3 tablespoons butter, melted
> 1 tablespoon finely chopped onion
> 1 garlic clove, minced
> 1/8 teaspoon dried rosemary, crushed

Dash pepper

Broil the steaks 4-6 in. from the heat for 5-7 minutes on each side or until meat reaches desired doneness (for medium-rare, a meat thermometer should read 145°; medium, 160°; well-done, 170°).

In a small bowl, combine the remaining ingredients; sprinkle over the steaks. Broil 2 minutes longer or until the topping is golden brown. **Yield:** 2 servings.

BACON 'N' ONION CARROTS

Catherine Troost, Chatham, Virginia

Besides being colorful, this side dish is fitting for a host of harvesttime meals—from busy weekday dinners to special holiday feasts. It also complements a variety of roasted meats, including pork, beef and poultry. The subtle taste of the carrots is really enhanced by the bacon and onion combination.

> 4 medium carrots, sliced
> 2 bacon strips, diced
> 1/4 cup chopped onion
> 4 teaspoons brown sugar
> 1/8 teaspoon pepper

Place carrots in a small saucepan; cover with water. Bring to a boil. Reduce heat; cover and simmer for 7-9 minutes or until tender.

Meanwhile, in a small skillet, cook the bacon over medium heat until crisp. Remove the bacon with a slotted spoon to the paper towels; drain, reserving 2 teaspoons drippings. Saute the onion in the drippings. Stir in the brown sugar and pepper until the brown sugar is melted.

Drain carrots; toss with onion mixture. Top with bacon. **Yield:** 2 servings.

RED ONION RINGS

Mary Lou Wayman, Salt Lake City, Utah

"Delicious and yummy" describes these onion rings. Not only does the batter coat the onions well, it also fries up light and crunchy. It has a little kick from the secret ingredient, cayenne.

> 1/2 large red onion
> 2 tablespoons plus 1/2 cup all-purpose
>   flour, *divided*
> 1 egg white
> 1/4 cup buttermilk
> 1/4 teaspoon salt
> 1/8 teaspoon cayenne pepper

Oil for deep-fat frying

Cut onion into 1/4-in. slices; separate into rings. In a shallow bowl, whisk 2 tablespoons flour, egg white, buttermilk, salt and cayenne until blended. Coat onion rings with remaining flour, then dip in buttermilk mixture.

In an electric skillet or deep-fat fryer, heat oil to 375°. Fry onion rings, a few at a time, for 1-2 minutes on each side or until golden brown. Drain on paper towels. **Yield:** 2 servings.

WARM CHOCOLATE-CARAMEL APPLES

Radelle Knappenberger, Oviedo, Florida

Every fall, my husband and I loved picking apples from the two apple trees in our backyard and then developing new recipes. This is just one of the many recipes we created that remain all-time favorites. Firm apples are recommended.

> 1/4 cup packed brown sugar
> 2 teaspoons butter, softened
> 2 medium Braeburn apples
> 1/4 cup orange juice
> 2 tablespoons chocolate syrup
> 2 tablespoons caramel ice cream topping
> 1/4 cup chopped walnuts

In a small bowl, combine brown sugar and butter. Core apples three-fourths of the way through; fill with brown sugar mixture.

Place in a small microwave-safe dish. Pour orange juice into dish. Microwave, uncovered, on high for 4-5 minutes or until apples are tender.

Transfer to dessert plates; top with chocolate syrup and caramel topping. Sprinkle with the walnuts. **Yield:** 2 servings.

Editor's Note: This recipe was tested in a 1,100-watt microwave.

Meals in Minutes

A hot home-cooked meal is just moments away with these recipes that can be made in half an hour or less.

Turn to Your Stove For Speedy Supper

YOU CAN CALL your family to dinner early when you serve this streamlined menu of recipes compiled by our Test Kitchen. By using your stovetop rather than your oven, you can have these dishes on the table in half an hour or less.

Creamy Tortellini Carbonara sent in by Cathy Croyle of Davidsville, Pennsylvania calls for only five ingredients and comes together in minutes. Simply simmer the bacon and Parmesan sauce in one pan, boil packaged tortellini in another, then combine them for a memorable main dish. Cathy recommends, "Add additional cheese or parsley to the sauce to fit your family's taste."

Serve this classic pasta toss with Apricot-Glazed Green Beans from Nancy Mueller. "I like to add a little extra flavor to homegrown beans, and this is one of our favorite treatments," she writes from Bloomington, Minnesota. Apricot preserves make the tasty coating for the veggies.

It's easy to complete this made-in-minutes meal with refreshing Fruit Medley. "This recipe is an adaptation of a fruit salad from my husband's aunt," says Becky Hughes of Las Cruces, New Mexico. "The original recipe calls for a home-made glaze, but I substitute canned peach pie filling to speed up preparation.

"Since my husband, son and I have busy schedules, we are often in a rush to get dinner on the table. This medley can be whipped up in no time and makes a great side salad or dessert," she remarks. "It disappears quickly at potlucks."

TORTELLINI CARBONARA

1 package (9 ounces) refrigerated cheese tortellini
8 bacon strips, cooked and crumbled
1 cup heavy whipping cream
1/2 cup minced fresh parsley
1/2 cup grated Parmesan cheese

Cook tortellini according to package directions. Meanwhile, in a large saucepan, combine the bacon, cream, parsley and cheese; cook over medium heat until heated through.

Drain tortellini; toss with cream sauce. Serve immediately. **Yield:** 4 servings.

APRICOT-GLAZED GREEN BEANS

1 pound fresh green beans, cut into 3-inch pieces
1/3 cup apricot preserves
1 tablespoon butter
1/4 teaspoon salt

Place beans in a steamer basket in a saucepan over 1 in. of water. Bring to a boil; cover and steam for 7-8 minutes or until crisp-tender.

In a microwave-safe bowl, combine the preserves, butter and salt. Cook, uncovered, on high for 30 seconds or until the butter is melted; stir until smooth.

Transfer beans to a serving bowl; add apricot mixture and toss to coat. **Yield:** 4 servings.

FRUIT MEDLEY

1 can (21 ounces) peach pie filling
1 can (20 ounces) pineapple chunks, drained
1 can (11 ounces) mandarin oranges, drained
1 jar (10 ounces) maraschino cherries, drained
2 medium firm bananas, sliced
1/2 cup chopped pecans

In a large bowl, combine the pie filling, pineapple, oranges, cherries and bananas. Cover and refrigerate. Just before serving, stir in pecans. **Yield:** 8-10 servings.

Down-Home Dishes Are Fast, Delicious

SEARCHING for quick fare with old-fashioned appeal? Look no further than this time-saving trio of dishes shared by family cooks.

Our food editors pulled together this comforting menu that takes advantage of both the microwave and the stove. So you can have a home-cooked dinner on the table in half an hour.

Start by preparing the meaty main dish sent in by Karen Kurtz. "When my daughters were little, the only meats they wanted to eat were hot dogs and hamburgers," recalls the Muskegon, Michigan cook. "But when I served Microwave Stroganoff, they loved it. They are now adults and still request it for their birthday dinners."

To complement the effortless entree, toss together a bowl of Wilted Lettuce Salad from Cheryl Newendorp of Pella, Iowa. The warm, tangy dressing takes just minutes to create when you cook the bacon in the microwave. With slices of hard-cooked egg, it all adds classic appeal to salad greens.

To cap off the meal, serve dishes of ice cream topped with warm Apricot Pecan Sauce. In Rosenort, Manitoba, Eleanor Martens needs just six ingredients to stir together this speedy, flavorful sauce made with vanilla and rum extracts.

"I like trying new recipes," Eleanor writes. "And I enjoy fixing this simple dessert as a treat for all of our grandchildren."

MICROWAVE STROGANOFF

    2 tablespoons butter
1-1/2 pounds boneless beef sirloin steak, cut
       into thin strips
  1/4 cup all-purpose flour
    1 envelope onion soup mix
2-1/4 cups hot water
    1 can (4 ounces) mushroom stems and
       pieces, drained
  1/2 cup sour cream
Hot cooked noodles

Melt the butter in a 2-qt. microwave-safe dish; arrange the meat evenly in dish. Microwave, uncovered, on high for 4-1/2 minutes, stirring once. Remove the meat with a slotted spoon and keep warm.

Stir flour and soup mix into drippings until blended. Gradually add water, stirring until smooth. Add mushrooms and beef.

Cover and microwave on high for 13-14 minutes or until the meat is tender and the sauce is thickened, stirring several times. Stir in the sour cream. Serve with noodles. **Yield:** 6-8 servings.

Editor's Note: This recipe was tested in a 1,100-watt microwave.

WILTED LETTUCE SALAD

    6 cups torn leaf lettuce
    3 tablespoons finely chopped onion
    3 bacon strips, diced
    2 tablespoons red wine vinegar
2-1/4 teaspoons sugar
1-1/2 teaspoons water
Salt and pepper to taste
    1 hard-cooked egg, sliced

In a large salad bowl, combine the lettuce and onion; set aside.

Place bacon on a microwave-safe plate lined with paper towels. Cover with another paper towel; microwave on high for 5-7 minutes or until crisp. Transfer bacon strips to paper towels.

In a small microwave-safe dish, combine 1-1/2 teaspoons bacon drippings, vinegar, sugar and water. Microwave, uncovered, on high for 45 seconds or until sugar is dissolved; stir until smooth.

Pour over lettuce; sprinkle with salt and pepper. Add bacon and hard-cooked egg; toss to coat. **Yield:** 6 servings.

Editor's Note: This recipe was tested in a 1,100-watt microwave.

APRICOT PECAN SAUCE

  1/2 cup apricot spreadable fruit
  1/2 cup heavy whipping cream
    2 tablespoons butter
  1/2 cup chopped pecans
  1/2 teaspoon vanilla extract
  1/4 to 1 teaspoon rum extract, optional
Vanilla ice cream

In a large saucepan, combine the spreadable fruit, cream and butter. Bring to a boil. Reduce heat; simmer, uncovered, for 3-5 minutes or until blended. Stir in pecans, vanilla and rum extract if desired. Remove from the heat. Serve over ice cream. **Yield:** 1 cup.

WHEN the holiday season is just around the corner, fuss-free meals are a busy cook's dream come true. That's why our home economists combined the following recipes into this delicious, streamlined supper that can be on the table in a half hour or less. It's special enough to serve to company or quick enough to enjoy after a long day at work.

The flavorful entree and side dish depend on everyday ingredients, so you can avoid last-minute trips to the grocery store. And if you keep a pound cake in the freezer, you'll have a head start on the luscious dessert.

From High Point, North Carolina, food lover Barbara Arbuckle shares her secret for moist Curry Chicken Breasts. The palate-pleasing sauce combines the savory flavors of curry powder, Worcestershire sauce, garlic, chili sauce, onion and hot pepper sauce. It's ready in no time.

For an easy accompaniment to the tender chicken, try pretty Lemon-Pepper Veggies. Submitted by Linda Bernhagen of Plainfield, Illinois, it's a breeze to make in the microwave.

"Guests are surprised that this quick dish is so flavorful," says Linda. "The lemon-pepper seasoning gives it zing."

Karen Gardiner finishes off the made-in-moments meal with Quick Coffee Torte. "This easy-to-prepare dessert really hits the spot," writes the Eutaw, Alabama cook.

She divides prepared pound cake into three layers, then jazzes it up with coffee and rum extract. Whipped topping sprinkled with grated chocolate complete the irresistible treat.

CURRY CHICKEN BREASTS

  4 boneless skinless chicken breast halves
    (4 ounces *each*)
  1 tablespoon canola oil
1/4 cup Worcestershire sauce
  4 teaspoons chili sauce
  1 to 2 teaspoons curry powder
  1 teaspoon garlic salt *or* garlic powder
1/4 teaspoon hot pepper sauce

1/4 cup chopped onion
Hot cooked rice

In a large skillet, brown chicken on both sides in oil. Combine the Worcestershire sauce, chili sauce, curry powder, garlic salt and hot pepper sauce. Pour over chicken. Add onion. Reduce the heat; cover and simmer for 9-11 minutes or until a meat thermometer reads 170°. Serve with rice. **Yield:** 4 servings.

LEMON-PEPPER VEGGIES

    2 cups fresh broccoli florets
    2 cups cauliflowerets
    1 cup sliced carrots
    2 tablespoons water
4-1/2 teaspoons butter, melted
    1 teaspoon lemon-pepper seasoning
  1/2 teaspoon garlic powder

In a microwave-safe bowl, combine the broccoli, cauliflower, carrots and water. Cover and microwave on high for 3-6 minutes or until the vegetables are crisp-tender; drain. Combine the remaining ingredients; drizzle over vegetables and toss to coat. **Yield:** 4 servings.

Editor's Note: This recipe was tested in a 1,100-watt microwave.

QUICK COFFEE TORTE

  1/4 cup sugar
  1/4 cup water
    1 tablespoon instant coffee granules
1-1/2 teaspoons butter
  1/8 teaspoon rum extract
    1 frozen pound cake (10-3/4 ounces),
      thawed
    1 carton (8 ounces) frozen whipped
      topping, thawed
Grated chocolate, optional

In a small saucepan, combine the sugar, water and coffee. Bring to a boil; cook for 3 minutes, stirring occasionally. Remove from the heat; stir in butter and rum extract. Cool slightly.

Split cake into three horizontal layers. Place bottom layer on a serving plate. Brush with about 1 tablespoon coffee mixture; spread with 1 cup whipped topping. Repeat layers. Brush remaining coffee mixture over cut side of remaining cake layer; place coffee side down over topping. Spread remaining whipped topping over top of torte. Garnish with grated chocolate if desired. Chill until serving. **Yield:** 6-8 servings.

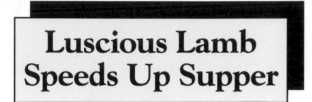

Luscious Lamb Speeds Up Supper

DAYS are jam-packed with activity for Ruth Lee, who lives in the close-knit farming village of Troy, Ontario. Ruth and her husband Doug are busy running an electric fencing business that's open 24 hours a day, 7 days a week.

Besides sharing many of the duties of their home-based business, Doug also works at a local brewery. "Since he works there full-time, it's usually my job to take care of the business, which includes repairing machines, selling supplies, doing estimates and installing fences," Ruth notes.

Ruth also belongs to an agricultural society and chairs a public-speaking contest. "I help with church dinners and various committees, and can over 150 jars of homegrown produce," she adds.

But spending time with family is important to Ruth, too. "We have two grown children and six grandchildren. They love to help in the kitchen when I'm preparing meals for get-togethers. It's time well spent!"

One of the streamlined suppers Ruth might serve at a family function is savory Lamb with Sauteed Veggies. "My parents raised sheep for more than 30 years, so I have several lamb recipes," she shares. "Not only are these chops tender, but they cook quickly."

"Partner it with delicious Seasoned Couscous, and you have a winner," Ruth says. Flecked with basil and parsley, the speedy stovetop side dish comes together in a snap.

Ruth caps off dinner with luscious Brownie Sundaes. "With prepared brownies, I can fix this sweet treat in a flash," she notes. "For extra flair, I roll the scoops of ice cream in pecans before placing them on top of the brownies."

LAMB WITH SAUTEED VEGGIES

  3 tablespoons olive oil, *divided*
  2 tablespoons Dijon mustard
  2 tablespoons balsamic vinegar
  2 teaspoons dried thyme
  2 garlic cloves, minced
1/4 teaspoon salt
1/4 teaspoon pepper
 12 lamb loin chops (1 inch thick and 6 to 7 ounces *each*)
  1 medium sweet red pepper, thinly sliced
  2 small zucchini, thinly sliced
  1 medium sweet onion, thinly sliced

Combine 2 tablespoons oil, mustard, vinegar, thyme, garlic, salt and pepper; set aside 1 tablespoon. Place chops on a broiler pan. Spread remaining mustard mixture over both sides of chops. Broil 4-6 in. from heat for 4-6 minutes on each side or until meat reaches desired doneness (for medium-rare, a meat thermometer should read 145°; medium, 160°; well-done, 170°).

Meanwhile, in a large skillet, saute the red pepper, zucchini and onion in the remaining olive oil until crisp-tender. Stir in reserved mustard mixture; toss to coat. Serve with lamb chops. **Yield:** 6 servings.

SEASONED COUSCOUS

  2 cups water
  1 tablespoon butter
  1 tablespoon dried parsley flakes
  2 teaspoons chicken bouillon granules
1/2 teaspoon dried minced onion
1/2 teaspoon dried basil
1/4 teaspoon pepper
1/8 teaspoon garlic powder
  1 package (10 ounces) couscous

In a large saucepan, combine the first eight ingredients; bring to a boil. Remove from the heat; stir in the couscous. Cover and let stand 5 minutes or until the liquid is absorbed. Fluff with a fork. **Yield:** 6 servings.

BROWNIE SUNDAES

3/4 cup semisweet chocolate chips
1/2 cup evaporated milk
  2 tablespoons brown sugar
  2 teaspoons butter
1/2 teaspoon vanilla extract
  6 prepared brownies (3 inches square)
  6 scoops vanilla *or* chocolate fudge ice cream
1/2 cup chopped pecans

In a large saucepan, combine the chocolate chips, milk and brown sugar. Cook and stir over medium heat for 5 minutes or until chocolate is melted and sugar is dissolved. Remove from the heat; stir in butter and vanilla until smooth.

Spoon 2 tablespoons warm chocolate sauce onto each dessert plate. Top with a brownie and scoop of ice cream. Drizzle with more sauce if desired; sprinkle with pecans. **Yield:** 6 servings.

Our Most Memorable Meals

*All-time family favorites still bring
folks together for dinner memories.*

Flavorful Menu Full of Fun

▪▪▪▪▪▪▪▪▪▪▪▪▪

VEGETABLE SOUP MEAT LOAF

Lola Miller, Puyallup, Washington

I found this recipe in a booklet that came with my new Hotpoint stove that was purchased in 1950. Mom first tried the recipe, and it's been a family favorite since. We also enjoy cold slices for sandwiches.

     2 slices white bread, torn
     1 can (10-1/2 ounces) condensed
        vegetarian vegetable soup, undiluted
     1 small onion, chopped
     1 eggs, lightly beaten
   1/2 teaspoon salt
   1/8 teaspoon pepper
 1-1/2 pounds lean ground beef
     1 can (8 ounces) tomato sauce

In a large bowl, soak bread in soup for 5 minutes. Stir in the onion, egg, salt and pepper. Crumble beef over mixture and mix well. Shape into an 8-in. x 4-in. oval.

Line an 11-in. x 7-in. baking dish with foil and grease the foil. Place meat loaf in pan; top with tomato sauce.

Bake, uncovered, at 350° for 50-60 minutes or until a meat thermometer reads 160° and meat is no longer pink. Let stand for 10 minutes before slicing. **Yield:** 6 servings.

▪▪▪▪▪▪▪▪▪▪▪▪▪

WILTED ICEBERG LETTUCE

Margaret Mitchell, Lincoln, Montana

My dad's mother brought this recipe with her from Czechoslovakia and turned it into her grandchildren's favorite. This warm salad is a good choice to accompany a meaty entree, such as roasts, chops or steaks.

     1 medium head iceberg lettuce, chopped
     6 bacon strips, diced
     1 small onion, chopped
     3 tablespoons all-purpose flour
     1 cup water
     1 cup white vinegar
     2 tablespoons sugar
   1/2 teaspoon salt
   1/4 teaspoon pepper

Place lettuce in a large salad bowl; set aside. In a small skillet, cook bacon over medium heat until crisp. Using a slotted spoon, remove to paper towels. Drain, reserving 2 tablespoons drippings.

Saute onion in drippings over medium heat until tender. Stir in flour until blended; cook and stir until lightly browned. Combine the water, vinegar, sugar, salt and pepper; gradually stir into onion mixture. Bring to a boil, stirring constantly; cook and stir 1 minute longer or until thickened.

Pour the hot dressing over the lettuce; toss to coat. Top with bacon and serve immediately. **Yield:** 6 servings.

▪▪▪▪▪▪▪▪▪▪▪▪▪

TWO-CHEESE MACARONI CASSEROLE

Martha Flowers, Bluffton, Indiana

This recipe was given to me by a dear friend years ago. I have shared it with everyone since it's a good dish to prepare on a busy day...very simple and easy.

 2-1/4 cups water
   1/4 cup butter, cubed
     4 cups (16 ounces) shredded cheddar
        cheese
     2 cups uncooked elbow macaroni
     1 cup (8 ounces) 4% cottage cheese
   1/8 teaspoon pepper
Pinch salt

In a large saucepan, bring water and butter to a boil. Remove from the heat; carefully stir in the remaining ingredients.

Transfer to a greased 2-qt. baking dish. Cover and bake at 350° for 45 minutes. Uncover; bake

10 minutes longer or until bubbly and macaroni is tender. **Yield:** 6 servings.

★░★░★░★░★░★

FROSTED CHOCOLATE MAYONNAISE CAKE

Deanna Blair, Brantford, Ontario

In my family this cake is also known as wartime cake. I was a child during World War II and still remember my mother making this cake as a treat, when eggs, butter and sugar were rationed. It's rich and moist, a little goes a long way and it never fails.

```
3/4 cup mayonnaise
  1 cup sugar
  1 teaspoon vanilla extract
  2 cups all-purpose flour
1/4 cup baking cocoa
  2 teaspoons baking soda
1/2 teaspoon salt
  1 cup water
```

CHOCOLATE FROSTING:

```
    2 tablespoons butter, softened
1-1/2 cups confectioners' sugar
    2 tablespoons baking cocoa
    2 tablespoons warm milk
    1 teaspoon vanilla extract
Pinch salt
```

In a large bowl, beat the mayonnaise, sugar and vanilla until smooth. Combine the flour, cocoa, baking soda and salt; add to the mayonnaise mixture alternately with water, beating well after each addition.

Pour into a greased 9-in. square baking pan. Bake at 350° for 25-30 minutes or until a tooth-pick inserted near the center comes out clean. Cool on a wire rack.

For frosting, in a small bowl, beat butter until light and fluffy. Gradually beat in confectioners' sugar, cocoa, milk, vanilla and salt. Frost cake. Store in the refrigerator. **Yield:** 9 servings.

Editor's Note: Reduced-fat or fat-free mayonnaise is not recommended for this recipe.

Festive Outdoor Party Fare

▰▰▰▰▰▰▰▰▰▰▰▰

BARBECUED HAMBURGERS

Marci Carl, Northern Cambria, Pennsylvania

When I got married, I asked my Aunt Jean for this recipe. She always made hamburgers this way for family picnics and the occasional church supper. I like them because they are very moist and taste great.

- 1/2 cup crushed saltines (about 15 crackers)
- 1 cup milk
- 1 teaspoon salt
- 1/4 teaspoon pepper
- 2 pounds ground beef
- 1-1/2 cups ketchup
- 1 large onion, chopped
- 1/3 cup Worcestershire sauce
- 3 tablespoons sugar
- 3 tablespoons cider vinegar
- 12 hamburger buns, split

In a large bowl, combine the saltines, milk, salt and pepper. Crumble beef over mixture and mix well. Shape into 12 patties. In a large skillet over medium heat, brown patties in batches on both sides. Place in a large roasting pan.

Combine the ketchup, onion, Worcestershire sauce, sugar and vinegar; pour over the patties. Cover and bake at 350° for 40-45 minutes or until a meat thermometer reads 160°. Serve on buns. **Yield:** 12 servings.

▰▰▰▰▰▰▰▰▰▰▰▰

CREAMY HERBED POTATO SALAD

Joan Ganey, West Hills, California

I came across this recipe in a magazine in an ortho-dontist's office over 25 years ago. It's still my favorite version of potato salad.

- 2 pounds red potatoes, cubed
- 4 green onions, chopped
- 1/2 cup chopped sweet pickles
- 1/4 cup chopped green pepper
- 1 hard-cooked egg, chopped

DRESSING:
- 1/2 cup mayonnaise
- 1/4 cup half-and-half cream
- 1 tablespoon minced fresh parsley
- 1 tablespoon lemon juice
- 1 teaspoon salt
- 1/2 teaspoon dill weed
- 1/2 teaspoon dried savory
- 1/4 teaspoon dried marjoram
- 1/4 teaspoon pepper

Place potatoes in a large saucepan and cover with water. Bring to a boil. Reduce heat; cover and simmer for 15-20 minutes or until tender. Drain and cool.

In a large bowl, combine the potatoes, onions, pickles, green pepper and egg. In a small bowl, combine the dressing ingredients. Pour over the salad and toss to coat. Cover and refrigerate for at least 1 hour before serving. **Yield:** 8 servings.

▰▰▰▰▰▰▰▰▰▰▰▰

COUNTRY BEAN BAKE

Tall Pines Farm, Gloria Jarrett, Loveland, Ohio

This recipe of my mom's makes the best baked beans I've ever eaten. I've taken them to many parties.

- 2 pounds bulk pork sausage
- 1 can (16 ounces) Boston baked beans
- 1 can (16 ounces) kidney beans, rinsed and drained
- 1 can (15-1/4 ounces) lima beans, rinsed and drained
- 1 can (15 ounces) butter beans, rinsed and drained
- 1 can (8 ounces) unsweetened crushed pineapple, drained
- 1 medium tart apple, peeled and shredded
- 1 small onion, diced
- 1/2 cup ketchup
- 1/2 cup molasses
- 1 tablespoon lemon juice
- 1 cup (4 ounces) shredded cheddar cheese

In a large skillet, cook the sausage over medium heat until no longer pink; drain. In a large bowl, combine the sausage, beans, pineapple, apple, onion, ketchup, molasses and lemon juice.

Transfer to a greased 3-qt. baking dish. Cover and bake at 325° for 60-70 minutes or until thickened and bubbly.

Uncover; sprinkle with cheese. Bake 5 minutes or until cheese is melted. **Yield:** 15 servings.

▰▰▰▰▰▰▰▰▰▰▰▰

CHERRY-BERRY PEACH PIE

Amy Hartke, Elgin, Illinois

I knew this pie was a keeper when I received compli-ments on it from my mother and grandmother.

2-1/2 cups all-purpose flour
   2 tablespoons sugar
  1/2 teaspoon salt
   1 cup cold butter, cubed
   4 to 6 tablespoons cold water

FILLING:
   2 cups fresh *or* frozen sliced peaches,
     thawed
1-3/4 cups pitted fresh dark sweet cherries *or*
   1 can (15 ounces) pitted dark sweet
   cherries, drained
   1 cup fresh *or* frozen blueberries, thawed
   1 teaspoon almond extract
   1 teaspoon vanilla extract
1-1/2 cups sugar
  1/4 cup all-purpose flour
  1/4 cup quick-cooking tapioca
  1/2 teaspoon salt
  1/2 teaspoon ground nutmeg
   1 tablespoon butter

In a large bowl, combine the flour, sugar and salt; cut in the butter until crumbly. Gradually add water, tossing with a fork until dough forms a ball. Divide the dough in half. Roll out one portion to fit a 9-in. deep-dish pie plate; transfer to a pie plate. Trim pastry even with edge of plate; set aside.

In a large bowl, combine the peaches, cherries, blueberries and extracts. Combine the sugar, flour, quick-cooking tapioca, salt and nutmeg; sprinkle over the fruit and gently toss to coat. Let stand for 15 minutes.

Spoon filling into crust. Dot with butter. Roll out remaining pastry; make a lattice crust. Seal and flute edges.

Bake at 375° for 50-55 minutes or until crust is golden brown and filling is bubbly. Cover edges with foil during the last 15 minutes to prevent overbrowning if necessary. Cool on a wire rack.
Yield: 6-8 servings.

A Casual Buffet Of Flavor

▼▼▼▼▼▼▼▼▼▼▼▼▼

TURNIP HASH PASTIES

Heidi Godfrey, Burnsville, West Virginia

This is a great winter recipe. It includes nutritious vegetables and meat as well. It's an old-fashioned pasty with lots of filling to make it a hearty meal.

>   2 cups all-purpose flour
>   3/4 teaspoon salt
>   2/3 cup shortening
>   6 to 7 tablespoons water
> FILLING:
>   1 pound ground beef
>   1-1/2 cups shredded peeled potatoes
>   1-1/2 cups shredded peeled turnips
>   1 medium onion, diced
>   2 tablespoons butter, melted
>   1 teaspoon salt
>   1/2 teaspoon pepper

In a large bowl, combine flour and salt; cut in shortening until crumbly. Gradually add water, tossing with a fork until dough forms a ball. Cover and refrigerate for 30 minutes.

For the filling, in a large skillet, cook beef over medium heat until no longer pink; drain. Transfer to a large bowl; stir in the potatoes, turnips, onion, butter, salt and pepper.

Divide dough into four equal portions. On a lightly floured surface, roll one portion into a 9-in. circle. Mound 1-1/2 cups of filling on half of circle. Moisten edges with water; fold dough over filling and press edges with a fork to seal.

Place on a greased baking sheet. Repeat with remaining dough and filling. Cut slits in tops of pasties. Bake at 375° for 40-45 minutes or until golden brown. **Yield:** 4 servings.

▼▼▼▼▼▼▼▼▼▼▼▼▼

HONEY HARVARD BEETS

Judy Nichols, Madisonville, Tennessee

This rich, sweet dish was served on my first visit to my in-laws 40 years ago. It's a colorful family favorite compatible with other fresh garden vegetables such as cabbage and green beans.

>   2 cans (14-1/2 ounces *each*) sliced beets
>   2 tablespoons cornstarch

>   1/2 cup white vinegar
>   1/2 cup honey
>   1/2 teaspoon salt
>   1/4 cup butter, cubed

Drain beets, reserving 1/2 cup juice; set beets aside. In a large saucepan, combine cornstarch and reserved juice until smooth. Stir in vinegar, honey and salt. Bring to a boil; cook and stir for 2 minutes or until thickened. Stir in butter and beets; heat through. **Yield:** 4-6 servings.

■■■■■■■■■■■■■

MONTEREY CORN BAKE

Irene Redick, Trenton, Ontario

I am happy to share this 50-year-old recipe. It came from my mother-in-law, who taught me how to cook. It is one of my family's favorite dishes, yielding enough for a group.

>   1 medium onion, chopped
>   1 garlic clove, minced
>   5 tablespoons butter, *divided*
>   2 cups sliced fresh mushrooms
>   1 medium sweet red pepper, chopped
>   1/2 teaspoon salt
>   1/4 teaspoon pepper
>   1 package (16 ounces) frozen corn, thawed
>   2 cups (8 ounces) shredded
>   Colby-Monterey Jack cheese
>   2 teaspoons brown sugar
>   1/2 cup dry bread crumbs
>   2 tablespoons minced fresh parsley

In a large skillet, saute the onion and garlic in 2 tablespoons butter until tender. Add the sliced mushrooms, chopped red pepper, salt and pepper; cook and stir for 5 minutes or until the vegetables are tender. Drain.

In a greased 2-qt. baking dish, layer half of the corn, mushroom mixture, cheese and brown sugar; repeat layers.

Melt the remaining butter; toss with the dry bread crumbs and fresh minced parsley. Sprinkle the bread crumb mixture over the casserole. Bake, uncovered, at 375° for 25-30 minutes or until golden brown. **Yield:** 4-6 servings.

FREEZING BELL PEPPERS

To freeze diced bell peppers, wash and dry them, remove the stems and seeds, then chop. Packed into freezer bags, they can keep up to 6 months. Use them directly from the freezer.

CARAMEL-FROSTED POTATO CAKE

Phyllis Schmidt, Manitowoc, Wisconsin

I am 90 years old and have been baking this cake every Christmas for 65 years! My sister-in-law gave me the recipe in 1941, and it has been in demand since. My grandchildren still don't know why it is called a potato cake, since it doesn't taste like potatoes!

3/4 cup butter, softened
2 cups sugar
4 eggs, *separated*
1 cup mashed potatoes (without added milk and butter)
2 ounces German sweet chocolate, melted
2 cups all-purpose flour
2 teaspoons baking soda
1 teaspoon ground nutmeg
1 teaspoon ground cloves
1/2 cup milk
1 cup chopped walnuts
FROSTING:
1/4 cup butter
1/2 cup packed brown sugar
1-1/4 cups confectioners' sugar
1/4 teaspoon vanilla extract
2 to 4 tablespoons milk

In a large bowl, cream the butter and sugar until light and fluffy. Beat in the egg yolks, potatoes and melted chocolate. Combine the flour, baking soda, ground nutmeg and cloves; add to the creamed mixture alternately with the milk, beating well after each addition. Stir in the chopped walnuts.

In a small bowl, beat egg whites until stiff peaks form; fold into batter. Pour into a greased and floured 10-in. fluted tube pan.

Bake at 350° for 55-60 minutes or until cake springs back when lightly touched. Cool for 10 minutes before removing from pan to a wire rack to cool completely.

For the frosting, in a small saucepan, melt the butter. Add the brown sugar; cook and stir over low heat for 2 minutes. Remove from the heat; cool for 3 minutes. Stir in the confectioners' sugar, vanilla and enough milk to achieve a thick pouring consistency. Pour over the cake. **Yield:** 12-16 servings.

Tasty Supper Is A Breeze

▰▰▰▰▰▰▰▰▰▰

GLAZED PORK CHOPS

Lisa Polson, San Rafael, California

When I saw this recipe in the newspaper years ago, I thought it sounded so good, I immediately went out and bought all the ingredients. Not only was it easy, the kids even raved about it. Almost everyone who has tasted it asks for the recipe.

  6 bone-in pork loin chops (8 ounces *each*)
  1 tablespoon canola oil
1/4 cup chopped onion
1/4 cup water
1/4 cup maple syrup
  1 tablespoon cider vinegar
  1 tablespoon Worcestershire sauce
  1 teaspoon salt
1/2 teaspoon chili powder
1/8 teaspoon pepper
  1 tablespoon cornstarch
  3 tablespoons cold water

In a large skillet, brown pork chops in oil on both sides. Transfer to a shallow 3-qt. baking dish. In a small bowl, combine the onion, water, syrup, vinegar, Worcestershire sauce, salt, chili powder and pepper; pour over chops.

Cover and bake at 350° for 30 minutes. Uncover; bake 15 minutes longer or until tender. Transfer to a serving platter or until a meat thermometer reads 160°.

Pour pan juices into a small saucepan. Combine cornstarch and cold water until smooth; stir into juices. Bring to a boil; cook and stir for 2 minutes or until thickened. Serve with pork chops. **Yield:** 6 servings.

▰▰▰▰▰▰▰▰▰▰

CHERRY-CHEESE GELATIN SALAD

Karen Ann Bland, Gove, Kansas

This recipe was in a community cookbook compiled by our high school's booster club 22 years ago. The measurements and directions were vague so I kept experimenting until I got it right. This is a pretty salad to serve at luncheons, and the flavor is light.

  1 can (20 ounces) unsweetened
    pineapple chunks

  1 can (15 ounces) pitted dark sweet
    cherries
  1 package (3 ounces) cherry gelatin
  1 package (3 ounces) cream cheese,
    softened
1/2 teaspoon sugar
  2 tablespoons chopped pecans
  1 drop almond extract
  5 lettuce leaves

Drain pineapple and cherries, reserving juices in a 2-cup measuring cup; add enough water to measure 2 cups. Set fruit aside.

In a small saucepan, bring juice mixture to a boil over medium heat. Remove from the heat; stir in gelatin until dissolved. Cover and refrigerate until partially set.

In a small bowl, combine the cream cheese, sugar, pecans and extract. Shape into 3/4-in. balls. Gently fold cheese balls and cherries into gelatin mixture. Transfer to five 1-cup molds coated with cooking spray. Refrigerate until firm.

Unmold the salad onto lettuce-lined plates; arrange the pineapple chunks around gelatin. **Yield:** 5 servings.

▰▰▰▰▰▰▰▰▰▰

BAVARIAN NOODLES

Frances Rosselet, Defiance, Ohio

I found this recipe in a farm newspaper, thought it sounded good and it was. I have used it for years. I often fix it instead of potatoes. If the apple skins are tough, I peel the apples. Otherwise, keep the skin on.

  2 cups uncooked egg noodles
  1 medium apple, chopped
1/4 teaspoon caraway seeds
  2 tablespoons butter
  2 tablespoons honey
  1 tablespoon Dijon mustard

Cook noodles according to package directions. Meanwhile, in a large skillet, saute apple and caraway in butter until apple is crisp-tender. Stir in the honey and mustard.

EASY-TO-CLEAN COLANDER

Cooked noodles can leave a sticky, difficult-to-remove residue on a colander. To make cleaning this important piece of equipment simple, before draining the noodles, spray the colander with cooking spray. It makes cleanup a lot faster and easier.

Drain the egg noodles; stir into the cooked and seasoned apple mixture. Cook until heated through. **Yield:** 5 servings.

POLISH BEET CAKE

Patricia Skalitzky, Oxford, Wisconsin

I make this cake a lot because everyone loves it. It's a hit for all occasions. The secret is not to tell anyone it's a beet cake. The beet flavor doesn't take over but makes the cake nice and moist.

1-1/2 cups sugar
    1 can (15 ounces) diced beets, drained
    1 cup canola oil
    3 eggs
    2 squares (1 ounce *each*) unsweetened chocolate, melted and cooled
    1 teaspoon vanilla extract
1-3/4 cups all-purpose flour
    1 teaspoon baking soda
1/2 teaspoon salt
FROSTING:
    1 cup butter, softened
    1 cup sugar
    3/4 teaspoon vanilla extract
1/2 cup warm milk (110° to 115°)

In a large bowl, beat the sugar, beets, oil, eggs, chocolate and vanilla until well blended. Combine the flour, baking soda and salt; gradually beat into sugar mixture until blended. Pour into a greased and floured 10-in. fluted tube pan.

Bake at 350° for 45-55 minutes or until a toothpick inserted near the center comes out clean. Cool for 10 minutes before removing from pan to a wire rack to cool completely.

For frosting, in a large bowl, beat butter and sugar until fluffy. Beat vanilla. Gradually beat in milk, 1 tablespoon at a time, until smooth. Frost top and sides of cake. Refrigerate leftovers. **Yield:** 12 servings.

This Dinner Is Simply Divine

■▼■▼■▼■▼■▼■▼■

TOMATO APPLE PORK ROAST

Barb Mitchell, Alvinston, Ontario

Here's a very tender, fall-off-your-fork roast. For a one-pot meal, add new potatoes and baby carrots.

    1 boneless whole pork loin roast
      (4 to 5 pounds)
    3 medium apples, peeled and chopped
    2 medium tomatoes, seeded and chopped
    1 small onion, chopped
    2 tablespoons brown sugar
    2 tablespoons cider vinegar
    1 garlic clove, minced
  1/4 teaspoon ground mustard
  1/4 teaspoon minced fresh gingerroot
Dash salt

Place roast on a rack in shallow roasting pan. Add about 1 in. of water to pan. Combine remaining ingredients; press onto roast. Bake, uncovered, at 350° for 1-1/4 to 1-3/4 hours or until a meat thermometer reads 160°. Let stand for 10 minutes before slicing. **Yield:** 12 servings.

■▼■▼■▼■▼■▼■▼■

"EVERYTHING" MASHED POTATO CASSEROLE

Pamela Shank, Parkersburg, West Virginia

This tasty bake evolved over the course of a year. It's topped with sour cream, bacon, cheese and chives.

    3 pounds potatoes (about 9 medium),
      peeled and quartered
    1 package (8 ounces) cream cheese,
      cubed
  1/2 cup butter, cubed
  1/2 cup milk
  1/4 teaspoon salt
  1/4 teaspoon pepper
    2 cups (16 ounces) sour cream
    2 cups (8 ounces) shredded cheddar
      cheese
    3 bacon strips, cooked and crumbled
    1 tablespoon minced chives

Place the potatoes in a large pot; cover with water. Bring to a boil. Reduce heat; cover and

simmer for 15-20 minutes or until tender. Drain. In a large bowl, mash the potatoes. Beat in the cream cheese, butter, milk, salt and pepper until fluffy. Transfer to a greased 3-qt. baking dish. Spread the sour cream over the top.

Bake, uncovered, at 350° for 10 minutes. Sprinkle with cheddar cheese, bacon and chives. Bake 5 minutes longer or until heated through and cheese is melted. **Yield:** 12 servings.

■▼■▼■▼■▼■▼■▼■

SIMPLE SAUTEED ZUCCHINI

Christy Maestri, Ozark, Arkansas

This simple vegetable side dish can be cooked in just a few minutes and is a great accent to any entree.

    12 cups thinly sliced zucchini (about
        10 medium)
   3/4 teaspoon dried thyme
   3/4 teaspoon dried rosemary, crushed
   1/2 teaspoon dill weed
     3 tablespoons olive oil
Salt and pepper to taste

In a Dutch oven, saute the zucchini, thyme, rosemary and dill in oil until crisp-tender. Reduce heat to medium; cover and cook for 5-7 minutes or until tender, stirring occasionally. Season with salt and pepper. **Yield:** 10-12 servings.

■▼■▼■▼■▼■▼■▼■

SWEET POTATO POUND CAKE

Diane Mannix, Helmville, Montana

Originally from Texas, we love sweet potatoes, but this pound cake deserves to be a tradition in any home.

    1 cup butter, softened
    2 cups sugar
    4 eggs
    1 teaspoon vanilla extract
    3 cups all-purpose flour
    2 teaspoons baking powder
    1 teaspoon ground cinnamon
  1/2 teaspoon baking soda
  1/4 teaspoon salt
  1/4 teaspoon ground nutmeg
    2 cups cold mashed sweet potatoes
GLAZE:
    1 cup confectioners' sugar
    1 teaspoon grated orange peel
    3 to 5 teaspoons orange juice

In a large bowl, cream butter and sugar until light and fluffy. Add eggs, one at a time, beating well after each addition. Beat in vanilla. Combine

the flour, baking powder, cinnamon, baking soda, salt and nutmeg; add to creamed mixture alternately with sweet potatoes. Beat just until combined (batter will be stiff).

Pour into a greased and floured 10-in. fluted tube pan. Bake at 350° for 50-60 minutes or until a toothpick inserted near the center comes out clean. Cool for 10 minutes before removing from pan to a wire rack to cool completely.

In a small bowl, combine confectioners' sugar, peel and enough juice to achieve desired consistency. Drizzle over cake. **Yield:** 12 servings.

The Best of Country Cooking 2009

Make Meals Special Again

⬛⬛⬛⬛⬛⬛⬛

GOLDEN CORNISH HENS

Mary Lee Allred, Paris, Idaho

I clipped this recipe out of a newspaper many years ago, altering it to fit my family's taste by mainly increasing the amount of both the pineapple and raisins. This is an easy, hearty entree with a nice old-fashioned flavor to fix for the holidays.

- 1 package (6 ounces) long grain and wild rice mix
- 1 can (8 ounces) unsweetened crushed pineapple
- 1/2 cup raisins
- 6 Cornish game hens (20 ounces *each*)
- 2 tablespoons butter, melted
- 1/4 teaspoon salt
- 1/4 teaspoon pepper
- 3 tablespoons honey

Prepare rice mix according to package directions. Drain pineapple, reserving juice; set aside. Stir pineapple and raisins into rice.

Just before baking, loosely stuff each hen with 3/4 cup rice mixture; tie legs together with kitchen string. Place hens, breast side up, on a rack in a shallow roasting pan. Brush with butter; sprinkle with salt and pepper.

Bake, uncovered, at 350° for 1-3/4 to 2 hours or until a meat thermometer reads 180° for hens and 165° for stuffing.

In a small saucepan, bring honey and reserved pineapple juice to a boil. Remove from the heat. Baste over the hens. Bake 15 minutes longer or until golden brown. **Yield:** 6 servings.

⬛⬛⬛⬛⬛⬛⬛

GREEN BEANS DELUXE

Lucy Martin, Dallas, Texas

We have belonged to a dinner/bridge group for many years, and this green bean dish has always been a favorite. The pinch of nutmeg enhances the flavor, which is creamy and rich. It goes well with a holiday meal, both in color and taste.

- 1 package (16 ounces) frozen French-style green beans
- 1 small onion, chopped
- 2 tablespoons butter
- 1 tablespoon all-purpose flour
- 3/4 cup sour cream
- 1/2 teaspoon salt
- 1/4 teaspoon pepper
- Pinch ground nutmeg
- 1/4 cup shredded cheddar cheese

Prepare green beans according to the package directions. Meanwhile, in a large skillet, saute the onion in butter until tender. Reduce heat; stir in the flour until blended. Add the sour cream, salt, pepper and nutmeg; heat through (do not boil).

Drain the beans; stir into sour cream mixture. Transfer to a greased 1-qt. baking dish. Bake, uncovered, at 350° for 15-20 minutes or until heated through. Sprinkle with the cheese; bake 5 minutes longer or until cheese is melted. **Yield:** 4-6 servings.

⬛⬛⬛⬛⬛⬛⬛

CREAMY CRANBERRY GELATIN

Mary Fitch, Ransomville, New York

I picked up this recipe at the gas company when I was a teen in the fifties. I modified it slightly, entered it in a newspaper contest and won $100! It was a delight to our family's taste buds.

- 1 cup orange juice
- 1 package (3 ounces) pineapple gelatin
- 1 package (3 ounces) cream cheese, softened
- 1 can (16 ounces) jellied cranberry sauce

In a small saucepan, bring the orange juice to a boil. Place the gelatin in a small bowl; add the orange juice and stir until dissolved. Refrigerate until slightly thickened.

In a small bowl, beat cream cheese until fluffy. Add cranberry sauce; beat until smooth. Beat in gelatin mixture. Pour into six 1/2-cup gelatin molds coated with cooking spray. Refrigerate for several hours or overnight. Unmold onto serving plates. **Yield:** 6 servings.

⬛⬛⬛⬛⬛⬛⬛

SOUTHERN HONEY-PECAN PIE

Allie Smith, New Orleans, Louisiana

Chock-full of pecans and honey, classic pecan pie is made even sweeter with honey. I like a piece with a hot cup of fresh-brewed coffee.

- 1/4 cup sugar
- 3 tablespoons all-purpose flour
- 3 eggs, lightly beaten

1 cup honey
1/3 cup butter, melted
1 teaspoon vanilla extract
1/4 teaspoon salt
1 cup chopped pecans
1 unbaked pastry shell (9 inches)
1/2 cup pecan halves

In a small bowl, combine the sugar and flour. Stir in the eggs, honey, butter, vanilla and salt. Add the chopped pecans and mix well. Pour into the pastry shell. Arrange the pecan halves around the edge and center of pie.

Cover the edges loosely with foil. Bake at 350° for 25 minutes. Remove the foil; bake for 20-25 minutes longer or until a knife blade inserted near the center of the pie comes out clean. Cool completely on a wire rack. Store in the refrigerator. **Yield:** 6-8 servings.

General Recipe Index

A

APPETIZERS & SNACKS

Cold Appetizers
Calla Lily Tea Sandwiches, 12
Caprese Tomato Bites, 7
Cold Vegetable Pizza, 14
Party Pitas, 11
Pickled Mushrooms, 14

Dips & Spreads
Bean and Pineapple Salsa, 12
Catfish Spread, 6
Chorizo Bean Dip, 13
Creamy Red Pepper Dip, 5
Fruit 'n' Nut Spread, 8
Pineapple Pecan Cheese Ball, 17
Turkey Cheese Ball, 9

Hot Appetizers
Bacon Water Chestnut Wraps, 6
Cheddar-Veggie Appetizer
    Torte, 16
Chili Chicken Strips, 17
Oysters Rockefeller, 10
Pepper Jack Cheese Sticks, 9
Pizza Roll-Ups, 15
Shrimp 'n' Mushroom Lettuce
    Wraps, 10
Spinach-Stuffed Portobellos, 5

Snacks
No-Bake Salted Pumpkin
    Seeds, 17

APPLES
Apple Harvest Cake, 128
Apple Pie, 112
Apple Pie Bars, 105
Apple Pie Dessert, 137
Apple Spice Drops, 107
✓Apple Tuna Sandwiches, 34
Cheddar Apple Pizza, 68
Cinnamon Poached Apples, 125
Citrus Cider Punch, 14
Coconut-Cranberry Apple
    Crisp, 129

Honey-Apple Turkey Breast, 68
Potato Brunch Medley, 73
Six-Fruit Salad, 39
Sweet Potato Waldorf Salad, 23
Tomato Apple Pork Roast, 168
Warm Chocolate-Caramel
    Apples, 150

APRICOTS
Apricot-Glazed Green Beans, 152
Apricot Pecan Sauce, 154
Apricot Sunshine Coffee Cake, 86
Fruity Chocolate Tortilla
    Cups, 134

ARTICHOKES
Artichoke Stuffing, 77
Lemon Artichoke Romaine
    Salad, 28
Stuffed Artichokes, 149

ASPARAGUS
Asparagus Cream Cheese
    Omelet, 57
Chicken Asparagus Bundles, 148
Crumb-Topped Asparagus
    Casserole, 76
Lemony Vegetables and Pasta, 47
Mock Hollandaise, 79

B

BANANAS
All-American Banana Split, 135
Banana Cheesecake, 130
Banana Fritters, 120
Banana Ice Cream, 114
Chocolate Banana Smoothies, 139
Six-Fruit Salad, 39

BARLEY & BULGUR
Mediterranean Bulgur Salad, 19
Mushroom Barley Soup, 137

BARS & BROWNIES
Apple Pie Bars, 105
Black Walnut Brownies, 101
Brenda's Lemon Bars, 99
Brownie Sundaes, 158
Caramel Pecan Bars, 106
Chewy Date Nut Bars, 104
Chippy Blond Brownies, 103
Chocolate Peanut Squares, 102
Cereal Cookie Bars, 100
Double Chocolate Orange
    Brownies, 99
Ginger Cranberry Bars, 102
Marble Brownies, 108
Peanut Butter Brownie Bars, 105
Raspberry Patch Crumb Bars, 104

BEANS, LENTILS & TOFU
Basil Polenta with Beans 'n'
    Peppers, 77
Bean and Pineapple Salsa, 12
Calypso Burritos, 53
Chorizo Bean Dip, 13
Country Bean Bake, 162
Hominy Meatball Stew, 23
✓Lentil Soup, 31
Mediterranean Bulgur Salad, 19
Southwestern Chicken Packets, 64
Thai Tofu Lettuce Wraps, 56

BEEF (also see Ground Beef & Ground Buffalo)
Beef Burgundy Stew, 146
Beef Potpie, 46
Cajun Pepper Steak, 52
Chorizo Bean Dip, 13
Double-Cheese Beef Panini, 35
Flank Steak Fajitas, 66
Italian Beef Sandwiches, 19
Microwave Stroganoff, 154
Oven Swiss Steak, 145
Pinwheel Flank Steaks, 60
Reuben Sandwiches, 40
Savory Pot Roast, 44

Sizzling Country Steak, 150
Steaks with Shallot Sauce, 62
Tex-Mex Scramble, 63

BEETS
Honey Harvard Beets, 164
Polish Beet Cake, 167

BEVERAGES
Citrus Cider Punch, 14
✓Cran-Raspberry Iced Tea, 5
Flavored Mocha Drink Mix, 7
Hot Cocoa, 139
Orange Creme Sodas, 15
Orange Lemonade, 8
Pink Rhubarb Punch, 15

BISCUITS
Green Onion Drop Biscuits, 89
Zucchini Cheddar Biscuits, 88

BLACKBERRIES
Four-Berry Spinach Salad, 140
Fresh Blackberry Pie, 125

BLUE RIBBON RECIPES
Appetizers
Catfish Spread, 6
Cheddar-Veggie Appetizer
    Torte, 16
Chorizo Bean Dip, 13
Bars
Apple Pie Bars, 105
Chewy Date Nut Bars, 104
Peanut Butter Brownie Bars, 105
Raspberry Patch Crumb
    Bars, 104
Breads, Rolls & Muffins
Almond-Filled Butterhorns, 95
Cranberry Surprise Muffins, 87
Desserts
Apple Harvest Cake, 128
Banana Cheesecake, 130
Cherry Walnut Cake, 114
Chocolate Cherry Lincoln
    Log, 122

Chocolate Peanut Butter
    Dessert, 111
Cream Cheese Ice Cream, 124
Frosty Raspberry Parfaits, 128
Frozen Cheesecake Bites, 133
Lemonade Dessert, 118
Maine Blueberry Cake, 130
Maple Cream Meringue Pie, 135
Peanut Ice Cream Delight, 121
Rhubarb Dessert Cake, 132
Strawberry Mallow Pops, 122
Main Dishes
Beef Potpie, 46
Chicken 'n' Corn Bread Bake, 48
Citrus Baked Fish, 68
Easy Chicken Potpie, 43
Grilled Turkey Tenderloins, 60
Honey-Dijon Pork Tenderloin, 43
Leek and Herb Stuffed
    Chicken, 71
Lemony Vegetables and
    Pasta, 47
Over-the-Top Mac 'n' Cheese, 49
Pinwheel Flank Steaks, 60
Roasted Pepper Chicken
    Penne, 54
Skillet Sea Scallops, 55
Side Dishes
Creamed Spinach, 74
Crumb-Topped Asparagus
    Casserole, 76
Grilled Chiles Rellenos, 82
Mushroom Rice Medley, 79
White 'n' Sweet Mashed
    Potatoes, 83
Soups, Salads & Sandwiches
✓Apple Tuna Sandwiches, 34
Chipotle Butternut Squash
    Soup, 32
Double-Cheese Beef Panini, 35
Grandma's Potato Salad, 33
Grilled Veggie Tortilla
    Wraps, 41
Herbed Raspberry-Hazelnut
    Salad, 40
Next-Generation German
    Potato Salad, 31
Rainbow Pasta Salad, 22
Ranch Turkey Burgers, 25

Spicy Chicken Salad with
    Mango Salsa, 20
Thai Tofu Lettuce Wraps, 56
Winter Salad, 39
Zesty Gazpacho, 27

BLUEBERRIES
Blueberry Lemon Cake, 113
✓Blueberry Orange Smoothies, 11
Cherry-Berry Peach Pie, 162
Four-Berry Spinach Salad, 140
Maine Blueberry Cake, 130
Old-Fashioned Blueberry
    Muffins, 97
Six-Fruit Salad, 39

BREADS & ROLLS
(also see Biscuits; Muffins)
Almond-Filled Butterhorns, 95
Brown Rice Yeast Rolls, 92
Cinnamon Swirl Quick Bread, 94
Flaxseed Bread, 95
Lemon Currant Loaves, 86
Little Snail Rolls, 89
Mother's Rolls, 86
Parmesan-Ranch Pan Rolls, 96

BROCCOLI & CAULIFLOWER
Broccoli and Noodles, 145
Frosted Cauliflower, 142
Lemon-Pepper Veggies, 156

BURGERS (see Sandwiches)

C

CABBAGE & SAUERKRAUT
Creamy Pineapple Coleslaw, 145
Reuben Sandwiches, 40
Skillet Cabbage Rolls, 69
Sweet-and-Sour Red Cabbage, 78

✓*Recipe includes Nutrition Facts
and Diabetic Exchanges*

CAKES, COFFEE CAKES & CHEESECAKES

(also see Cupcakes)
Almond Coffee Cake, 90
Apple Harvest Cake, 128
Apricot Sunshine Coffee Cake, 86
Banana Cheesecake, 130
Basketball Cake, 127
Blue-Ribbon Butter Cake, 111
Blueberry Lemon Cake, 113
Burger 'n' Hot Dog Cake, 126
Buttery Almond Pear Cake, 85
California Lemon Pound Cake, 132
Caramel-Frosted Potato Cake, 165
Cherry Walnut Cake, 114
Chocolate Cherry Lincoln Log, 122
Chocolate Raspberry Tea Cakes, 129
Cinnamon-Walnut Coffee Cake, 88
Cranberry-Sour Cream Coffee
    Cake, 91
Cream-Filled Cinnamon Coffee
    Cake, 85
Frosted Chocolate Mayonnaise
    Cake, 161
Frozen Cheesecake Bites, 133
Jam-Topped Mini Cheesecakes, 112
Maine Blueberry Cake, 130
Orange-Date Coffee Cake, 91
Polish Beet Cake, 167
Poppy Seed Chiffon Cake, 115
Rhubarb Dessert Cake, 132
Sour Cream Chocolate Cake, 124
Sweet Potato Pound Cake, 168

CARROTS

Bacon 'n' Onion Carrots, 150
Calypso Burritos, 53
Carrot Cake Pancakes, 44
Carrot Zucchini Saute, 81
✓Lentil Soup, 31
Orange Carrot Muffins, 92

CASSEROLES

Brunch Egg Bake, 70
Chicken 'n' Corn Bread Bake, 48
Crumb-Topped Asparagus
    Casserole, 76
"Everything" Mashed Potato
    Casserole, 168

Kielbasa and Pepper Casserole, 55
Over-the-Top Mac 'n' Cheese, 49
Sausage Rice Casserole, 146
Tomato and Cheese Strata, 51
Tuna 'n' Pea Casserole, 65
Two-Cheese Macaroni
    Casserole, 160

CHEESE

Asparagus Cream Cheese
    Omelet, 57
Bacon-Topped Grilled Cheese, 38
Blue Cheese Pear Salad, 138
Brunch Egg Bake, 70
Caprese Tomato Bites, 7
Cheddar 'n' Pea Tossed Salad, 30
Cheddar Apple Pizza, 68
Cheddar-Veggie Appetizer
    Torte, 16
Cheesy Chicken Chowder, 37
Cherry Cheese Blintzes, 57
Cherry-Cheese Gelatin Salad, 166
Cream Cheese Ice Cream, 124
Creamy Cheese Rice, 148
Crustless Four-Cheese Quiche, 51
Double-Cheese Beef Panini, 35
"Everything" Mashed Potato
    Casserole, 168
Fresh Mozzarella Tomato Salad, 21
Gouda Muffins, 96
Hearty Cheese Soup, 138
Lemon Ricotta Pancakes, 50
Omelet Wedges with Cheese
    Sauce, 52
Oven-Fried Parmesan Chicken, 48
Over-the-Top Mac 'n' Cheese, 49
Parmesan-Ranch Pan Rolls, 96
Parmesan Rice Pilaf, 140
Party Pitas, 11
Pepper Jack Cheese Sticks, 9
Pineapple Pecan Cheese Ball, 17
Pizza Roll-Ups, 15
Tomato and Cheese Strata, 51
✓Tomato Soup with Cheese
    Tortellini, 29
Turkey Cheese Ball, 9
Two-Cheese Macaroni
    Casserole, 160
Zucchini Cheddar Biscuits, 88

CHERRIES

Cherries over Creamy Fluff, 115
Cherry-Berry Peach Pie, 162
Cherry Cheese Blintzes, 57
Cherry-Cheese Gelatin Salad, 166
Cherry Walnut Cake, 114
Chicken with Cherry Sauce, 46
Chocolate Cherry Lincoln Log, 122
Chocolate-Covered Cherry
    Cookies, 100

CHICKEN & CORNISH HENS

Calla Lily Tea Sandwiches, 12
Cashew Chicken, 69
Cheesy Chicken Chowder, 37
Chicken 'n' Corn Bread Bake, 48
Chicken 'n' Fruit Salad, 38
Chicken Asparagus Bundles, 148
Chicken Dinner Packets, 141
Chicken Salad Pockets, 29
Chicken with Cherry Sauce, 46
Chili Chicken Strips, 17
Curry Chicken Breasts, 156
Dijon Chicken, 56
Easy Chicken Potpie, 43
Garlic Clove Chicken, 66
Golden Cornish Hens, 170
Green Chili Chicken
    Sandwiches, 22
Leek and Herb Stuffed
    Chicken, 71
Luncheon Salad, 26
Oven-Fried Chicken, 59
Oven-Fried Parmesan Chicken, 48
Roasted Pepper Chicken
    Penne, 54
Southwestern Chicken Packets, 64
Spicy Chicken Salad with Mango
    Salsa, 20

CHOCOLATE

Black Walnut Brownies, 101
Brownie Sundaes, 158
Chippy Blond Brownies, 103
Chocolate Banana Smoothies, 139
Chocolate Cherry Lincoln
    Log, 122

Chocolate Chip Cheesecake
    Dessert, 145
Chocolate-Covered Cherry
    Cookies, 100
Chocolate Macadamia
    Macaroons, 119
Chocolate Mousse, 121
Chocolate Peanut Butter
    Dessert, 111
Chocolate Peanut Squares, 102
Chocolate Pecan Kisses, 129
Chocolate Raspberry Tea
    Cakes, 129
Double Chocolate Orange
    Brownies, 99
Flavored Mocha Drink Mix, 7
Frosted Chocolate Mayonnaise
    Cake, 161
Fruity Chocolate Tortilla
    Cups, 134
German Chocolate Toffee
    Cookies, 106
Graduation Caps, 107
Hot Cocoa, 139
Jumbo Chocolate Chip
    Cookies, 101
Marble Brownies, 108
Peanut Butter Brownie Bars, 105
Sour Cream Chocolate Cake, 124
Warm Chocolate-Caramel
    Apples, 150

COCONUT
Chocolate Macadamia
    Macaroons, 119
Coconut-Cranberry Apple
    Crisp, 129
Orange Coconut Meringue
    Pie, 131

CONDIMENTS
Acorn Squash with Caramel
    Sauce, 73
Apricot Pecan Sauce, 154
✓Baked Flounder with Tartar
    Sauce, 62
Mock Hollandaise, 79
Pork Tenderloin Medallions, 65

COOKIES & CANDY
Apple Spice Drops, 107
Baby Pacifier Favors, 108
Chocolate-Covered Cherry
    Cookies, 100
Chocolate Macadamia
    Macaroons, 119
Chocolate Pecan Kisses, 129
Chunky Hazelnut Oatmeal
    Cookies, 99
Cookie Pudding Pots, 127
Double Butterscotch Cookies, 109
German Chocolate Toffee
    Cookies, 106
Graduation Caps, 107
Honey Maple Cookies, 103
Jumbo Chocolate Chip
    Cookies, 101
Ladybug Cookies, 109
Peanut Butter Ice Cream
    Sandwiches, 119

CORN & CORNMEAL
Basil Polenta with Beans 'n'
    Peppers, 77
Beef Potpie, 46
Chicken 'n' Corn Bread Bake, 48
Corn Chowder with
    Dumplings, 37
Monterey Corn Bake, 164
Southwestern Chicken Packets, 64

CRANBERRIES
Coconut-Cranberry Apple
    Crisp, 129
✓Cran-Raspberry Iced Tea, 5
Cranberry-Sour Cream Coffee
    Cake, 91
Cranberry Surprise Muffins, 87
Creamy Cranberry Gelatin, 170
Fruit 'n' Nut Spread, 8
Ginger Cranberry Bars, 102
Luncheon Salad, 26
Pork Tenderloin Medallions, 65

CUPCAKES
Chocolate Raspberry Tea
    Cakes, 129

Elvis Cupcakes, 117
Root Beer Cupcakes, 116
Surprise Red Cupcakes, 116

D

DEEP FRYER RECIPES
Banana Fritters, 120
Orlando Orange Fritters, 88
Pepper Jack Cheese Sticks, 9
Red Onion Rings, 150

DESSERTS (also see Bars &
Brownies; Cakes, Coffee Cakes
& Cheesecakes; Cookies & Candy;
Cupcakes; Ice Cream; Pies; Pudding
& Mousse)
Apricot Pecan Sauce, 154
Banana Fritters, 120
Cherries over Creamy Fluff, 115
Chocolate Chip Cheesecake
    Dessert, 145
Chocolate Peanut Butter
    Dessert, 111
Cinnamon Poached
    Apples, 125
Coconut-Cranberry Apple
    Crisp, 129
Frosty Raspberry Parfaits, 128
Fruit Medley, 152
Fruity Chocolate Tortilla
    Cups, 134
Lemonade Dessert, 118
Mango Delight Gelatin
    Mold, 118
Maple Pears, 133
Orlando Orange Fritters, 88
Peaches 'n' Cream, 147
Quick Coffee Torte, 156
Spiced Pear Dessert, 142
Strawberry Rhubarb Cream, 139
Strawberry Rhubarb Tart, 113
Warm Chocolate-Caramel
    Apples, 150

✓*Recipe includes Nutrition Facts
and Diabetic Exchanges*

E

EGGS
Asparagus Cream Cheese Omelet, 57
Brunch Egg Bake, 70
✓Calico Pepper Frittata, 50
Country Brunch Pie, 64
Country Pizza Pie, 63
Crustless Four-Cheese Quiche, 51
Grandma's Potato Salad, 33
Maple Cream Meringue Pie, 135
Omelet Wedges with Cheese Sauce, 52
Orange Coconut Meringue Pie, 131
Tex-Mex Scramble, 63
Tomato and Cheese Strata, 51

F

FISH & SEAFOOD
✓Apple Tuna Sandwiches, 34
✓Baked Flounder with Tartar Sauce, 62
Catfish Spread, 6
Citrus Baked Fish, 68
Mustard-Crusted Salmon, 141
New England Clam Chowder, 36
Oysters Rockefeller, 10
Salmon with Fettuccine Alfredo, 59
Savory Orange Salmon, 49
✓Seafood Salad Pitas, 33
Shrimp 'n' Mushroom Lettuce Wraps, 10
Shrimp Chowder, 36
Skillet Sea Scallops, 55
Thai Tilapia, 147
Tuna 'n' Pea Casserole, 65
✓Zippy Tomato-Topped Snapper, 149

FRUIT (also see specific kinds)
Chicken 'n' Fruit Salad, 38
Chewy Date Nut Bars, 104
Fruit 'n' Nut Spread, 8
Fruit Medley, 152
Fruity Chocolate Tortilla Cups, 134

Orange-Date Coffee Cake, 91
Spiced Pork Loin with Plums, 58

G

GELATIN (see Salads & Dressings)

GREEN BEANS
Apricot-Glazed Green Beans, 152
Barbecue Green Bean Bake, 83
Green Beans Deluxe, 170
Green Beans with Herbs, 75
String Bean Salad, 142

GRILLED RECIPES
Bacon-Topped Grilled Cheese, 38
Barbecued Hamburgers, 162
Double-Cheese Beef Panini, 35
Green Chili Chicken Sandwiches, 22
Grilled Chiles Rellenos, 82
Grilled Deli Sandwiches, 27
Grilled Potatoes, 82
Grilled Turkey Tenderloins, 60
Grilled Veggie Tortilla Wraps, 41
Individual Campfire Stew, 61
Marinated Pork Chops, 61
Pinwheel Flank Steaks, 60
Ranch Turkey Burgers, 25
Thai Tilapia, 147

GROUND BEEF & GROUND BUFFALO
Barbecued Hamburgers, 162
Buffalo-Stuffed Bell Peppers, 48
Burgers with Garden Sauce, 24
Farmhouse Chili Dogs, 66
Homemade Meatballs, 70
Hominy Meatball Stew, 23
Individual Campfire Stew, 61
Meatballs Stroganoff, 45
Open-Faced Hamburgers, 25
Pizza Roll-Ups, 15
Skillet Cabbage Rolls, 69
Turnip Hash Pasties, 164
Vegetable Soup Meat Loaf, 160

H

HAM & BACON
Bacon 'n' Onion Carrots, 150
Bacon Mashed Potatoes, 76
Bacon-Topped Grilled Cheese, 38
Bacon Water Chestnut Wraps, 6
BLT Pizza, 71
✓BLT Tortillas, 32
Brunch Egg Bake, 70
Grilled Deli Sandwiches, 27
Next-Generation German Potato Salad, 31
Old-Fashioned Glazed Ham, 54
Party Pitas, 11
Tortellini Carbonara, 152
Wild Rice and Ham Chowder, 36

HOT DOGS (see Sausage)

I

ICE CREAM
All-American Banana Split, 135
Banana Ice Cream, 114
Brownie Sundaes, 158
Cream Cheese Ice Cream, 124
Orange Creme Sodas, 15
Peanut Butter Ice Cream Sandwiches, 119
Peanut Ice Cream Delight, 121
Pumpkin Ice Cream Pie, 115
Strawberry Mallow Pops, 122

L

LAMB
Lamb with Sauteed Veggies, 158

LEMONS & LIMES
Apricot Pecan Sauce, 154
Blueberry Lemon Cake, 113
Brenda's Lemon Bars, 99
California Lemon Pound Cake, 132
Citrus Cider Punch, 14

Lemon Artichoke Romaine
    Salad, 28
Lemon Currant Loaves, 86
Lemon-Pepper Veggies, 156
Lemon Ricotta Pancakes, 50
Lemonade Dessert, 118
Lemony Vegetables and Pasta, 47
Orange Lemonade, 8

M

MANGOES
Mango Delight Gelatin Mold, 118
Spicy Chicken Salad with Mango
    Salsa, 20

MEATBALLS & MEAT LOAF
Homemade Meatballs, 70
Hominy Meatball Stew, 23
Meatballs Stroganoff, 45
Vegetable Soup Meat Loaf, 160

MICROWAVE RECIPES
Catfish Spread, 6
Lemon-Pepper Veggies, 156
Microwave Stroganoff, 154
No-Bake Salted Pumpkin
    Seeds, 17
Red Potato Skewers, 81
Spiced Pear Dessert, 142

MUFFINS
Brown Sugar Rhubarb Muffins, 96
Cranberry Surprise Muffins, 87
Gouda Muffins, 96
Old-Fashioned Blueberry
    Muffins, 97
Orange Carrot Muffins, 92

MUSHROOMS
Fettuccine with Mushrooms and
    Tomatoes, 45
Mushroom Barley Soup, 137
Mushroom Burgers, 24
Mushroom Rice Medley, 79

Pickled Mushrooms, 14
Shrimp 'n' Mushroom Lettuce
    Wraps, 10
Spinach-Stuffed Portobellos, 5
Wild Rice Turkey Soup, 41

N

NUTS & PEANUT BUTTER
Almond Coffee Cake, 90
Almond-Filled Butterhorns, 95
Apricot Pecan Sauce, 154
Black Walnut Brownies, 101
Buttery Almond Pear Cake, 85
Caramel Pecan Bars, 106
Cashew Chicken, 69
Cherry Walnut Cake, 114
Chewy Date Nut Bars, 104
Chocolate Macadamia
    Macaroons, 119
Chocolate Peanut Butter
    Dessert, 111
Chocolate Peanut Squares, 102
Chocolate Pecan Kisses, 129
Chunky Hazelnut Oatmeal
    Cookies, 99
Cinnamon-Walnut Coffee Cake, 88
Elvis Cupcakes, 117
Fruit 'n' Nut Spread, 8
Herbed Raspberry-Hazelnut
    Salad, 40
Peach-Almond Spinach Salad, 35
Peanut Butter Brownie Bars, 105
Peanut Butter Ice Cream
    Sandwiches, 119
Peanut Ice Cream Delight, 121
Pear Praline Pie, 120
Pineapple Pecan Cheese Ball, 17
Southern Honey-Pecan Pie, 170
Winter Salad, 39

O

OATS
Cereal Cookie Bars, 100
Chunky Hazelnut Oatmeal
    Cookies, 99

ONIONS, SHALLOTS & LEEKS
Bacon 'n' Onion Carrots, 150
Carzalia Sweet Onion Salad, 38
Green Onion Drop Biscuits, 89
Leek and Herb Stuffed Chicken, 71
Red Onion Rings, 150
Steaks with Shallot Sauce, 62
Zucchini-Stuffed Onions, 75

ORANGES
✓Blueberry Orange Smoothies, 11
Citrus Baked Fish, 68
Double Chocolate Orange
    Brownies, 99
Orange Carrot Muffins, 92
Orange Coconut Meringue Pie, 131
Orange Creme Sodas, 15
Orange-Date Coffee Cake, 91
Orange Lemonade, 8
Orlando Orange Fritters, 88
Savory Orange Salmon, 49
Six-Fruit Salad, 39
Spinach Salad with Red Currant
    Dressing, 33

OVEN ENTREES (also see
Casseroles; Pizza)
✓Baked Flounder with Tartar
    Sauce, 62
Buffalo-Stuffed Bell Peppers, 48
Beef Potpie, 46
Burgers with Garden Sauce, 24
Chicken Asparagus Bundles, 148
Chicken Dinner Packets, 141
Citrus Baked Fish, 68
Country Brunch Pie, 64
Crustless Four-Cheese Quiche, 51
Dijon Chicken, 56
Easy Chicken Potpie, 43
Glazed Pork Chops, 166
Golden Cornish Hens, 170
Homemade Meatballs, 70
Honey-Apple Turkey Breast, 68
Lamb with Sauteed Veggies, 158

*✓Recipe includes Nutrition Facts
and Diabetic Exchanges*

OVEN ENTREES (*continued*)
Leek and Herb Stuffed
    Chicken, 71
Mustard-Crusted Salmon, 141
Old-Fashioned Glazed Ham, 54
Omelet Wedges with Cheese
    Sauce, 52
Open-Faced Hamburgers, 25
Oven-Fried Chicken, 59
Oven-Fried Parmesan Chicken, 48
Oven Swiss Steak, 145
Savory Pot Roast, 44
Sizzling Country Steak, 150
Southwestern Chicken Packets, 64
Tomato Apple Pork Roast, 168
Turnip Hash Pasties, 164
Venison Tortilla Lasagna, 58
✓Zippy Tomato-Topped
    Snapper, 149

P

PANCAKES
Carrot Cake Pancakes, 44
Cherry Cheese Blintzes, 57
Lemon Ricotta Pancakes, 50
Zucchini Potato Pancakes, 80

PASTA
Bavarian Noodles, 166
Broccoli and Noodles, 145
Fettuccine with Mushrooms
    and Tomatoes, 45
Italian Stew, 26
Lemony Vegetables and Pasta, 47
Over-the-Top Mac 'n' Cheese, 49
Rainbow Pasta Salad, 22
Roasted Pepper Chicken
    Penne, 54
Salmon with Fettuccine
    Alfredo, 59
Seasoned Couscous, 158
✓Tomato Soup with Cheese
    Tortellini, 29
Tortellini Carbonara, 152
Tuna 'n' Pea Casserole, 65
Two-Cheese Macaroni
    Casserole, 160

PEACHES
Cherry-Berry Peach Pie, 162
Fruity Chocolate Tortilla Cups, 134
Luncheon Salad, 26
Peach-Almond Spinach Salad, 35
Peaches 'n' Cream, 147

PEARS
Blue Cheese Pear Salad, 138
Buttery Almond Pear Cake, 85
Maple Pears, 133
Pear Praline Pie, 120
Spiced Pear Dessert, 142
Sweet Potato and Pear Soup, 34
Winter Salad, 39

PEAS
Cheddar 'n' Pea Tossed Salad, 30
Tuna 'n' Pea Casserole, 65

PEPPERS
Basil Polenta with Beans 'n'
    Peppers, 77
Buffalo-Stuffed Bell Peppers, 48
Bean and Pineapple Salsa, 12
Cajun Pepper Steak, 52
✓Calico Pepper Frittata, 50
Chorizo Bean Dip, 13
Creamy Red Pepper Dip, 5
Green Chili Chicken
    Sandwiches, 22
Grilled Chiles Rellenos, 82
Italian Beef Sandwiches, 19
Kielbasa and Pepper Casserole, 55
Mexican Pork Roast, 53
Roasted Pepper Chicken Penne, 54
Roasted Red Pepper Soup, 19

PIES
Apple Pie, 112
Apple Pie Dessert, 137
Cherry-Berry Peach Pie, 162
Country Brunch Pie, 64
Fluffy Pumpkin Pie, 123
Fresh Blackberry Pie, 125
Maple Cream Meringue Pie, 135

Orange Coconut Meringue Pie, 131
Pear Praline Pie, 120
Pumpkin Ice Cream Pie, 115
Southern Honey-Pecan Pie, 170
Strawberry Cheesecake Pie, 134

PINEAPPLE
Bean and Pineapple Salsa, 12
Cherry-Cheese Gelatin Salad, 166
Creamy Pineapple Coleslaw, 145
Pineapple Pecan Cheese Ball, 17
Pink Rhubarb Punch, 15

PIZZA
BLT Pizza, 71
Cheddar Apple Pizza, 68
Cold Vegetable Pizza, 14
Country Pizza Pie, 63
Greek Spinach Pizza, 43
Pizza Roll-Ups, 15

PORK (*also see Ham & Bacon;
Sausage & Hot Dogs*)
Glazed Pork Chops, 166
Homemade Meatballs, 70
Honey-Dijon Pork Tenderloin, 43
Marinated Pork Chops, 61
Mexican Pork Roast, 53
Pork Tenderloin Medallions, 65
Spiced Pork Loin with Plums, 58
Tomato Apple Pork Roast, 168

**POTATOES &
SWEET POTATOES**
Bacon Mashed Potatoes, 76
Beef Potpie, 46
Caramel-Frosted Potato Cake, 165
Cheesy Chicken Chowder, 37
Corn Chowder with Dumplings, 37
Creamy Herbed Potato Salad, 162
Crunchy Sweet Potato Bake, 74
"Everything" Mashed Potato
    Casserole, 168
Grandma's Potato Salad, 33
Grilled Potatoes, 82
Homemade Meatballs, 70
Individual Campfire Stew, 61

Kielbasa and Pepper Casserole, 55
Mashed Potato Roses, 78
Next-Generation German Potato
    Salad, 31
Potato Brunch Medley, 73
Red Potato Skewers, 81
Sausage and Kale Soup, 21
Shrimp Chowder, 36
String Bean Salad, 142
Sweet Potato and Pear Soup, 34
Sweet Potato Pound Cake, 168
Sweet Potato Waldorf Salad, 23
Three-Potato Salad, 29
Turnip Hash Pasties, 164
White 'n' Sweet Mashed
    Potatoes, 83
Wild Rice and Ham Chowder, 36
Zucchini Potato Pancakes, 80

PUDDINGS & MOUSSE
Biltmore's Bread Pudding, 123
Bread Pudding with Butter
    Sauce, 143
Chocolate Mousse, 121
Cookie Pudding Pots, 127

PUMPKIN
Fluffy Pumpkin Pie, 123
No-Bake Salted Pumpkin Seeds, 17
Pumpkin Ice Cream Pie, 115

R

RASPBERRIES
Chocolate Raspberry Tea
    Cakes, 129
✓Cran-Raspberry Iced Tea, 5
Four-Berry Spinach Salad, 140
Frosty Raspberry Parfaits, 128
Herbed Raspberry-Hazelnut
    Salad, 40
Raspberry Patch Crumb Bars, 104

RHUBARB
Brown Sugar Rhubarb Muffins, 96
Pink Rhubarb Punch, 15

Rhubarb Dessert Cake, 132
Strawberry Rhubarb Cream, 139
Strawberry Rhubarb Tart, 113

RICE
Brown Rice Yeast Rolls, 92
Creamy Cheese Rice, 148
Mushroom Rice Medley, 79
Oven Rice Supreme, 76
Parmesan Rice Pilaf, 140
Sausage Rice Casserole, 146
Spicy Spanish Rice, 81
Wild Rice and Ham Chowder, 36
Wild Rice Turkey Soup, 41

S

SALADS & DRESSINGS
Dressing
French Dressing with
    Tomatoes, 80
Fruit & Gelatin Salads
Blue Cheese Pear Salad, 138
Cherry-Cheese Gelatin
    Salad, 166
Creamy Cranberry Gelatin, 170
Fruit Medley, 152
Luncheon Salad, 26
Mango Delight Gelatin
    Mold, 118
Six-Fruit Salad, 39
Green Salads & Coleslaw
Cheddar 'n' Pea Tossed
    Salad, 30
Creamy Pineapple Coleslaw, 145
Four-Berry Spinach Salad, 140
Herbed Raspberry-Hazelnut
    Salad, 40
Lemon Artichoke Romaine
    Salad, 28
Peach-Almond Spinach
    Salad, 35
Spinach Salad with Red
    Currant Dressing, 33
Wilted Iceberg Lettuce, 160
Wilted Lettuce Salad, 154
Winter Salad, 39

Main-Dish Salads
Chicken 'n' Fruit Salad, 38
Chicken Salad Pockets, 29
✓Seafood Salad Pitas, 33
Spicy Chicken Salad with
    Mango Salsa, 20
Pasta & Bulgur Salads
Mediterranean Bulgur Salad, 19
Rainbow Pasta Salad, 22
Potato Salads
Creamy Herbed Potato
    Salad, 162
Grandma's Potato Salad, 33
Next-Generation German
    Potato Salad, 31
String Bean Salad, 142
Sweet Potato Waldorf Salad, 23
Three-Potato Salad, 29
Vegetable Salads
Avocado Tomato Salad, 35
Carzalia Sweet Onion Salad, 38
Fresh Mozzarella Tomato
    Salad, 21

SANDWICHES
Burgers
Barbecued Hamburgers, 162
Burgers with Garden Sauce, 24
Mushroom Burgers, 24
Open-Faced Hamburgers, 25
Ranch Turkey Burgers, 25
Sandwiches
✓Apple Tuna Sandwiches, 34
Bacon-Topped Grilled Cheese, 38
✓BLT Tortillas, 32
Calla Lily Tea Sandwiches, 12
Calypso Burritos, 53
Chicken Salad Pockets, 29
Farmhouse Chili Dogs, 66
Flank Steak Fajitas, 66
Green Chili Chicken
    Sandwiches, 22
Grilled Deli Sandwiches, 27

*✓Recipe includes Nutrition Facts
and Diabetic Exchanges*

SANDWICHES (*continued*)
Grilled Veggie Tortilla
  Wraps, 41
Hot Italian Patties, 30
Italian Beef Sandwiches, 19
Reuben Sandwiches, 40
✓Seafood Salad Pitas, 33
Shredded Venison
  Sandwiches, 20
Shrimp 'n' Mushroom Lettuce
  Wraps, 10
Thai Tofu Lettuce Wraps, 56
Turkey Dijon Melts, 137

SAUSAGE
Chorizo Bean Dip, 13
Country Bean Bake, 162
Country Brunch Pie, 64
Country Pizza Pie, 63
Farmhouse Chili Dogs, 66
Hot Italian Patties, 30
Italian Stew, 26
Kielbasa and Pepper Casserole, 55
Sausage and Kale Soup, 21
Sausage Rice Casserole, 146

SIDE DISHES (*also see*
Condiments; Salads & Dressings)
Acorn Squash with Caramel
  Sauce, 73
Apricot-Glazed Green Beans, 152
Artichoke Stuffing, 77
Bacon 'n' Onion Carrots, 150
Bacon Mashed Potatoes, 76
Barbecue Green Bean Bake, 83
Basil Polenta with Beans 'n'
  Peppers, 77
Bavarian Noodles, 166
Broccoli and Noodles, 145
Carrot Zucchini Saute, 81
✓Colorful Vegetable Medley, 78
Country Bean Bake, 162
Creamed Spinach, 74
Creamy Cheese Rice, 148
Crumb-Topped Asparagus
  Casserole, 76
Crunchy Sweet Potato Bake, 74

"Everything" Mashed Potato
  Casserole, 168
Frosted Cauliflower, 142
Green Beans Deluxe, 170
Green Beans with Herbs, 75
Grilled Chiles Rellenos, 82
Grilled Potatoes, 82
Honey Harvard Beets, 164
Lamb with Sauteed Veggies, 158
Lemon-Pepper Veggies, 156
Mashed Potato Roses, 78
Monterey Corn Bake, 164
Mushroom Rice Medley, 79
Oven Rice Supreme, 76
Parmesan Rice Pilaf, 140
Potato Brunch Medley, 73
Red Onion Rings, 150
Red Potato Skewers, 81
Seasoned Couscous, 158
Simple Sauteed Zucchini, 168
Special Garden Medley, 73
Spicy Spanish Rice, 81
Stuffed Artichokes, 149
Summer Squash Medley, 140
Sweet-and-Sour Red Cabbage, 78
Tangy Zucchini Saute, 74
Two-Cheese Macaroni
  Casserole, 160
White 'n' Sweet Mashed
  Potatoes, 83
Zucchini-Stuffed Onions, 75

SLOW COOKER RECIPES
Flank Steak Fajitas, 66
Garlic Clove Chicken, 66
Italian Beef Sandwiches, 19
Mexican Pork Roast, 53
Shredded Venison Sandwiches, 20

SMOOTHIES
✓Blueberry Orange Smoothies, 11
Chocolate Banana Smoothies, 139
Strawberry Flax Smoothies, 149

SOUPS & STEWS
Beef Burgundy Stew, 146
Cheesy Chicken Chowder, 37

Chipotle Butternut Squash
  Soup, 32
Corn Chowder with Dumplings, 37
Creamy Zucchini Soup, 39
✓Curried Turkey Vegetable
  Soup, 28
Hearty Cheese Soup, 138
Hominy Meatball Stew, 23
Individual Campfire Stew, 61
Italian Stew, 26
✓Lentil Soup, 31
Mushroom Barley Soup, 137
New England Clam Chowder, 36
Roasted Red Pepper Soup, 19
Sausage and Kale Soup, 21
Shrimp Chowder, 36
Sweet Potato and Pear Soup, 34
✓Tomato Soup with Cheese
  Tortellini, 29
Wild Rice and Ham Chowder, 36
Wild Rice Turkey Soup, 41
Zesty Gazpacho, 27

SPINACH & KALE
Chipotle Butternut Squash
  Soup, 32
Creamed Spinach, 74
✓Curried Turkey Vegetable
  Soup, 28
Four-Berry Spinach Salad, 140
Greek Spinach Pizza, 43
Party Pitas, 11
Peach-Almond Spinach Salad, 35
Sausage and Kale Soup, 21
Spinach Salad with Red Currant
  Dressing, 33
Spinach-Stuffed Portobellos, 5

STOVETOP ENTREES
(*also see Pancakes; Sandwiches;*
Soups & Stew)
Asparagus Cream Cheese
  Omelet, 57
Cajun Pepper Steak, 52
✓Calico Pepper Frittata, 50
Carrot Cake Pancakes, 44
Cashew Chicken, 69
Chicken with Cherry Sauce, 46

Chili Chicken Strips, 17
Curry Chicken Breasts, 156
Fettuccine with Mushrooms
  and Tomatoes, 45
Honey-Dijon Pork Tenderloin, 43
Lemony Vegetables and Pasta, 47
Meatballs Stroganoff, 45
Pork Tenderloin Medallions, 65
Roasted Pepper Chicken Penne, 54
Salmon with Fettuccine Alfredo, 59
Savory Orange Salmon, 49
Skillet Cabbage Rolls, 69
Skillet Sea Scallops, 55
Spiced Pork Loin with Plums, 58
Steaks with Shallot Sauce, 62
Tex-Mex Scramble, 63
Tortellini Carbonara, 152

STRAWBERRIES
Four-Berry Spinach Salad, 140
Fruity Chocolate Tortilla Cups, 134
Six-Fruit Salad, 39
Spinach Salad with Red Currant
  Dressing, 33
Strawberry Cheesecake Pie, 134
Strawberry Flax Smoothies, 149
Strawberry Mallow Pops, 122
Strawberry Rhubarb Cream, 139
Strawberry Rhubarb Tart, 113

T

TOMATOES
Avocado Tomato Salad, 35
BLT Pizza, 71
✓BLT Tortillas, 32
Caprese Tomato Bites, 7

Fettuccine with Mushrooms
  and Tomatoes, 45
French Dressing with Tomatoes, 80
Fresh Mozzarella Tomato Salad, 21
Mediterranean Bulgur Salad, 19
Special Garden Medley, 73
Tomato and Cheese Strata, 51
Tomato Apple Pork Roast, 168
✓Tomato Soup with Cheese
  Tortellini, 29
Zesty Gazpacho, 27
✓Zippy Tomato-Topped
  Snapper, 149

TURKEY
✓Curried Turkey Vegetable
  Soup, 28
Grilled Turkey Tenderloins, 60
Honey-Apple Turkey Breast, 68
Ranch Turkey Burgers, 25
Turkey Cheese Ball, 9
Turkey Dijon Melts, 137
Wild Rice Turkey Soup, 41

V

VEGETABLES
(also see specific kinds)
Avocado Tomato Salad, 35
Burgers with Garden Sauce, 24
Cheddar-Veggie Appetizer
  Torte, 16
Cold Vegetable Pizza, 14
✓Colorful Vegetable Medley, 78
✓Curried Turkey Vegetable
  Soup, 28

Easy Chicken Potpie, 43
Grilled Deli Sandwiches, 27
Grilled Veggie Tortilla Wraps, 41
Lamb with Sauteed Veggies, 158
Lemon-Pepper Veggies, 156
Lemony Vegetables and Pasta, 47
Rainbow Pasta Salad, 22
Special Garden Medley, 73
Vegetable Soup Meat Loaf, 160

VENISON
Shredded Venison Sandwiches, 20
Venison Tortilla Lasagna, 58

Z

ZUCCHINI & SQUASH
Acorn Squash with Caramel
  Sauce, 73
Calypso Burritos, 53
Carrot Zucchini Saute, 81
Cheddar-Veggie Appetizer
  Torte, 16
Chipotle Butternut Squash
  Soup, 32
✓Colorful Vegetable Medley, 78
Creamy Zucchini Soup, 39
Grilled Veggie Tortilla Wraps, 41
Italian Stew, 26
Lamb with Sauteed Veggies, 158
Simple Sauteed Zucchini, 168
Summer Squash Medley, 140
Tangy Zucchini Saute, 74
Zucchini Cheddar Biscuits, 88
Zucchini Potato Pancakes, 80
Zucchini-Stuffed Onions, 75

*✓Recipe includes Nutrition Facts
and Diabetic Exchanges*

Alphabetical Recipe Index

A

Acorn Squash with Caramel Sauce, 73
All-American Banana Split, 135
Almond Coffee Cake, 90
Almond-Filled Butterhorns, 95
Apple Harvest Cake, 128
Apple Pie, 112
Apple Pie Bars, 105
Apple Pie Dessert, 137
Apple Spice Drops, 107
✓Apple Tuna Sandwiches, 34
Apricot-Glazed Green Beans, 152
Apricot Pecan Sauce, 154
Apricot Sunshine Coffee Cake, 86
Artichoke Stuffing, 77
Asparagus Cream Cheese Omelet, 57
Avocado Tomato Salad, 35

B

Baby Pacifier Favors, 108
Bacon 'n' Onion Carrots, 150
Bacon Mashed Potatoes, 76
Bacon-Topped Grilled Cheese, 38
Bacon Water Chestnut Wraps, 6
✓Baked Flounder with Tartar Sauce, 62
Banana Cheesecake, 130
Banana Fritters, 120
Banana Ice Cream, 114
Barbecue Green Bean Bake, 83
Barbecued Hamburgers, 162
Basil Polenta with Beans 'n' Peppers, 77
Basketball Cake, 127
Bavarian Noodles, 166
Bean and Pineapple Salsa, 12
Beef Burgundy Stew, 146
Beef Potpie, 46
Biltmore's Bread Pudding, 123
Black Walnut Brownies, 101
BLT Pizza, 71
✓BLT Tortillas, 32
Blue Cheese Pear Salad, 138

Blue-Ribbon Butter Cake, 111
Blueberry Lemon Cake, 113
✓Blueberry Orange Smoothies, 11
Bread Pudding with Butter Sauce, 143
Brenda's Lemon Bars, 99
Broccoli and Noodles, 145
Brown Rice Yeast Rolls, 92
Brown Sugar Rhubarb Muffins, 96
Brownie Sundaes, 158
Brunch Egg Bake, 70
Buffalo-Stuffed Bell Peppers, 48
Burger 'n' Hot Dog Cake, 126
Burgers with Garden Sauce, 24
Buttery Almond Pear Cake, 85

C

Cajun Pepper Steak, 52
✓Calico Pepper Frittata, 50
California Lemon Pound Cake, 132
Calla Lily Tea Sandwiches, 12
Calypso Burritos, 53
Caprese Tomato Bites, 7
Caramel-Frosted Potato Cake, 165
Caramel Pecan Bars, 106
Carrot Cake Pancakes, 44
Carrot Zucchini Saute, 81
Carzalia Sweet Onion Salad, 38
Cashew Chicken, 69
Catfish Spread, 6
Cereal Cookie Bars, 100
Cheddar 'n' Pea Tossed Salad, 30
Cheddar Apple Pizza, 68
Cheddar-Veggie Appetizer Torte, 16
Cheesy Chicken Chowder, 37
Cherries over Creamy Fluff, 115
Cherry-Berry Peach Pie, 162
Cherry Cheese Blintzes, 57
Cherry-Cheese Gelatin Salad, 166
Cherry Walnut Cake, 114
Chewy Date Nut Bars, 104
Chicken 'n' Corn Bread Bake, 48
Chicken 'n' Fruit Salad, 38
Chicken Asparagus Bundles, 148

Chicken Dinner Packets, 141
Chicken Salad Pockets, 29
Chicken with Cherry Sauce, 46
Chili Chicken Strips, 17
Chipotle Butternut Squash Soup, 32
Chippy Blond Brownies, 103
Chocolate Banana Smoothies, 139
Chocolate Cherry Lincoln Log, 122
Chocolate Chip Cheesecake Dessert, 145
Chocolate-Covered Cherry Cookies, 100
Chocolate Macadamia Macaroons, 119
Chocolate Mousse, 121
Chocolate Peanut Butter Dessert, 111
Chocolate Peanut Squares, 102
Chocolate Pecan Kisses, 129
Chocolate Raspberry Tea Cakes, 129
Chorizo Bean Dip, 13
Chunky Hazelnut Oatmeal Cookies, 99
Cinnamon Poached Apples, 125
Cinnamon Swirl Quick Bread, 94
Cinnamon-Walnut Coffee Cake, 88
Citrus Baked Fish, 68
Citrus Cider Punch, 14
Coconut-Cranberry Apple Crisp, 129
Cold Vegetable Pizza, 14
✓Colorful Vegetable Medley, 78
Cookie Pudding Pots, 127
Corn Chowder with Dumplings, 37
Country Bean Bake, 162
Country Brunch Pie, 64
Country Pizza Pie, 63
✓Cran-Raspberry Iced Tea, 5
Cranberry-Sour Cream Coffee Cake, 91

Cranberry Surprise Muffins, 87
Cream Cheese Ice Cream, 124
Cream-Filled Cinnamon Coffee
    Cake, 85
Creamed Spinach, 74
Creamy Cheese Rice, 148
Creamy Cranberry Gelatin, 170
Creamy Herbed Potato Salad, 162
Creamy Pineapple Coleslaw, 145
Creamy Red Pepper Dip, 5
Creamy Zucchini Soup, 39
Crumb-Topped Asparagus
    Casserole, 76
Crunchy Sweet Potato Bake, 74
Crustless Four-Cheese Quiche, 51
✓Curried Turkey Vegetable
    Soup, 28
Curry Chicken Breasts, 156

D

Dijon Chicken, 56
Double Butterscotch Cookies, 109
Double-Cheese Beef Panini, 35
Double Chocolate Orange
    Brownies, 99

E

Easy Chicken Potpie, 43
Elvis Cupcakes, 117
"Everything" Mashed Potato
    Casserole, 168

F

Farmhouse Chili Dogs, 66
Fettuccine with Mushrooms
    and Tomatoes, 45
Flank Steak Fajitas, 66
Flavored Mocha Drink Mix, 7
Flaxseed Bread, 95
Fluffy Pumpkin Pie, 123
Four-Berry Spinach Salad, 140
French Dressing with Tomatoes, 80
Fresh Blackberry Pie, 125
Fresh Mozzarella Tomato Salad, 21
Frosted Cauliflower, 142
Frosted Chocolate Mayonnaise
    Cake, 161
Frosty Raspberry Parfaits, 128
Frozen Cheesecake Bites, 133
Fruit 'n' Nut Spread, 8

Fruit Medley, 152
Fruity Chocolate Tortilla Cups, 134

G

Garlic Clove Chicken, 66
German Chocolate Toffee
    Cookies, 106
Ginger Cranberry Bars, 102
Glazed Pork Chops, 166
Golden Cornish Hens, 170
Gouda Muffins, 96
Graduation Caps, 107
Grandma's Potato Salad, 33
Greek Spinach Pizza, 43
Green Beans Deluxe, 170
Green Beans with Herbs, 75
Green Chili Chicken
    Sandwiches, 22
Green Onion Drop Biscuits, 89
Grilled Chiles Rellenos, 82
Grilled Deli Sandwiches, 27
Grilled Potatoes, 82
Grilled Turkey Tenderloins, 60
Grilled Veggie Tortilla Wraps, 41

H

Hearty Cheese Soup, 138
Herbed Raspberry-Hazelnut
    Salad, 40
Homemade Meatballs, 70
Hominy Meatball Stew, 23
Honey-Apple Turkey Breast, 68
Honey-Dijon Pork Tenderloin, 43
Honey Harvard Beets, 164
Honey Maple Cookies, 103
Hot Cocoa, 139
Hot Italian Patties, 30

I

Individual Campfire Stew, 61
Italian Beef Sandwiches, 19
Italian Stew, 26

J

Jam-Topped Mini
    Cheesecakes, 112
Jumbo Chocolate Chip
    Cookies, 101

K

Kielbasa and Pepper Casserole, 55

L

Ladybug Cookies, 109
Lamb with Sauteed Veggies, 158
Leek and Herb Stuffed
    Chicken, 71
Lemon Artichoke Romaine
    Salad, 28
Lemon Currant Loaves, 86
Lemon-Pepper Veggies, 156
Lemon Ricotta Pancakes, 50
Lemonade Dessert, 118
Lemony Vegetables and Pasta, 47
✓Lentil Soup, 31
Little Snail Rolls, 89
Luncheon Salad, 26

M

Maine Blueberry Cake, 130
Mango Delight Gelatin Mold, 118
Maple Cream Meringue Pie, 135
Maple Pears, 133
Marble Brownies, 108
Marinated Pork Chops, 61
Mashed Potato Roses, 78
Meatballs Stroganoff, 45
Mediterranean Bulgur Salad, 19
Mexican Pork Roast, 53
Microwave Stroganoff, 154
Mock Hollandaise, 79
Monterey Corn Bake, 164
Mother's Rolls, 86
Mushroom Barley Soup, 137
Mushroom Burgers, 24
Mushroom Rice Medley, 79
Mustard-Crusted Salmon, 141

N

New England Clam Chowder, 36
Next-Generation German
    Potato Salad, 31
No-Bake Salted Pumpkin
    Seeds, 17

O

Old-Fashioned Blueberry
    Muffins, 97
Old-Fashioned Glazed Ham, 54

✓*Recipe includes Nutrition Facts
and Diabetic Exchanges*

Omelet Wedges with Cheese Sauce, 52
Open-Faced Hamburgers, 25
Orange Carrot Muffins, 92
Orange Coconut Meringue Pie, 131
Orange Creme Sodas, 15
Orange-Date Coffee Cake, 91
Orange Lemonade, 8
Orlando Orange Fritters, 88
Oven-Fried Chicken, 59
Oven-Fried Parmesan Chicken, 48
Oven Rice Supreme, 76
Oven Swiss Steak, 145
Over-the-Top Mac 'n' Cheese, 49
Oysters Rockefeller, 10

P

Parmesan-Ranch Pan Rolls, 96
Parmesan Rice Pilaf, 140
Party Pitas, 11
Peach-Almond Spinach Salad, 35
Peaches 'n' Cream, 147
Peanut Butter Brownie Bars, 105
Peanut Butter Ice Cream Sandwiches, 119
Peanut Ice Cream Delight, 121
Pear Praline Pie, 120
Pepper Jack Cheese Sticks, 9
Pickled Mushrooms, 14
Pineapple Pecan Cheese Ball, 17
Pink Rhubarb Punch, 15
Pinwheel Flank Steaks, 60
Pizza Roll-Ups, 15
Polish Beet Cake, 167
Poppy Seed Chiffon Cake, 115
Pork Tenderloin Medallions, 65
Potato Brunch Medley, 73
Pumpkin Ice Cream Pie, 115

Q

Quick Coffee Torte, 156

R

Rainbow Pasta Salad, 22
Ranch Turkey Burgers, 25
Raspberry Patch Crumb Bars, 104
Red Onion Rings, 150

Red Potato Skewers, 81
Reuben Sandwiches, 40
Rhubarb Dessert Cake, 132
Roasted Pepper Chicken Penne, 54
Roasted Red Pepper Soup, 19
Root Beer Cupcakes, 116

S

Salmon with Fettuccine Alfredo, 59
Sausage and Kale Soup, 21
Sausage Rice Casserole, 146
Savory Orange Salmon, 49
Savory Pot Roast, 44
✓Seafood Salad Pitas, 33
Seasoned Couscous, 158
Shredded Venison Sandwiches, 20
Shrimp 'n' Mushroom Lettuce Wraps, 10
Shrimp Chowder, 36
Simple Sauteed Zucchini, 168
Six-Fruit Salad, 39
Sizzling Country Steak, 150
Skillet Cabbage Rolls, 69
Skillet Sea Scallops, 55
Sour Cream Chocolate Cake, 124
Southern Honey-Pecan Pie, 170
Southwestern Chicken Packets, 64
Special Garden Medley, 73
Spiced Pear Dessert, 142
Spiced Pork Loin with Plums, 58
Spicy Chicken Salad with Mango Salsa, 20
Spicy Spanish Rice, 81
Spinach Salad with Red Currant Dressing, 33
Spinach-Stuffed Portobellos, 5
Steaks with Shallot Sauce, 62
Strawberry Cheesecake Pie, 134
Strawberry Flax Smoothies, 149
Strawberry Mallow Pops, 122
Strawberry Rhubarb Cream, 139
Strawberry Rhubarb Tart, 113
String Bean Salad, 142
Stuffed Artichokes, 149
Summer Squash Medley, 140

Surprise Red Cupcakes, 116
Sweet-and-Sour Red Cabbage, 78
Sweet Potato and Pear Soup, 34
Sweet Potato Pound Cake, 168
Sweet Potato Waldorf Salad, 23

T

Tangy Zucchini Saute, 74
Tex-Mex Scramble, 63
Thai Tilapia, 147
Thai Tofu Lettuce Wraps, 56
Three-Potato Salad, 29
Tomato and Cheese Strata, 51
Tomato Apple Pork Roast, 168
✓Tomato Soup with Cheese Tortellini, 29
Tortellini Carbonara, 152
Tuna 'n' Pea Casserole, 65
Turkey Cheese Ball, 9
Turkey Dijon Melts, 137
Turnip Hash Pasties, 164
Two-Cheese Macaroni Casserole, 160

V

Vegetable Soup Meat Loaf, 160
Venison Tortilla Lasagna, 58

W

Warm Chocolate-Caramel Apples, 150
White 'n' Sweet Mashed Potatoes, 83
Wild Rice and Ham Chowder, 36
Wild Rice Turkey Soup, 41
Wilted Iceberg Lettuce, 160
Wilted Lettuce Salad, 154
Winter Salad, 39

Z

Zesty Gazpacho, 27
✓Zippy Tomato-Topped Snapper, 149
Zucchini Cheddar Biscuits, 88
Zucchini Potato Pancakes, 80
Zucchini-Stuffed Onions, 75

✓*Recipe includes Nutrition Facts and Diabetic Exchanges*